Nebuchadnezzar's Children

Nebuchadnezzar's Children

Conventions of Madness in

Middle English Literature

Penelope B. R. Doob

New Haven and London, Yale University Press, 1974

For Betsy, Tom, and Tony

Contents

Preface

The search for Nebuchadnezzar's children in Middle English literature is astonishingly fruitful. Madmen and wild men abound in literary forests and perhaps in real ones; they grace numerous manuscript margins, and occasionally, in the guise of Charles VI of France or Henry VI of England, they emerge from literary obscurity to sit in the highest places. They figure in cautionary tales from the pulpit and in sophisticated romances, in history and in lyric poetry, in drama and in saints' lives. Finding Nebuchadnezzar's children is easy, whether we look among kings or peasants, knights or pagan lords or priests. But knowing what their madness signifies is much harder: Is it a physical illness like any other? If so, does it have any spiritual significance? Is it God's vengeance on the wicked? Is it, on the contrary, a sign of grace? Does it generally bear a constant meaning in literature? Is Herod's madness in the drama akin to Lancelot's or Ywain's or Merlin's madness, or do these characters embody radically different sorts of insanity with totally different meanings? And why do episodes of madness or wildness attach themselves to so many medieval figures, literary and historical?

These are some of the questions that led me to undertake this study, and I hope I have provided tentative answers at least. But the subject of madness is so rich and complex that I have necessarily had to be selective in approaching it. I am writing neither a medical history nor a catalog of European or even English madmen, and so certain kinds of material have had to be excluded — those medical treatises with little relevance for literature, for example, and most of the abundant literary material in French and German. And I have said very

ix

little about several illustrious literary madmen — Tristram, Lancelot, perhaps even Will in *Piers Plowman*.

What I have tried to do is focus attention on what seem to me to be the two most important problems for a study of the literary uses of madness in Middle English literature. First, what does madness generally *mean* in medieval society and literature? A precise answer is difficult, for the word was used very loosely to describe virtually any kind of irrational behavior, and I have chosen to explore medieval meanings of the word rather than to impose my own definition upon the material. One can, however, determine what expectations a fourteenth-century Englishman might have had of a real or literary madman in regard to the causes of his disease, his symptoms, his prognosis, and — most important — his moral status, and this I have tried to do. Second, how do medieval attitudes affect the literary uses and meanings of madness? Specifically, what are the conventional methods of representing madmen, especially the more famous ones like Nebuchadnezzar and Herod, and how can an understanding of these conventions and attitudes illuminate appropriate literary works? In answering these questions, I have drawn evidence from all periods from biblical times through the fifteenth century, but instead of presenting a chronological development of ideas, I have tried to show only what ways of looking at madness were available in late medieval England. To this end, I have used a variety of sources: the Bible and Apocrypha, commentaries, saints' lives, penitential handbooks, sermons, exemplum books, romances, plays, physiological and psychological treatises, encyclopedias, lyric poetry, and the works of the great Ricardians Chaucer, Gower, Langland, and the *Pearl*-poet.[1] Obviously a comprehensive study of all relevant texts would be the work of a lifetime, but I trust that I have provided a representative late medieval view of madness and its conventions. Those who wish further documentation of most points made in the present study may delve

---

1. The useful term *Ricardian* is J. A. Burrow's: *Ricardian Poetry: Chaucer, Gower, Langland, and the 'Gawain' Poet* (London: Routledge & Kegan Paul, 1971; New Haven: Yale University Press, 1971).

into its earlier and considerably lengthier incarnation as a dissertation.[2]

Perhaps a few technical details should be mentioned here. In the interest of brevity, I have provided only the translations of Latin texts except when the original language is important. Middle English passages have usually not been translated, but the more obscure words have been glossed. In both Latin and Middle English, I have silently corrected obvious typographical errors, and I have repunctuated where the sense seemed to demand it. Biblical quotations throughout are from the Douay-Rheims translation, always checked against the Vulgate. In my text I generally use the most familiar form of biblical proper names — for example, *Nebuchadnezzar* instead of *Nabuchodonosor* — but references to books of the Bible are given in the less common Douay forms. Dates of authors and works have been taken from such usual sources as standard editions and the *New Catholic Encyclopedia*.

Toronto
May 1973

---

2. Penelope Billings Reed Doob, *Ego Nabugodonosor: A Study of Conventions of Madness in Middle English Literature* (Ph.D. diss., Stanford University, 1969); available from University Microfilms, order no. 70-18, 397. The dissertation also includes much fuller treatment of such subjects as the historical and medical aspects of madness and of disease in general, the varieties of madness in medieval literature, the treatment of Nebuchadnezzar in biblical commentaries, and the development of the Herod figure in medieval literature. Another dissertation of interest is Judith S. Neaman's "The Distracted Knight: A Study of Insanity in the Arthurian Romances" (Ph.D. diss., Columbia University, 1968). Neaman occasionally covers some of the same material as I do, but our approaches, emphases, and conclusions usually differ. Neaman's medical and social history of insanity in the Middle Ages will be published by Doubleday in 1975.

Acknowledgments

I should like to thank here those whose generous advice has improved this book considerably. As supervisor of the dissertation on which this book is based, as adviser, and as friend, Professor V. A. Kolve has been an unfailing source of wisdom and kindness. Professor A. G. Rigg has given freely of his time and learning for many years; his assistance with my Latin translations and his close criticism of the manuscript have been invaluable. I am also indebted to Professor R. W. Ackerman, Professor Herbert D. Meritt, Professor John Leyerle, Professor Chauncey Wood, and Thomas Reed, Jr., all of whom have graciously read the manuscript in various stages, offering many suggestions for its improvement. Many people have offered bibliographical assistance along the way and deserve my thanks: Professors Richard Atkinson, Julian Brown, Angus Cameron, Michael Cummings, Roberta Frank, Charlotte Morse, and Wesley Trimpi. To the late Professor Michael Galton of the Dartmouth Medical School I owe a special debt: the many months I spent as his research assistant stimulated a continued interest in medicine which finds one rather perverse expression in this book. I am also grateful to the librarians and staff of the British Museum, the Bodleian Library, the Warburg Institute, the Index of Christian Art at Princeton, and the Library of the Pontifical Institute for Medieval Studies, Toronto, all of whom have been unfailingly helpful in my research.

I owe thanks for more material assistance to the Kent Fellowship Program of the Danforth Foundation, to Stanford and York universities for providing travel and research grants at appropriate moments, and to the Canada Council, which generously supported the final stages of manuscript preparation.

I am grateful to Pat Hope for suffering through three separate versions of the manuscript, typing them all with skill and good cheer. And finally I want to thank A. N. Doob for dealing efficiently and good-naturedly with the usual crises and catastrophes that arise during the writing of a book.

Acknowledgment is gratefully made to the following institutions for permission to reprint illustrations from their collections: trustees of the British Museum (pls. 1, 2, 3, 4, 5, 7, 11, 12, 13, 14, 15); National Monuments Record, London (pls. 6, 10, 16); Öffentliche Bibliothek der Universität Basel (pl. 8); Stiftsbibliothek Lilienfeld and Akademische Druck-u. Verlagsanstalt, Graz (pl. 9). The Council of the Early English Text Society kindly granted permission to quote from their various texts.

Abbreviations

AM　　　　　　Burton, Robert. *The Anatomy of Melancholy.* Edited by Floyd Dell and Paul Jordan-Smith. New York: Farrar and Rinehart, 1927.

ANCL　　　　　Ante-Nicene Christian Library.

AT　　　　　　Banks, Mary MacLeod, ed. *An Alphabet of Tales.* EETS, os 126, 127. 1904–05. Citations to this work are given in the text by exemplum number.

Bartholomeus　Bartholomeus Anglicus. *De proprietatibus rerum.* Ca. 1260. Citations in the text are to book and chapter in John Trevisa's translation (ca. 1398), printed at Westminster, ?1495, by Wynkyn de Worde.

CG　　　　　　Augustine. *The City of God.* In *Basic Writings of St. Augustine,* edited by Whitney J. Oates. New York: Random House, 1948. Book and chapter references are given first, followed in parentheses by volume and page references to the Oates edition.

CT　　　　　　Chaucer, Geoffrey. *Canterbury Tales.* In *Works,* edited by Fred N. Robinson. 2d ed. Boston: Houghton Mifflin, 1957. All citations from Chaucer are to this edition, and standard abbreviations of other titles have been used.

EETS, es　　　Publications of the Early English Text Society, extra series.

EETS, os — Publications of the Early English Text Society, original series.

GO — *Biblia sacra cum glossa ordinaria . . . et postilla Nicolai Lyrani.* 7 vols. Paris, 1590. Citations to J. P. Migne's edition of the *Glossa ordinaria* are indicated by references to *PL* 113 and 114.

"Hairy Anchorite" 1 and 2 — Williams, Charles Allyn. "Oriental Affinities of the Legend of the Hairy Anchorite, Part 1: Pre-Christian," and "Oriental Affinities . . . , Part 2: Christian." *University of Illinois Studies in Language and Literature* 10 and 11 (1925–26): 187–242 and 427–509.

JA and *JW* — Josephus. *Jewish Antiquities* and *The Jewish War.* In *Works,* edited and translated by H. St. John Thackeray, Ralph Marcus, Allen Wikgren, and Louis H. Feldman. LCL. 9 vols. London: William Heinemann, 1926–65. References are to title (*JA* or *JW*), book, and section.

LCL — Loeb Classical Library. London: William Heinemann; Cambridge: Harvard University Press.

LF — Library of Fathers.

Piers — Langland, William. *The Vision of William concerning Piers the Plowman.* Edited by W. W. Skeat. 2 vols. Oxford, 1886.

PL — Migne, J. P., ed. *Patrologiae cursus completus: Patrologia Latina.* 221 vols. Paris, 1844–64.

Saturn and Melancholy — Klibansky, Raymond; Panofsky, Erwin; and Saxl, Fritz. *Saturn and Melancholy: Studies in the History of Natural Philosophy, Re-*

ligion, and Art. New York: Basic Books, 1964.

ST   Aquinas, Thomas. *Summa Theologica.* In *Basic Writings of St. Thomas Aquinas,* edited by Anton C. Pegis. 2 vols. New York: Random House, 1945. References to part, question, and article are followed in parentheses by volume and page references to the Pegis edition.

Standard *PMLA* abbreviations are used for periodicals.

1 Backgrounds: Medieval Attitudes toward Madness

> We, as long as we are ruled by reason, correct our inordinate appetite, and conform ourselves to God's word, are as so many living saints: but if we give reins to lust, anger, ambition, pride, and follow our own ways, we degenerate into beasts, transform ourselves, overthrow our constitutions, provoke God to anger, and heap upon us this of *Melancholy*, and all kinds of incurable diseases, as a just and deserved punishment of our sins.
>
> Robert Burton, *The Anatomy of Melancholy*

Disease and madness have traditionally been associated with sin and guilt: Job's friends and counsellors through the ages unhesitatingly attribute his affliction to his own shortcomings. Perhaps it is simply a fact of human nature that we are loathe to acknowledge that misfortune comes by chance rather than by desert;[1] but whatever the reason, medical theory from pagan antiquity through the Renaissance assigned moral as well as physical causes to disease, and religious remedies were proposed in conjunction with more purely physiological ones.[2] For the Middle Ages,

1. See Melvin J. Lerner, "The Desire for Justice and Reactions to Victims," in *Altruism and Helping Behavior*, ed. Jacqueline R. Macaulay and Leonard Berkowitz (New York: Academic Press, 1970), pp. 205–29.
2. Useful medical histories include the following: Franz G. Alexander and Sheldon T. Selesnick, *The History of Psychiatry* (New York: Harper and Row, 1966); Wilfrid Bonser, *The Medical Background of Anglo-Saxon England: A Study in History, Psychology, and Folklore* (London: Wellcome Historical Medical Library, 1963); *Saturn and Melancholy*; John S. Scarborough, *Roman Medicine* (London: Thames & Hudson, 1969); Henry E.

the connection between sin and disease was inevitable. Admired Greek and Roman authorities often linked madness with transgression: Heracles, Ajax, and Orestes are all driven mad by angry gods, and Cicero finds that evil passions cause mental disturbance and insanity.[3] More important, the Bible continually attributes disease to sin, not only providing such colorful examples as the mad Saul (1 Kings 15–16) but also giving more explicit warning to the wicked: "But if thou wilt not hear the voice of the Lord thy God, to keep and to do all his commandments and ceremonies, which I command thee this day, all these curses shall come upon thee and overtake thee. . . . The Lord strike thee with madness and blindness and fury of mind" (Deut. 28:15, 28). With such precedents, it is not surprising that medieval commentators often interpret specific diseases as the product of appropriate sins; thus Rabanus Maurus (d. 856) writes, "Sickness is a disease caused by vice. . . . Fever is a fleshly desire, burning insatiably. . . . Swelling leprosy is puffed-up pride. . . . He has scabs on his body whose mind is ruined by lusts of the flesh." [4] This moral bias in considering mental or physical illness is evident even in purely medical texts. In the extremely popular Salernitan medical treatise *Flos medicine,* the verb *pecco* ("offend, sin") is used to describe a humoural alteration leading to disease, while in English works the names of many diseases suggest sin: erysipelas is called "the fyere of helle," epilepsy is "goddis wrath," and madness and

---

Sigerist, *A History of Medicine,* 2 vols. (New York: Oxford University Press, 1951, 1961); Charles Hugh Talbot, *Medicine in Medieval England* (London: Oldbourne History of Science Library, 1967); Lynn Thorndike, *History of Magic and Experimental Science during the First Thirteen Centuries of Our Era,* 2 vols. (New York: Macmillan, 1923); Agnes Carr Vaughan, *Madness in Greek Thought and Custom* (Baltimore: J. H. Furst, 1919); Ilza Veith, *Hysteria: The History of a Disease* (Chicago: University of Chicago Press, 1965); and Gregory Zilboorg and George W. Henry, *A History of Medical Psychology* (New York: W. W. Norton, 1941).

3. *Tusculan Disputations,* trans. J. E. King, LCL (London, 1950), 3. 2, 3. 5, and 4. 10.

4. *De universo, PL* 111:501–03.

other diseases are "deofolseocnes" ("devil-sickness").[5] Bartholomeus, in Trevisa's 1398 translation, links epilepsy with "the *vyce* of the heed" and warns against "the *malyce*" of some humours and the *"euyll* dedely qualytees" of melancholy (4. 4, 8, 11; italics mine). Such use of moral terminology in allegedly scientific treatises indicates how pervasive the religious view of disease was in the Middle Ages; even if medical writers used such terms in a strictly physiological sense, their readers might well feel free to pursue the moral implications of medical texts.

GENERAL CAUSES AND PURPOSES OF DISEASE

Medieval theoreticians recognized many possible reasons for the association of disease with sin. Ultimately, they believed, all disease comes by the will of God, and the most common moral justification for disease is that God in his justice inflicts disease on the unrepentant sinner as a punishment. Thus, for example, Abbot Leofstan of Bury Saint Edmunds was afflicted when he and a fellow monk tried to discover whether King Edmund's severed head was truly joined to his body as legend told. Leofstan took the head, the monk took the feet, and both pulled as hard as they could, but the body remained intact. As punishment for this impiety, Leofstan's hands were paralyzed, and he became blind, dumb, and mad, according to various versions of the story.[6] It was commonly recognized in the Middle Ages that disease was a fitting punishment for the wicked because it inflicted misery in life as a token of the pains of hell, it symbolized the deformity of a sinful soul, it provided a forceful example to deter others, and it conveniently dispatched one to the greater punishments of death and hell.

5. *Flos medicine* 7. 2480, in *Collectio Salernitana,* ed. Salvatore de Renzi (Naples, 1859), vol. 5; George Henslow, ed., *Medical Works of the Fourteenth Century* (London, 1899), p. 84; Bartholomeus 7. 10; and Bonser, *Medical Background,* p. 257.

6. See Abbo, *Passio Sancti Eadmundi,* and Abbot Samson, *Opus de miraculis sancti Ædmundi,* in *Memorials of St. Edmund's Abbey,* ed. Thomas Arnold, Rolls Series, no. 96 (London, 1890), 1:23 and 134.

But there are other important justifications for disease, as might be expected from man's need to explain why some people recover and why even saints occasionally suffer. In an extremely important passage the *Glossa ordinaria* (ca. twelfth–thirteenth century) codifies medieval thought on the subject: God uses disease "for testing, or for improving the just, or for damning the wicked" (*GO* 3:2164). Although the view of disease as a punishment to damn the wicked was extremely popular, still more common were the optimistic views of illness as purgation or as test. According to the Bible, "Whom the Lord loveth, he chastiseth; and he scourgeth every son whom he receiveth" (Heb. 12:6). For medieval theory, this meant that truly fortunate men would be purged of their sins here and now on earth, and illness is one of those earthly afflictions that, borne meekly, constitute earthly purgatory and entitle a soul to "pardon with Peers Plouhman *a pena et a culpa*" (*Piers* C 10. 186). Illness may thus be a means of grace as well as punishment, and the *Ancrene Riwle* (ca. 1200) emphasizes the purgative and testing aspects of disease.

> God proves His beloved and chosen people as a goldsmith tries gold in the fire. There the false gold perishes and the true comes out the brighter. Illness is a fire of which we must endure the heat, but nothing purifies gold so well as illness cleanses the soul. Illness which is sent by God, and not that which is caught by some through their own foolishness, does these six things: washes away sins previously committed; protects against those that were threatening; tests our patience; keeps us humble; increases our reward; puts the patient sufferer on a level with the martyrs. Thus bodily illness is the health of the soul, salve for its wounds, a shield against further wounds, which God sees it would receive did not illness prevent it.[7]

7. M. B. Salu, trans. (London: Burns & Oates, 1963), p. 80. The popular metaphor in the first paragraph comes ultimately from Wisdom 3:6.

Thus physical and mental affliction might be salutary, and men of great sanctity often prayed for it, as a very popular tale illustrates. A monk, noted for his ability to cast out demons, grew proud and his powers failed him. Repenting, he prayed that he might himself be possessed and become as lowly as those he had cured. All came to pass as he had asked, and for five months he was chained as a maniac; then, sufficiently punished and purified by suffering, he regained his sanity and his powers (*AT* 739).

Few people have the presence of mind to pray for suffering, of course, so usually purgative disease is inflicted on the heedless sinner as both a token of his guilt and a means of penance. The whole process of sin, disease, self-knowledge, repentance, and cure is illustrated by Lancelot in Malory's *Tale of the Sankgreal*.[8] Half-asleep outside a chapel, Lancelot hears a sick knight praying for a cure of his long illness. Thanks to his penitent suffering, the knight's sin is forgiven, and he is cured by the Grail; but Lancelot, "overtakyn with synne," is stricken with sudden paralysis when he tries to approach. The sick knight's squire explains Lancelot's trouble: "I dare well sey . . . that he dwellith in som dedly synne whereof he was never confessed." Seized by guilt, Lancelot confesses to a hermit, thereby curing body and soul. Both the sick knight and Lancelot are made aware of their sins by means of their afflictions; both acknowledge the penitential aspect of their suffering, and both intend to reform so that they may be whole in body and soul. Unfortunately Lancelot habitually falls back into his old sins: his first madness, in *The Book of Sir Tristram de Lyones,* is followed by his paralysis at the chapel; and later sins lead to a long trance at Corbenic, which he rightly interprets as "ponyshemente for the four-and-twenty yere that he had bene a synner, wherefore oure Lorde

---

8. In *Works,* ed. Eugène Vinaver, 2d ed., 3 vols. (Oxford: Clarendon Press, 1967), 2:894–99 (Caxton 13. 18–20). For the trance at Corbenic, see *Works,* 2:1015–17 (Caxton 17. 15–16); for Lancelot's final illness, see *Works,* 3:1257 (Caxton 21. 12).

put hym in penaunce the four-and-twenty dayes and nyghtes."
Later, after still more sins, he dies in a sickness that he brings
upon himself by fasting as he apparently realizes once again
the penitential nature of illness.

The third major purpose of disease is to test the saint. Job
is the classic example of the suffering just man, but his friends,
responding in the normal human way to any misfortune,
assume that disease is always punishment for sin and fail to
distinguish between what Gregory calls the trial of proba-
tion and the trial of purification.[9] In literature too the distinction is seldom made, and there are relatively few examples
of disease as test. Saints' legends — especially those of the
desert fathers — and treatments of Christ's Passion are exceptions in which undeserved suffering is given prominence, and
there are also occasional references to a kind of melancholy
madness afflicting holy contemplatives and giving them the
opportunity to increase their merit through trial.[10] But there
are few such exceptions, and we must conclude that the interpretation of disease as a test from God was less attractive to
medieval authors than the views of disease as punishment and
as purgation. Given the predominantly didactic view of literature in the Middle Ages, this is to be expected: tales of
tyrants slaughtered and knights purified by disease are far
more constructive morally than stories encouraging a sick man
to see himself as a saint being tested by God.

Disease, then, has three major functions in God's plan.
First, it is punitive, leading to death and damnation. Second,
it is monitory and purgative, at once a visible token of sin,
a punishment for sin, and a means of expiation. Third, it is
a test to prove the elect and increase their merit. Thus the
traditional association of sin and disease holds in two of these
three categories; and the third category — disease as test —
seldom operates in literature or, as Job's case shows, is recognized in life. In general, then, disease in literature is seen as

9. *Morals on the Book of Job,* trans. James Bliss, LF, 3 vols. (Oxford,
1844–50), 1:343.
10. See *Saturn and Melancholy,* pp. 74–77.

punishment or purgation, and its infliction is morally justified by the sick man's guilt.

If we turn from the three purposes or final causes of disease to the efficient causes — the exact mechanisms and agencies that cause disease — we find the same close relationship of sin with disease whether we consider originating or instrumental causes. To deal with first things first: as Robert Burton puts it, "The impulsive cause of these miseries in man, this privation or destruction of God's image, the cause of death and diseases, of all temporal and eternal punishments, was the sin of our first parent Adam." [11] For some authorities, Original Sin seems simply to have opened a Pandora's Box of miseries including disease; thus the *Miroure of Mans Saluacionne* explains:

And if man had alway / kept gods commandment
He ne had neuer felt of deth / nor of none othere tourment
He ne shuld neuer hafe bene waike / nor felt of werynesse
Nor neuer hafe felt a poynt / of vnhelth, nor sekenesse.[12]

But many authors wish to explain precisely how Original Sin caused disease; after all, God often acts through some physical agency, and consequently the alteration brought about by Original Sin should be explicable scientifically. According to such reasoning, Adam and Eve were created in perfect humoural balance and made in the image of God in that reason ruled will and the passions. They could suffer no disease until they themselves destroyed their delicately interrelated physiological, psychological, and moral balance by sin. With the Fall, however, corruption and disorder entered body and soul. From a moral and psychological point of view man became increasingly susceptible to sin and madness.

11. *AM*, p. 114. Although Burton's work is later than our period of investigation — the first edition appeared in 1621 — it codifies and is thoroughly representative of medieval views of madness and disease.

12. Alfred H. Huth, ed. (London, 1888), p. 14. The *Miroure* is a fifteenth-century translation of the influential *Speculum humanae salvationis* (ca. 1324), a long poem in which events in the life of Christ are linked with other biblical or mythological events that prefigure them.

Ideally, all man's actions should be ruled by reason; to the
extent that he departs from reason and its judgments of
what is good, man is mad (seen psychologically) and sinful
(seen morally).[13] An important consequence of the Fall was
that reason was weakened, and the passions, sensitive appetite,
and will grew stronger. According to Chaucer, "For as
muche as the resoun of man ne wol nat be subget ne obeisant
to God, that is his lord by right, therfore leseth it the lordshipe that it sholde have over sensualitee, and eek over the
body of man. And why? For sensualitee rebelleth thanne
agayns resoun, and by that way leseth resoun the lordshipe
over sensualitee and over the body. For right as resoun is
rebel to God, right so is bothe sensualitee rebel to resoun
and the body also" (CT 10. 263–65). The punishment fits the
crime, and the destruction of due order between God and
man caused — and continues to cause with every sin — psychological, moral, and physiological disorder. Both mind and
body rebel against reason, and this continuing rebellion was
augmented in Eden by a change in man's physical constitution. The perfect sanguine temperament of prelapsarian man
was lost, the unending humoural strife that causes death and
disease and that can predispose man to sin began, and, as if
this disorder were not enough, Hildegard of Bingen (d. 1179)
theorized that the Fall led to the creation of the melancholy
humour, that chief fount of madness and disease.[14] The dread-

13. For the interrelationship of madness, sin, and reason see *ST* 1–2. Q.
74 and 77 (2:601–16, 630–43). For modern summaries, applicable to medieval as well as to Renaissance thought, see Lawrence Babb, *The Elizabethan Malady: A Study of Melancholia in English Literature from 1580
to 1642* (East Lansing: Michigan State University Press, 1951), pp. 1–20;
J. B. Bamborough, *The Little World of Man* (London: Longmans, Green,
1952), pp. 9–51 and passim; and Lily B. Campbell, *Shakespeare's Tragic
Heroes: Slaves of Passion* (Cambridge, 1930; reprinted New York: Barnes
and Noble, 1966), pp. 79–83 and 93–102.

14. *Causae et curae*, ed. Paul Kaiser, Bibliotheca Scriptorum Graecorum
et Romanorum Teubneriana (Leipzig, 1909), pp. 33, 36, 38, 143. For the
sanguine temperament as the ideal, see William of Conches (d. 1160), *De
philosophia*, *PL* 172:93 (attributed to Honorius of Autun by Migne; for
correct ascription, see *Saturn and Melancholy*, p. 102n111).

ful consequences of the Fall are, of course, transmitted to every man in his very conception, "sithen we of such mater / byn mad, in which synne is regnyng." [15] Thus Original Sin not only brought about the first diseases but also created that physiological and psychological degeneration which would incline man to sin and serve as a mechanism through which additional sins might bring about earthly punishment — the appropriate disease — without God's direct intervention.

The intricate relationship between man's physical being (humours, organs, imagination, particular reason, memory, sensitive appetite, passions, etc.) and his incorporeal soul (reason, will) is too complex for full discussion here. [16] The most important thing to understand is not the precise mechanism of the interactions but the fact that in the Middle Ages one simply could not separate mental, moral, and physiological processes; each aspect of man interacts with every other aspect, and what one eats, for instance, usually affects one's mind and one's soul. As the popular treatise *Secreta secretorum* puts it, "Kynde [nature] is so grete a fellowe betwen body and Sowle, that the Passyons of body chaungyth the sowle; and the Passions of Sowle, chaungyth the body." [17] This means that just as Original Sin led to the possibility of disease, so each actual sin can have its deleterious effect on the body by bringing forth its own disease. To take one example, the passion of rage, which is often a sin, raises the body's temperature and dries the various bodily fluids (e.g. animal spirits that facilitate perception and thought). The result may well be fever and madness, compounded by the creation of the highly dangerous adust, or burnt, humours. Thus sin and disease are intimately connected as cause and effect; Original Sin changed

15. Francis A. Foster, ed., *A Stanzaic Life of Christ* (early fourteenth century), EETS, os 166 (1926), ll. 4561–62.

16. Throughout the present book I assume the reader's knowledge of the rudiments of medieval faculty psychology and humoural physiology such as may be gained from Bamborough's *Little World of Man*.

17. Robert Steele, ed., *Secreta secretorum: Three Prose Versions*, EETS, es 74 (1898), p. 219. This influential work, erroneously attributed to Aristotle, is cited in Yonge's 1422 translation, *The Gouernaunce of Prynces*.

every man's constitution, and individual sin leads to further
mental and physical degeneration. Therefore, we are all diseased, sinful, and mad; as Burton puts it, "Ask not with him
in the Poet, What madness ghosts this old man, but what
madness ghosts us all? For we are all mad, not once, but
always so, & ever and altogether as bad as he" (*AM*, p. 36).

Clearly, then, in the Middle Ages there was a strong
tendency to moralize disease, to see all disease as the consequence of Original Sin and most disease as the punishment
or purgation of individual sins. This moral attitude is especially marked in regard to madness, a term which I use as
freely as did medieval writers, to include any mental aberration from any cause. Although most forms of madness were
similar in kind to any other disease, caused by the same
mechanisms supernatural or natural and inflicted for the
same purposes, insanity was in some ways more horrible than
other diseases because it deprives men of reason — the image
of God.[18] Moreover, in that sin typically involves the overthrow or, worse, the perversion of reason by will and passion,[19] there is an especially close resemblance between sin
and madness, a resemblance that frequently becomes identity,
as we shall see. In some ways, then, madness is the most appropriate punishment for sin as well as its most fitting emblem;
as Burton puts it, "We, so long as we are ruled by reason,
correct our inordinate appetites, and conform ourselves to
God's word, are as so many living saints: but if we give reins
to lust, anger, ambition, pride, and follow our own ways, we
degenerate into beasts, transform ourselves, overthrow our
constitutions, provoke God to anger, and heap upon us this
[affliction] of *Melancholy,* and all kinds of incurable diseases,
as a just and deserved punishment of our sins" (*AM*, pp. 118–
19). The rest of this chapter will consider some of those rela-
tionships between sin and madness that underly the role of
the madman as the symbol of the sinner and the type of post-
lapsarian man.

18. See *CG* 12. 23 (2:205).
19. See, for instance, *ST* 1-2. Q. 77, A. 8 (2:642–43).

THE CAUSES OF MADNESS

A study of the instrumental causes of madness reveals that all have, or can be interpreted as having, a moral component. This is true regardless of whether the disease is overtly supernatural or apparently physiological in origin; the presence of a readily discernible physical cause does not at all preclude moral fault on the part of the sick man or God's hand at work through one of many available agencies. The model for the onset of disease seems to be this: a man sins; God determines to punish him; God inflicts disease either directly or through angelic or diabolic intermediaries, through the environment (season, stars), or through permitting a man's sins to modify his humours and cause illness (e.g. rage stimulates the growth of choler and fever, leading to frenzy). Supernatural causes are preferred in overtly religious and didactic works, while scientific explanations often function in more sophisticated literature such as the romances; but whatever the immediate cause of madness, the ultimate moral causes are always implicit. I should like now to consider some of the more important causes of insanity, giving a few examples from medieval literature and showing how sin is or may be involved in each case.

Frequently madness is caused directly by God. Sometimes such miracles are initiated by prayer, as in a case reported by the Knight of La Tour-Landry. A hermit's chapel was a popular resort for pilgrims, and one day, as the pilgrims chattered away during mass, the hermit noticed a devil writing down their foolish words. The hermit prayed that the pilgrims might know their sins, and "thanne sodenly all they that iangeled [chattered] beganne to crye lyke wode folke oute of her mynde." When reminded of their sins, "the pepill that were there oute of her mynde . . . cried, and pulled euer of her tyre [clothing]," showing some of the more common symptoms of madness. Finally they confessed, and when the hermit absolved them of their sins, "they were heled, and come againe into her witte, and thei kepte hem euer after

from iangelinge atte Goddes seruice." [20] The pattern here of
madness serving as penance and leading to self-knowledge,
confession, and reform is extremely common in literature, as
we shall see in later chapters.

In another and more serious case, God afflicts an impious
youth to punish rather than reform him. According to William of Malmesbury a crowd of people in Gloucester were
waiting for Bishop Wulfstan to finish dining so that he could
baptize and confirm their children. When they grew impatient, a boy asked rashly, "Why do ye tarry for the Bishop
who is filling his belly with the monks? Come: if any man
would have his child signed [with the cross], let him come to
me." Thereupon the boy smeared the children's heads with
mud as he intoned "unseemly words," unfortunately not pre-
served. In the midst of general hilarity, God acted: suddenly
the boy went mad, tearing his hair, grinning uncontrollably,
beating his head against the cemetery wall, and eventually
falling into a pit from which he was rescued with great difficulty. Later his madness was cured temporarily by Wulfstan's
blessing, but a few days later the boy died. The moral is clear:
thus end all who mock God, his bishops, and his sacraments;
thus is the madness of sacrilege made literal.[21] These two
examples are representative of many similar cases of madness
sent by God: the onset of the disease is sudden; its symptoms
are spectacular; and, whether the madness is purgative or
punitive, it is clearly symbolic of and caused by the madman's
sin.

An equally spectacular and still more common cause of
madness is demonic possession.[22] The popularity of possession
as an etiology stems from several factors. First, biblical tradi-

20. Thomas Wright, ed., *The Book of the Knight of La Tour-Landry*
(late fourteenth century, trans. early fifteenth century), rev. ed., EETS, os
33 (1906), pp. 40–41.

21. *Life of St. Wulfstan, Bishop of Worcester*, trans. J. H. F. Peile
(Oxford: Basil Blackwell, 1934), 2. 14 (pp. 53–55).

22. A full and useful discussion of possession is Traugott Konstantin
Oesterreich's *Possession*, trans. D. Ibberson (London: Kegan Paul, Trench,
Trübner, 1930). Demonic possession, of course, was a common cause of all
kinds of disease, not only of madness.

tion endorsed it — Saul, probably the best-known madman, was possessed by an unclean spirit, and so were many of the people cured by Christ.[23] Second, the onset of madness is so sudden, and it responds to physiological cure so seldom and to spiritual cure (if we are to believe saints and psychiatrists) so well, that it might well seem to be of supernatural origin. Finally, the common association of sin and devils, on one hand, and of sin and madness, on the other, may well have contributed to the linking of sin, devils, and madness.

Whatever the original reasons for its popularity, possession, like a direct act of God, has one overwhelming advantage as a cause of madness: it usually signifies quite unambiguously the moral turpitude of the possessed, since the fiend has no power in man unless God ordains it or man permits it by his own sins. Of course there are theoretical exceptions, and saints are frequently tempted by the devil who may also afflict them with assorted physical disorders. But temptation and physical disease are seldom extended to actual possession unless a man has sinned grievously like the proud exorcist described earlier; and, although Oesterreich finds that there was no unanimity on the moral status of the possessed, his extensive evidence suggests that possession was usually considered the result and token of sin.[24] In any case, the possessed are de facto servants of the devil so long as they are possessed, regardless of the reason for their affliction. Even the innocent serpent, possessed by the devil to tempt Eve, was punished, although the fault lay in the devil rather than in the beast he chose to use.[25] While some authorities acknowledged that possessed men might conceiv-

23. For Saul, see 1 Kings 16:14–23; for Christ's miracles, see, for instance, Matt. 8:28–33, 9:32–33, and 10:1, where Christ gives his disciples power over demons. The early church fathers also wrote often on possession: e.g. *CG* 19. 4, 19. 9, and 22. 8 (2:475, 483, 618–28).

24. *Possession*, passim.

25. Peter Comestor (d. 1180) notes that the serpent, like all possessed creatures, was ignorant of what the devil used him for, and so God did not question him after the Fall "because he had not done it of himself, but the devil acted through him" (*Historia scholastica, PL* 198:1073). Nevertheless, the serpent was punished.

ably be saved even though their madness led to suicide, in
practice a man once possessed was tainted for life: "If anyone is troubled by a devil, he may not touch the sacred
mysteries. If by the mercy of God and by fasting he is cleansed,
he shall after ten years be received into the office of the
clerics, not of the priests." [26]

One reason for this insistence on the wickedness of the
possessed may be that most biblical instances of possession
are explicitly related to sin, often both in the text and in
commentaries. An interesting example is the miracle of the
Gadarene swine, most fully recounted in Mark 5:1–15:

> And they came over the strait of the sea into the coun-
> try of the Gerasens. And as he went out of the ship,
> immediately there met him out of the monuments a man
> with an unclean spirit, Who had his dwelling in the
> tombs, and no man now could bind him, not even with
> chains. For having been often bound with fetters and
> chains, he had burst the chains, and broken the fetters
> in pieces, and no one could tame him. And he was always
> day and night in the monuments and in the mountains,
> crying and cutting himself with stones. And seeing Jesus
> afar off, he ran and adored him. And crying with a
> loud voice, he said: What have I to do with thee, Jesus
> the Son of the most high God? I adjure thee by God that
> thou torment me not. For he said unto him: Go out of the
> man, thou unclean spirit. And he asked him: What is thy
> name? And he saith to him: My name is Legion, for we
> are many. And he besought him much, that he would
> not drive him away out of the country. And there was
> there near the mountain a great herd of swine, feeding.

26. The Judgment of Clement (eighth century), in *Medieval Handbooks
of Penance*, trans. John McNeill and Helena Gamer (New York: Columbia
University Press, 1938), p. 273; on madness and suicide, see Penitential of
Theodore, ibid., p. 207. As we shall see, both Charles VI of France and
Thomas Hoccleve suffered from the similar assumption that a man once
mad was forever untrustworthy.

And the spirits besought him, saying: Send us into the swine, that we may enter into them. And Jesus immediately gave them leave. And the unclean spirits going out, entered into the swine: and the herd with great violence was carried headlong into the sea, being about two thousand, and were stifled in the sea. And they that fed them fled, and told it in the city and in the fields. And they went out to see what was done: And they come to Jesus, and they see him that was troubled with the devil, sitting, clothed, and well in his wits, and they were afraid.

Although in the Bible the man's possession is not explicitly related to his previous sins, the commentators are unanimous in concluding that this madness is punitive. An English sermon identifies the maniac as a great sinner: "Crist bad þe dewell goy owte of þe man; and he asked þe fende what was is name, and he seid Legio. Legio is asmoche to say as vj þousande vj hundreþ syxti and vj; so many devells were in on man for is synne." [27] The *Glossa ordinaria* goes still further in drawing a moral application: not only was the maniac a sinner, but so figuratively were the swine, who represent "men lacking speech and reason, given to filthy deeds, grazing on the mountain of pride. And unless a man lives thus like a pig, the devil receives no power over him, or rather, he receives power only to test him, not to destroy him." [28] The story of Mary Magdalene, certainly one of the most popular saints in the Middle Ages, teaches a similar lesson. The seven devils cast out of her by Christ represent "seven synnes mortale / Whilk out of hire voided penaunce and contricionne." [29] With such precedents, it is hardly sur-

27. Woodburn O. Ross, ed., *Middle English Sermons edited from B.M. MS Royal 18 B. xxiii*, EETS, os 209 (1940), p. 97.

28. PL 114:275. *The Ayenbite of Inwyt*, Dan Michel's translation (ca. 1340) of the *Somme des Vices et Vertues*, gives a similar interpretation of the swine as gluttons possessed as a punishment; ed. Richard Morris, re-ed. Pamela Gradon, EETS, os 23 (1965), p. 50.

29. *Miroure of Mans Saluacionne*, p. 53.

prising that possession usually signifies wickedness curable
only by exorcism, faith, and the good life.

Another factor contributing to the equation of possession
with sin may be the iconographical habit of representing sinners and possessed madmen in the same fashion. Possession
is usually indicated by a devil riding the possessed person,
hovering over his head, or entering his mouth; while the
cure is shown by the demon's issuing from the patient's
mouth (see plates 1 and 2, showing the possession of Saul
and the miracle of the Gadarene swine). But this iconography
was used not only for clear cases of possession; it was also
adapted to signify that someone was so evil that he might
well be possessed or that a given action was so mad that it
must have been inspired by the devil. Thus Herod ordering
the Slaughter of the Innocents is often depicted as possessed
(see plate 3), as are figures representing the sins of Luxury
(plate 4) and Avarice (plate 5).[30] Similarly the cure of sin
by confession may be related iconographically to the exorcism
of demons from a madman, as in a misericord in New College,
Oxford (plate 6). The fact that the same pictorial device was
used to indicate both sin and madness must have strengthened the traditional association of the two concepts; it is
possible, for example, that the presence of a demon in pictures
of Herod may have led some medieval dramatists to depict
Herod as mad. In any case, artistic tradition presumably bol-

30. Similar iconography is used to portray the murderers of Thomas
Becket (Norwich Cathedral, Cloister Boss no. 108 [National Monuments
Record numbering]); Adam and Eve eating the apple (British Museum
MS Royal 2 B. vii, fol. 3v); Herod and Herodias at the murder of John
the Baptist (Norwich Cathedral, Cloister Boss no. 100); and the Jewish
High Priests (see Oscar G. Farmer, *Fairford Church and Its Stained Glass
Windows*, 8th ed. [Bath: Harding and Curtis, 1965], pp. 35–39).

The comparison of sins to possessing devils is extremely common in literature; e.g. in *Wisdom*, ll. 909–10, we are told that every sinner has devils,
representing deadly sins, in his soul (Mark Eccles, ed., *The Macro Plays*,
EETS, os 262 [1969]); and a story in the *Gesta Romanorum*, ed. S. J.
Herrtage, EETS, es 33 (1879), p. 425, notes that there are seven devils —
the sins — blocking penitence in each man. The point of such stories is
that by sin one gives oneself over to the devil; to the extent that one sins,
one is indeed possessed.

stered the popularity of possession as a cause of madness quite clearly related to sin.

Not surprisingly, stories of possession are found most frequently in didactic contexts, where they are used to warn against sin: the devil will drive you mad if you don't watch out. Thus Gregory the Great tells of an old monk who stole some money while buying provisions for his monastery. When he returned, he was seized by an evil spirit; after the spirit had departed, his brothers, suspicious of the cause of his madness, asked whether he had perhaps stolen some money. He denied it vehemently, and the devil returned immediately. After going through the same cure-lie-possession sequence eight times, "he did penance, prostrated himself, admitted his sin and the evil spirit returned no more." [31] Perhaps the best story of devil-induced madness, if not actually of possession, is told by the Knight of La Tour-Landry, writing to instruct his daughters in good conduct. There was a lady who took so long dressing on Sundays that she continually delayed mass. One day, "in stede of the mirrour, the devell turned to her his ars, the whiche was so foule and orible that for ferde she was wode and oute of her mynde, and was so sike longe; and atte the laste God sent her her witte; & she was chastised, and wolde no more make folke to mouse [wait] after her, but wolde be sonner arraied and atte the Chirche thanne ani other." [32]

In concluding this brief discussion of possession as a cause of madness, I should like to stress that possession was almost always associated with sin in that the devil seldom could have power over a man unless he had consented to it in some way, usually by sinning. Those who are possessed are sinners, and by a curious expansion of the association, those who are sinners are possessed by the devil in one of three senses: a demon is in them and governing them; or they follow demonic promptings so thoroughly that they might as well be physically possessed; or by their evil actions they have given themselves

<hr />

31. *Epistles* 11. 44; cited in Oesterreich, *Possession*, p. 162.

32. *Book of the Knight of La Tour-Landry*, p. 45. Comparison with the friar in Chaucer's *Summoner's Prologue* is inevitable; see *CT* 3. 1704–05.

over to the devil in eternity, and this eventual punishment is signified by earthly possession. Saul illustrates possession in its strict sense; Herod, possession in its more general sense; and Adam and Eve, in the act of sin, possession in the last sense mentioned.[33]

33. A sermon hints at the possession of Adam and Eve: the blind, deaf, and dumb demoniac of Luke 11:14 "betokeneþ all mankeend þat com of Adam and Eve. Man was fulfilled of þe fend when þat he forsoke God and become þe feendes man"; *Middle English Sermons*, p. 146.

In this chapter the major concern is with those forms of madness and possession that carry clear religious and moral implications. But more secular forms of madness are worth mentioning briefly, for they figure occasionally in romances and legends and are related to religious varieties of possession in that the creatures who cause madness — fairies, elves, and other supernatural beings — were often incorporated into the Christian system as demons.

The Old English word *ilfig* ("mad, frantic") suggests that elves were thought to possess or madden people, and there is some evidence that satyrs, fauns, lamias, and other forest dwellers caused insanity in their beholders: see *CG* 15.23 (2:107); Bartholomeus 5. 2; M. D. Anderson, *The Medieval Carver* (Cambridge: Cambridge University Press, 1935), p. 100; Richard Bernheimer, *Wild Men in the Middle Ages: A Study in Art, Sentiment, and Demonology* (Cambridge: Harvard University Press, 1952), passim; Bonser, *Medical Background*, pp. 159 and 163; and Zilboorg and Henry, *History of Medical Psychology*, pp. 106ff. A representative case concerns Meilerius of Caerleon, who one day tried to make love to a beautiful young girl in the forest. As soon as he embraced her, she turned into "so shaggy, hairy, and rough a creature, so terribly deformed, that simply by looking at it he lost his mind and went mad" (Giraldus Cambrensis, *Itinerarium Cambriae*, in *Opera*, ed. James Dimock, Rolls Series, no. 21 [London, 1868], 6:57). Presumably this lady was a female counterpart of the incubus who seduced Merlin's and Sir Gowther's mothers. Another way to lose one's mind in the forest — perhaps through the agency of fairies — was to sleep under certain trees, particularly the ash or the elder: see Alexander Porteous, *Forest Folklore, Mythology, and Romance* (London: Allen and Unwin, 1928), pp. 85–86. On the association of the elder with witches and fairies, see Robert Graves, *The White Goddess: A Historical Grammar of Poetic Myth*, amended and enlarged ed. (New York: Noonday Press, 1969), p. 185.

Still another form of possession may be found in berserks and perhaps even in the many English romance heroes who fight madly in battle. "Wodan," or Odin, may possess such people so that they fight "wodely": see H. R. Ellis Davidson, *Gods and Myths of Northern Europe* (Harmonds-

Natural as opposed to supernatural causes of madness are less obviously related to the sick man's moral condition, but here too there is often a connection between sin and punishment. At first sight it might seem that there is no human fault in cases of astrologically induced madness: Is the individual responsible for the fact that certain planets correspond to the humours, so that Saturn might physiologically stimulate melancholy madness, while Mars could increase choler and produce frenzy and the madness of anger or war? Should a man be able to control the moon, which rules all bodily fluids — humours, spirits, the brain, the eye—and which induces madness by manipulating humours, passions, and illusions? [34] For the Middle Ages the answer was usually yes, even

---

worth: Penquin, 1964), pp. 66–69; and Bonser, *Medical Background*, pp. 127–28. The berserks' madness often has bad moral connotations; see Christopher Tolkien, ed., *Saga of King Heidrik the Wise* (London: Thomas Nelson, 1960), pp. 5–7, where the twelve berserks are called "inglorious." But there seems to be no such condemnation of English heroes who fight "wodely," even in so extreme and unfortunate a case as that of Gawain in the alliterative *Morte Arthure*, ed. Edmund Brock, 2d ed., EETS, os 8 (1871), ll. 3724–863.

Belief in the power of lamias, fairies, and such creatures to drive men mad was often condemned as superstition by the Church: thus the *Corrector and Physician* (ca. 1010), a penitential handbook by Burchard of Worms, forbids belief in "women of the wilds, called 'the sylvan ones,' who . . . when they wish show themselves to their lovers, and, they say, have taken delight with these, and then when they wish they depart and vanish"; *Medieval Handbooks of Penance*, p. 338. Robert of Brunne's *Handlyng Synne* (ed. F. J. Furnivall, EETS os 119, 123 [1901, 1903], ll. 479ff.) and Mirk's *Instructions to Parish Priests* (ed. Edward Peacock, rev. F. J. Furnivall, EETS, os 31 [1902], ll. 360ff.) forbid belief in witchcraft. Other penitentials forbid belief in maddening love potions and in women's power to take away men's minds by manipulating the moon, but apparently such beliefs persisted; even the Church occasionally adopted such folk superstitions as that "mathematici," or wizards, could drive men mad by summoning spirits to possess them; *Medieval Handbooks of Penance*, app. 1 and p. 277.

34. For planetary associations of the humours, see Roger Bacon, *Opus Majus*, ed. John Henry Bridges, 2 vols. (Oxford, 1897), 1:377–78, and *Saturn and Melancholy*, pp. 127–29. For the moon's powers, see Bartholomeus 5. 3 and 8. 18.

here a man may be responsible for his madness: although
the planets cannot work directly on the incorporeal soul, nonetheless they may lead a man into sin and madness by working
through the body, the imagination, the sensitive appetite, the
passions, and so forth. And if they do, it is the man's own
fault. As Aquinas puts it,

> . . . there is no reason why man should not be prone to
> anger or concupiscence, or some like passion, by reason
> of the influence of heavenly bodies, just as by reason of
> his natural temperament. Now the majority of men are
> led by the passions, which the wise alone resist. Conse-
> quently, in the majority of cases predictions about human
> acts, gathered from the observation of the heavenly bodies,
> are fulfilled. Nevertheless, as Ptolemy says, *the wise man
> governs the stars,* as though to say that by resisting his
> passions, he opposes his will, which is free and in no
> way subject to the movement of the heavens, to such
> effects of the heavenly bodies.[35]

Lunacy, then, often carries with it the moral condemnation
of the lunatic as a weak and passionate man; the lunatic boy
of the Gospels, far from being a victim of misfortune, symbolizes "those people who change like the moon, never stay-
ing in the same condition but waxing and waning through
various vices." [36]

The seasons too might predispose a man to madness. Since
each humour is increased in its season, spring tends to produce love-madness; summer, choleric madness; and autumn,
melancholy madness and despair. Thomas Hoccleve could,
like his friends, blame his madness on summer heat and
autumn weather, but he shuns that easy and irresponsible
explanation.[37] A man need not succumb to seasonal madness

35. *ST* 1–2. Q. 9, A. 5 (2:257).
36. *Glossa ordinaria, PL* 114:282.
37. See *Complaint,* ll. 2, 21, and 92ff., in *Hoccleve's Works: The Minor
Poems,* ed. Frederick J. Furnivall and I. Gollancz, rev. Jerome Mitchell
and A. I. Doyle, EETS es 61, 73 (1892, 1925; reprinted in one vol., 1970).

any more than to astrological madness, for he can rule his will and control his diet to rid himself of excess humours. Here again, a potentially neutral form of madness carries implicit moral condemnation of the madman; just as he could conquer sin and passion, so he could overcome the stars and seasons if he chose. Such environmental causes of madness may not always be guided by God's hand as a punishment for sin, but even when they are not, they gain power over a man thanks to his sin of omission in failing to control his passions by reason.

As the immediate cause of madness becomes more subject to man's control, the cause-and-effect relationship of sin to madness becomes more scientifically explicable and less supernatural. In the case of the boy baptizing children with mud, his sin justified his punishment but did not directly cause it — God was the immediate cause. But in madness caused by food and drink, for instance, the sin that *justifies* the punishment is often its immediate *physiological* cause as well, and the intricate interrelationship of morality, psychology, and physiology is clear. Gluttony is a sin, and it leads directly to punishment because, as Chaucer notes, "thurgh the grete habundaunce of his mete, the humours in his body been distempred" (*CT* 10. 825). Too much melancholy food might produce melancholy madness, while hot foods stimulate choleric madness and produce those dangerous adust or burnt humours. Alternatively, as Bartholomeus explains, excessively moist food and drink can stifle digestion and create "malycyous smoke" that "dystourblyth the substaunce & the vse of reason" (4. 5). Undue fasting, oddly enough, is also a cause of madness in that it dries the body and stimulates the imagination, causing hallucinations (Bartholomeus 4. 5). And, lest we assume that in these cases madness will afflict holy men, the *Alphabet of Tales* (26) demonstrates that fasting-madness comes from pride. The devil tempted a monk to eat only half a loaf of bread each day, and the monk succumbed. He grew weak, "and þer fell a swyngyllyng [ringing] in his hede þat he wex fonde with, & mad as a guse; & so he contynued vnto he deyid." Such stories are rare, however, and far more attention is paid

to gluttony and especially to drinking as causes of madness.
For most writers, drunkenness was simply a brief form of madness, as Chaucer's Pardoner explains:

Senec seith a good word doutelees;
He seith he kan no difference fynde
Bitwix a man that is out of his mynde
And a man which that is dronkelewe,
But that woodnesse [madness], yfallen in a shrewe [wicked
    person],
Persevereth lenger than doth dronkenesse.

[CT 6. 492–97]

But drunkenness, although it has the same physiological effects
as overeating, is even worse morally: not only is it gluttony,
but it is also the predictable and voluntary denial of reason,
the image of God. As the Parson notes, drunkenness "is the
horrible sepulture of mannes resoun; and therfore, whan a
man is dronken, he hath lost his resoun; and this is deedly
synne" (CT 10. 821). The madness of drink is not only the
punishment of sin but also another form of sin itself. It is
hardly surprising that the tavern is often presented as both
the devil's temple and bedlam, where sin, deformity, and madness are created and dwell:

At cherche kan god his uirtues sseawy [show] and do his
miracles; þe blinde to liȝte; þe crokede to riȝte; yelde þe
wyttes of þe wode [mad]; þe speche to þe dombe; þe
hierþe [hearing] to þe dyaue. Ac [but] þe dyeuel deþ al
ayenward [the contrary] ine þe taverne, vor huanne þe
glotoun geþ in to þe tauerne, ha geþ opriȝt; huanne he
comþ a-yen, he ne heþ uot [foot] þat him moȝe sostenyi
ne bere. Huanne he þerin geþ, he y-zycþ [sees] and y-herþ
and specþ wel and onderstant; huan he comþ ayen, he heþ
al þis uorlore [lost] ase þe ilke þet ne heþ wyt ne scele
[reason] ne onderstondinge.[38]

38. *Ayenbite of Inwyt*, p. 56.

Sin thus leads to the brief madness of drunkenness, just as habitual sin may bring on more permanent madness; and sin, in that it involves the denial or perversion of reason, is madness in a very real sense.

There are other more important physiological and psychological causes of madness, however, and in discussing these it is important to remember not only the intimate connections between body and soul but also the fact that all disorder and rebellion of body and corporeal mind (imagination, particular reason, memory, appetite, passions) derive from Original Sin; consequently, mental and spiritual diseases instigated by this rebellion are ultimately the punishment of sin. In dealing with some of the physiological and psychological causes of madness, I should like first to summarize Bartholomeus's findings: the scientific theory he presents was common knowledge in the late Middle Ages, and his discussion of the causes and characteristics of various forms of madness can often contribute to an understanding of literary madmen.

Bartholomeus reports that corrupt or adust humours, along with excesses of natural humours, are especially important causes of madness. Corrupt blood stops up passages of the body and brain and produces frenzy: this is proved by the fact that dogs who eat menstrual blood will go mad (4. 8). Corrupt phlegm stops up the brain and leads to senility, a relatively minor form of madness (4. 9). Unnatural choler produces wrath-madness and "wakynge, chaungynge of mynde, ferdful syȝtes in slepe . . . & fyry smoke that chaungyth the brayne & the vertue ymaginatyf" (4. 10). But corrupt melancholy is worst of all, and Bartholomeus's description of its effects is worth citing at length:

> þe pacient is feynt, ferdful in herte without cause. . . .
> And soo yf we aske of suche why they fere & wherfore they
> ben sory, they haue noon answere. Some wene that they
> sholde deye anone vnresonably; some drede enmyte of
> some woo; some loue & desyre deth. . . .
>   He dremyth dredful dremes of derknesse and ferdfull

to se, & of stynkynge sauoure and smelle. Of all thise comen passio malencolia.

Also it comyth in a madnes & of dysposycion of malencolye whan suche hath lykynge and laughe alwaye of sorowfull thynges, and make sorowe & dolour for Ioyefull thynges.

Also suche holden theyr peas whan they sholde speke and speke tomoche whan they shold be styll. Also some trowe that they ben erthyn vesselles and drede to be towched leest they breke. And some wene they close & conteyne the worlde in theyr hondes & alle thynge in theyr delynge, & therfore they put not theyr hondes to take mete: they drede the worlde sholde falle & be loste yf they streyghte out theyr hondes. . . .

Also some wene that they haue noo heedes, and some that [they] haue leden heedes or asse heedes, or some other euyll shapen faccion.

And yf they here cockes crowe, they rere vp theyr hondes & armes & wene that theymself ben cockes, and at the last thei ben hoors for grete cryeng & dompe also.

Also some fall in to full euyll suspeccions without recouer & therfore they hate & blame theyr frendes, and somtyme smite & slee theim.

Malencoly men fall into thyse & many other wonderful passyons . . . the whyche passyons it were to longe to rekene all. And thus we se all daye as it felle late of a nobleman that felle in to suche a madnes of malencolye that he in all wyse trowed that he was a catte. And therfore he wolde noo where reste but vnder beddes, there cattes wayted after myse.

More ouer in punishment of synne, Nabugodonosor was punysshed wyth suche a payne, as it is wryten in storyes, that .vii. yeres hym semyd that he was a beest thrugh dyuers shappes lyke a lyon, an egle, & other. [4. 11]

Although such madness is ostensibly physiological in origin, it is worth remembering that excess humours could be prevented by proper diet and phlebotomy, while corrupt humours, usually formed by the heat of passion, might be prevented by virtuous conduct. Humour-induced madness, then, could be considered as a consequence of sin, a possibility that Bartholomeus explicitly acknowledges in mentioning Nebuchadnezzar. And, as discussions of Herod, Ywain, and Hoccleve will show, choleric and melancholy madness often carry explicit moral condemnation of the madman.

Bartholomeus's specific discussion of the causes and cures of major forms of madness continues to associate sin with madness even as he gives most of his attention to the primarily physical causes and manifestations of insanity. Thus he identifies frenzy with the biblical "madness and fury of mind" (Deut. 28:28) with which God strikes the disobedient (7. 5). Then, having established the moral justification for the disease, he proceeds to discuss frenzy in purely physiological and psychological terms (we shall see later that treatments of Herod's madness often follow the same course). For Bartholomeus, there are two kinds of frenzy: true frenzy is an infection of the brain caused by a great excess of choler, while perafrenzy is a similar infection caused by "fumosyte & smoke" (presumably the result of overeating or of adust humours). Choleric frenzy is most likely to begin in the heat of summer, while perafrenzy may appear at any time, bringing with it a high fever, black skin, dryness, pain, fainting, and the evaporation of the spirits. Most of these symptoms are common to choleric frenzy as well as to perafrenzy, so the two diseases are rather hard to distinguish; but true frenzy involves greater infection of the brain and seems to have a wider range of symptoms, including these:

> Dyscolouryd vryne durynge the feuer, wyth woodnes and contynuall wakynge; meuynge and castynge abowte the eyen; Ragynge, stretchynge, and castynge of hondes; meuynge & waggynge of heed; gryndynge & knockynge togyders of teeth. Alwaye he wol aryse of his bedde; now he syngeth, now he laughyth; now he wepith, and bytith gladly and rentyth his warden and his leche [physician]. Selde is he stylle but he cryeth moche. This hath moost

peryllous sykenesse but he knoweth not that he is seke.
[7. 5]

Perafrenzy may easily be cured by a moderate diet and the
calming of the passions, but true frenzy requires that the
madman be kept in darkness as well: "Dyuerse shapes of faces
and semblaunt of payntynge shall not be shewed tofore hym,
leest he be encombryd wyth woodnesse. All that ben abowte
hym shall be commaundyd to by styll and in scylence: men
shall not answere to his nyce wordes." Phlebotomy and head
plasters are useful, but unless there is immediate improvement,
the prognosis is bad. Continual indulgence in passion and
anger is not an easy habit to break, and the frenzied man, even
if cured, is likely to bring his disease upon himself again.

Bartholomeus next discusses two diseases under the general name *amentia:* melancholia ("infeccion of the mydyll
celle of the hede with pryuacion of reason") and inania (infection of the imagination).[39] These diseases share somewhat
varied causes, many of which are clearly under individual
control.

> Thyse passyons come somtyme of malencoly meetes, &
> somtyme of drynke of stronge wyne that brenneth the
> humours & torneth theym into asshes; somtyme of pass-
> yons of the soule, as of besynes & grete thouȝtes, of sorowe
> & of to grete studye & of drede; somtyme of the bytynge
> of a wood hounde, other of some other venemous beest;
> somtyme of corrupte & pestylence ayre that is Infecte;
> somtyme of malyce of corrupt humour that hath the
> maystry in the body. [7. 6]

The symptoms are similar to those of frenzy, and suggested
cures include psychological and physiological components.

---

39. Traditionally, various sorts of madness were associated with injury
to various parts of the brain: mania was usually linked with the imagination, melancholia with the particular reason, and lethargy with memory;
but medical opinion varies widely in this as in other matters. See Alexander
and Selesnick, *History of Psychiatry*, p. 60; Isidore of Seville, *Etymologiarum
sive originum libri XX*, ed. W. M. Lindsay, 2 vols. (Oxford: Clarendon
Press, 1957), 4. 7. 5; and *Saturn and Melancholy*, pp. 92–93.

Some cryen, and lepe and hurte and wounde theymselfe
and other men, and derken & hyde themself in preuy and
secrete places. . . .
The medycynes of theym is that he be bounde that
he ne hurte not hymself and other men. And namely
suche shal be refresshyd and comfortyd, and wythdrawe
from cause of matere of besy thoughtes, and he shall
be gladded wyth Instrumentes of Musyk, and somdeale
be ocupyed. And atte the laste yf purgacions and electu-
aryes suffysen not, he shall be holpe wyth crafte of
Syrurgery. [7. 6]

The last varieties of madness Bartholomeus discusses are
stupor and lethargy, which he interprets as the punitive blindness of Deut. 28:28. Stupor is blindness of reason, while
lethargy is an aggravated form of stupor involving the infection of the memory with phlegm. The symptoms are essentially those of senility, and the proposed cures are rather
drastic: "that the seke man be layed in a lyght place and that
there be talkyng & grete spekyng & disputacion. And that he
be draw & halyd strongly by the heere of his berde & of his
heed . . . and that stynkynge thynge smokynge be put to the
nether parties, as guttes, horne brente, and such other" (7. 7).
Thus the three major types of madness — frenzy, amentia,
and stupor — are associated with excesses of three humours:
choler, melancholy, and phlegm. Each type may be associated
with sin, Original or actual, and the etiology of each is somewhat distinctive: frenzy comes from too much passion and
from overeating; amentia from adust melancholy and from
such passions as anxiety, fear, and grief; stupor from the
coldness of age or from drinking so much that the body's
natural heat is quenched (usually excess of drink increases
heat). Frenzy is characterized by raving and by swift emo-
tional changes, amentia by violence and fear, and stupor by
lack of responsiveness. In that frenzy and amentia are by far
the more colorful diseases, it is natural that they should be the
most common varieties of madness in literature. And the
fact that they are associated with punitive disease even in a

medical discussion bears witness to their strong moral connotations.

Although both medicine and literature accept the multiple
causation of disease — sin produces physiological alteration
which then produces madness — medicine tends to stress the
immediate physiological cause, as we have seen with Bartholomeus, while literature often stresses the initial moral
cause. Thus, in dealing with naturally caused madness, literature usually emphasizes the passions — which are sinful to the
extent that they are inordinate and voluntary[40] — rather than
the exact physiological changes they initiate. Burton is typical
of earlier writers in finding that passion leads to sin and
thence to madness, both literal and figurative: "All men are
carried away with passion, discontent, lust, pleasures, &c.; they
generally hate those virtues they should love, and love such
vices they should hate. Therefore more than melancholy, quite
mad, brute beasts, and void of reason (AM, p. 61). Although
all passions that conquer reason entail a brief fit of madness
lasting as long as the passion, several passions were thought
to lead to madness as their characteristic disease and punishment.

Such a passion is wrath, which is both a short form of madness and, if it is habitual, a cause of more lasting insanity like
that which periodically tortured the irate Saul. As the *Speculum Christiani* notes, anger is "pure wodneȝ or madnes,"
while the *Ayenbite of Inwyt* condemns the sin of ire because
it "makeþ þane man al oute of wytte zuo þet he no þing ne
yziȝþ, ne uor him, ne uor oþren, to lede." [41] This last comment on the inability of an angry man to lead anyone is particularly appropriate, for in much medieval literature it is
precisely the political leader, the proud king, who is prey
to both temporary and permanent forms of anger-madness.[42]

40. See *ST* 1–2. Q. 59, A. 2–3; and 1–2. Q. 77, A. 6–7 (2:450–53 and
639–42).

41. Gustaf Holmstedt, ed., *Speculum Christiani* (fourteenth century),
EETS, os 182 (1933), p. 62; and *Ayenbite of Inwyt*, p. 150.

42. Temporary anger-madness is especially common in romances: see,
for instance, the emperor's behavior in W. W. Skeat, ed., *William of Pa-*

This sort of madness — and it must be stressed that habitual anger *is* madness; it is not simply *like* madness — will be discussed further in relation to Herod in chapter 3.

Another group of related passions that often produce madness, as Bartholomeus notes, is fear, accidie, and grief. Sometimes the melancholy madness produced by fear is relatively brief and even beneficial, as with the woman terrified into madness and eventual reform by the devil in her mirror. But other sorts of fear and anxiety lead to destructive, long-term disease. Certain modes of life were considered particularly dangerous: the influential Roman physician Caelius Aurelianus warns against study, while Rufus of Ephesus condemns a life of reflection (*cogitatio*) and sadness. Constantinus Africanus (d. 1087), one of the most important medieval writers on madness, even provides a list of people in circumstances likely to produce excessive grief and hence madness: they are students "grieving over the failure of their minds, . . . those who lose their beloved possessions . . . or some precious things which cannot be restored," and the religious, who "incur this complaint and become drunk as it were with their excessive anxiety and vanity." [43] Cassian explains more fully the sort of melancholy madness or accidie that besets religious people: "It is akin to dejection and especially felt by wandering monks and solitaries, a persistent and obnoxious enemy to such as dwell in the desert, disturbing the monk especially about midday, like a fever mounting at a regular time. . . . And so some of the Fathers declare it to be the demon of

---

lerne, EETS, es 1 (1867), ll. 1974–76; and Athelstan's fury in *Athelstan,* ed. A. M. Trounce, EETS, os 224 (1951), ll. 453–55. Such temporary insanity often tends to add excitement and vividness to the narrative rather than to contribute to the major themes of the works or even to characterization.

43. For Caelius see *On Acute Diseases and on Chronic Diseases,* ed. and trans. I. E. Drabkin (Chicago: University of Chicago Press, 1950), p. 537; for Rufus see *Saturn and Melancholy,* p. 50; and for Constantinus see Thorndike, *History of Experimental Science,* 1:752. Chaucer may have had these statements in mind in the *House of Fame,* ll. 29–35, where he lists the possible causes of horrible dreams as study, melancholy fears, and contemplation.

noontide which is spoken of in the XCth Psalm. . . . One's mind is in an irrational confusion, like the earth befogged in a mist." [44] Such accidie, according to Cassian, grows into the greater madness of despair unless quietness of mind and pleasant labors banish it; and Hoccleve seems to follow a similar prescription when he turns to the business of writing to distract him from his own melancholy despair.

There is a second kind of grief-madness, suggested in Constantinus's second category of melancholics: the madness of loss, most often found when a beloved person has died or been untrue. It is this madness that Lancelot suffers when Guinevere finds him with Elaine, that Ywain suffers when Alundyne's ring is taken back, that Troilus suffers when Criseyde leaves. Such examples might be multiplied many times over: the *Motif-Index of the English Metrical Romances* lists numerous cases of grief leading to madness, with such symptoms as tearing the hair and face, beating one's head against a wall, swooning, and suicide.[45] As for the morality of such grief-madness, from a religious point of view it is questionable: as the Penitential of Saint Hubert (ca. 850) notes in regard to mourning, "If anyone lacerates himself over his dead with a sword or his nails, or pulls his hair, or rends his garments, he shall do penance for forty days." [46] Although literary judgments are seldom so harsh, we must still be aware of the possibility of moral fault in characters temporarily mad through grief such as Heurodis in *Sir Orfeo*, the Dreamer in *Pearl*, or Melibee, who, hearing of the injury to his wife and daughter, "lyk a mad man, rentynge his clothes, gan to wepe and crye" (*CT* 7. 973).

---

44. *Of Accidie*, in *The Desert Fathers*, trans. Helen Waddell (London: Constable, 1936), pp. 229–30. On accidie, see also Siegfried Wenzel, *The Sin of Sloth: Acedia in Medieval Thought and Literature* (Chapel Hill: University of North Carolina Press, 1967).

45. Gerald Bordman, FF Communications, no. 190 (Helsinki, 1963), F 1041. 21ff.

46. *Medieval Handbooks of Penance*, p. 294.

THE SYMPTOMS OF MADNESS

As the various causes of madness generally carry moral connotations that brand the madman as a sinner responsible for his own disease, so too the usual symptoms (most of which should be evident from examples given so far) often point to moral fault in at least two ways. First, the actions of many madmen — running about aimlessly, crying out, hiding under beds, tearing at one's garments, inappropriate singing and laughing, and so on — are grotesque, mechanical, absurd; as such, they naturally indicate a certain deformity of soul, a lack of the image of God, that is associated with moral depravity. Second, literary madmen suffer from a sort of guilt by association: the symptoms of literary madmen, which are astonishingly consistent throughout history, seem to be based primarily on accounts of biblical madmen — Saul, the demoniacs of the New Testament, Nebuchadnezzar — all of whom were thought to be notorious sinners in the throes of their punishment. Thus many symptoms commonly associated with madness may have been immediately, though presumably not ultimately, derived from literature rather than from direct observation. Perhaps this is one instance when literature influences perception: if literary tradition clearly defines certain standard symptoms of insanity, then a man will assume that anyone exhibiting those symptoms is mad, and a writer describing madness will tend to notice and mention only those symptoms traditionally associated with insanity. The point will become important later in discussions of Charles VI and of Thomas Hoccleve, but for the moment it is necessary to realize only that people with symptoms of madness will normally seem wicked, and wicked people in literature may well acquire some of the standard trappings of madness.[47]

47. Sometimes, of course, appearances are misleading, and there are some cases where madness does not imply moral fault at all. As Saint Paul noted, "If any man among you seem to be wise in this world, let him become a fool, that he may be wise. For the wisdom of this world is foolishness with God" (1 Cor. 3:18–19). Saints may seem mad to the world, for, as Aquinas comments, "The more our mind is raised to the contemplation of spiritual

At this point I should like to consider briefly some of these standard symptoms both in their biblical setting and in a few later examples. The miracle of the Gadarene swine quoted earlier includes the elements of running, living in the wilderness, violence, crying out, self-destructiveness, and nakedness. Additional common symptoms occur in the miracle of the dumb and lunatic boy, who is mute, falls down, foams at the mouth, grinds his teeth, faints, cries out, and mutilates him-

---

things, the more it is withdrawn from sensible things" (*Summa Contra Gentiles* 3. 47 [2:82]). Similarly, "A man may be virtuous without having full use of reason as to everything, provided he have it with regard to those things which have to be done virtuously. . . . Hence even those who seem to be simple, through lack of worldly shrewdness, can be prudent" (*ST* 1–2. Q. 58, A. 4 [2:446]). What society deems madness may be sanity to God, for in relation to the love of God man's will should dominate his reason (*ST* 1. Q. 82, A. 3 [1:781]).

Very holy people may also be mad in a more literal sense when they are in a state of ecstasy. Thus true prophets may be mad when prophesying, but they can be distinguished from victims of demonic possession by the fact that true prophets, like Daniel, have control over the onset of their prophetic trance; see Albert the Great, *Commentaria in librum Danielis*, in *Opera omnia*, ed. Augustus Borgnet (Paris, 1893), 18:512. Those saints graced with the sight of God are also mad in a blessed way, for, as Caesarius of Heisterbach claims, "When the mind reaches God in contemplation, the rational sense fails"; *The Dialogue on Miracles*, trans. H. von E. Scott and C. C. Swinton Bland, 2 vols. (London: Routledge, 1929), 8. 4 (2:5). Jacques de Vitry describes "devote wommen, þat was so hugelie ravissid with thoght of holy liffyng, þat of all þe day þer was no witt in þaim vnto none oute-ward thyng . . ." (*AT* 670); and Margery Kempe claims that what seemed to others to be fits of madness were in fact divine visions; Sanford Brown Meech and Hope Emily Allen, eds., *The Book of Margery Kempe*, EETS, os 212 (1940), pp. 68–70. Henry VI of England was also accused of madness thanks to his occasional fits when he was totally unconscious of himself and his surroundings. But for Henry and his biographer John Blacman, these fits were actually visions of Christ, Mary, and John the Baptist; thus the king was not constitutionally insane but "a man in a trance or on the verge of heaven; having his conversation in heaven"; *Henry the Sixth: A Reprint of John Blacman's Memoir*, ed. and trans. M. R. James (Cambridge: Cambridge University Press, 1919), pp. 38 and 43. Thus the visionary may be mad in a sense, but his madness signals sanctity rather than guilt.

self (Mark 9:16–17; Luke 9:39). Such symptoms — and others associated with Nebuchadnezzar, to be discussed in the next chapter — recur constantly in literary madmen, and examples abound in this study. Let me give only two here. One, from the *Alphabet of Tales* (36) deals with an adulterer punished by demonic possession in which he "skratt & bete hym selfe, & went in-to þe kurk, & þer he was so mad þat now he wold clymbe vp als hye as he myght, & sodanlie fall down agayn vnto þe erth, & þus he did ewhile he swelte [died] aforn all þe pepull." In the second example, Lydgate combines the madman's conventional speechlessness with his traditional violence and habitation in the wilderness to create a chilling picture of the coming of Doomsday:

> The tenthe day, from kavernys & ther kavys
>   Men shal come out, lyk folk that kan no good,
> And renne abrood lyk drounke men þat Ravys
>   Or as they weren frentyk, outhir wood,
>   Dedly pale, and devoyde of blood;
> Nat speke a woord Oon vnto anothir,
>   As witles peple of resoun and of mood [mind],
> No queyntaunce maad, brothir vnto brothir.[48]

Even if the context of these examples did not point to the sinfulness of the madmen, the symptoms themselves would be enough. The notorious mystic Margery Kempe should not have been surprised when people responded to her cryings and roarings as less than a token of sanctity: "For summe seyd it was a wikkyd spiryt vexid hir; sum seyd it was a sekenes; sum seyd sche had dronkyn to mech wyn." [49] Clearly, then, the symptoms of madness are dramatic and colorful, which may explain some of the popularity of madness in literature quite apart from considerations of madness as moral symbolism.

48. "The Fiftene Toknys Aforn the Doom," ll. 49–56, in *The Minor Poems: Part I*, ed. Henry Noble MacCracken, EETS, es 107 (1911), p. 119.
49. *The Book of Margery Kempe*, p. 69.

Madness and Responsibility

As we have seen, both the usual causes of madness and its typical symptoms generally imply that the sick man is morally at fault and thus responsible for his disease, whatever its precise etiology. At this point it is worth considering a further problem: granted that most madmen are responsible for their madness, to what extent are they responsible for acts committed while mad? If Herod is possessed by a demon when he orders the Slaughter of the Innocents, can he then be blamed for that deed? Generally the insane were not thought to be legally at fault for any crimes they committed,[50] but morally the issue is more complicated, in theory at least. According to the Church, men are responsible only for "human acts" — voluntary acts moved by the will and assented to by reason.[51] Or, from the point of view of sin, an act is sinful only when both will and reason err in pursuing something they should avoid or in loving temporal things more than God; mortal sin, in particular, demands that reason be capable of functioning freely but that it then be perverted, so that it knowingly and willfully makes the wrong choice.[52] Consequently, to determine if an act is sinful, we must determine if it is rational and voluntary. If it is wholly voluntary, it is sinful; if it is wholly involuntary and could not have been prevented by reasonable foresight, it is not sinful. But most sins, especially those involving passion, fall somewhere in between; man's reason is often somewhat befuddled by his desires.

Nevertheless, even a man quite overwhelmed with passion is responsible for acts committed in the heat of passion if

50. For an excellent discussion of both civil and canon law, see R. Colin Pickett, *Mental Affliction and Church Law* (Ottawa: University of Ottawa Press, 1952), pp. 1–70. Pickett considers the legal categories of insanity, the status of the insane with regard to the sacrments, etc. On legal treatment of the insane in England, see Talbot, *Medicine in Medieval England*, pp. 180–82.

51. Pickett, *Mental Affliction and Church Law*, pp. 3–7.

52. See *ST* 1–2. Q. 74 and 77 (2:601–16, 630–43).

that passion was initially voluntary. Aquinas draws an analogy to the state of drunkenness which is willingly entered into, so that a drunken man is responsible for the sins he commits when drunk even though he did not directly and voluntarily approve those particular acts. Similar reasoning applies to certain types of madness, as Aquinas explains:

> For a passion is sometimes so strong as to take away the use of reason altogether, as in the case of those who are mad through love or anger; and then, if such a passion is voluntary from the beginning, the act is reckoned a sin, because it is voluntary in its cause, as we have stated with regard to drunkenness. If, however, the cause be not voluntary but natural, for instance, if anyone through sickness or some such cause fall into such a passion as deprives him of the use of his reason, his act is rendered wholly involuntary, and he is entirely excused from sin. Sometimes, however, the passion is not such as to take away the use of reason altogether. In that case reason can drive the passion away by turning to other thoughts, or it can prevent it from having its full effect, since the members are not put to work except by the consent of reason. . . . Therefore such a passion does not excuse from sin altogether.[53]

A totally involuntary act (e.g. a murder committed by a man maddened by a blow on the head) is not sinful; a partly voluntary act (a murder committed by a man maddened by passion so strong it could have been resisted only with the greatest difficulty) is a sin, but its seriousness is somewhat diminished; and a technically voluntary act (a murder committed by a drunk) is completely sinful. Thus a man who is voluntarily mad is responsible for his actions, but a man who is involuntarily mad (a congenital fool or someone with an injured brain or a fever) is not responsible. The moral status of a man whose madness is in one sense involuntary (it is caused by a fever, say) but in another sense voluntary (the

53. *ST* 1–2. Q. 77, A. 7 (2:641).

fever is caused by sin) is dubious. However, the common notion that madness is a predictable consequence of sin and hence somewhat voluntary is found in early church law: the Council of Worms (868) decreed that a madman who killed someone and later regained his sanity should receive some punishment because the insanity was itself believed to be the result of his past sins. Nevertheless, the council recognized the principle of diminished responsibility for crimes committed while insane: the madman's penance should be lighter than that of someone who had committed murder while sane.[54] To some extent, then, even a completely mad man was responsible for his actions if his sin had caused his madness in the first place.

CURES FOR MADNESS

To the extent that disease is seen in moral terms as a punishment for sin or a test from God, the cure too usually has a moral component. It was widely believed that no purely physical cure would be effective unless the sin that originally caused the disease were forgiven. The actions of Christ as physician gave suitable precedent for this view: as the fourteenth-century English physician John Mirfeld explains, "The Lord, when about to cure the man sick of the palsy, first loosed from off him the bonds of his sins, saying unto him, 'Man, thy sins are forgiven thee,' in order that He might show him that it was due to the fetters of his iniquities that he was condemned to weakness of the joints, and that unless these were first unbound, he could not be made whole." [55] Consequently, the cure of any illness must involve

54. Canon 28, in *Sacrorum Consiliorum Nova et Amplissima Collectio* ed. Joannes Dominicus Mansi (Venice, 1770; facsimile reprint, Paris, Leipzig: H. Welter, 1902), 15:874; mentioned by Pickett, *Mental Affliction and Church Law*, p. 45. For the opinion that the madman is *not* responsible for his actions, see *Saturn and Melancholy*, p. 74, on William of Auvergne.

55. *Florarium*, in *Johannes de Mirfeld of St. Batholomew's Smithfield: His Life and Works*, ed. Percival Horton-Smith Hartley and Harold Richard Aldridge (Cambridge: University Press, 1936), p. 127. Mirfeld wrote two major works: the *Breviarium Bartholomei*, a medical text, and

spiritual treatment, and this requirement was formalized in canon law, as Mirfeld reports: "The physician, when called in to attend the sick, ought, before everything else, to warn them, and to persuade them at the outset to call in physicians of the soul, that is to say, Confessors; and then, when provision has been made for their spiritual health, he may lawfully proceed to apply his remedy to the body and make use of medicine." [56] Confession and penance are normal prerequisites for any cure, and if spiritual remedies are not applied, purely physical treatment has no chance of success.[57]

---

the *Florarium Bartholomei*, a theological treatise, one of whose chapters deals with medicine.

Church spokesmen often condemned the use of any but spiritual medicine, but in general the Church upheld the value of earthly medicine, relying heavily on Ecclus. 38:1–15, which reads in part, "Honour the physician for the need thou hast of him, for the most High hath created him. . . . Let him not depart from thee, for his works are necessary. . . . He that sinneth in the sight of his Maker, shall fall into the hands of the physician."

56. *Florarium*, in *Works*, p. 127. The provision of a confessor is not solely for the purpose of giving extreme unction, as is made clear by a similar passage in Comestor's *Historia scholastica*: "Because . . . it is established that when a man grows sick, it is sometimes on account of his sins, the physician visiting a sick man ought first to warn him to repent and confess, lest the poultice be applied in vain because of sin remaining like iron in a wound" (*PL* 198:1567).

57. In many cases both spiritual and physical treatments were presumably applied, since the Church was responsible for the care of the sick, including the insane. Contrary to widespread belief, the care of madmen seems often to have been quite considerate: see Talbot, *Medicine in Medieval England*, pp. 180–85; and Rotha Mary Clay, *The Medieval Hospitals of England* (London: Methuen, 1909), pp. 32–34. Of course, there were exceptions: madmen seem to have been permitted to wander without care, and some apparently lived like wild men in the forests; see Zilboorg and Henry, *History of Medical Psychology*, p. 141; Bernheimer, *Wild Men*, p. 12; and J. S. P. Tatlock, "Geoffrey of Monmouth's *Vita Merlini*," *Speculum* 18 (1943): 280. Michel Foucault notes that German madmen were sometimes banished from cities or put aboard real ships of fools to be carried out of the neighborhood or perhaps to pilgrimage shrines where their wits might be restored; *Madness and Civilization: A History of Insanity in the Age of Reason*, trans. Richard Howard (New York: Random House, Pantheon Books, 1965), pp. 8–9.

In treating cases of madness, of course, spiritual physicians
face one major problem: the madman is incapable of confession, and preliminary treatment is needed to bring him to his
senses so he can acknowledge his sin. But even though the
proper order of treatment — spiritual and then physical —
could not always be followed in such cases, there was a full
range of spiritual, psychological, and physiological cures, and
frequently we find all three sorts used in one case.[58] Moreover,
overtly physiological remedies often carried spiritual overtones just as with overtly physiological causes of disease.

Many physiological treatments are based on humoural theory: if the balance of humours is corrected, the disease should
disappear. Thus phlebotomy is often recommended for love-
madness in spring, for choleric madness in summer, and for
melancholy madness in autumn; Bartholomeus too enjoins
phlebotomy for frenzy and amentia (7. 5–6). Similarly, purgation — often by means of hellebore — is commonly prescribed,
and the diet might be restricted to reduce the quantity of
offending humours (Bartholomeus 7. 5–6). On the other
hand, a deficiency of blood might cause melancholy madness,
and a common but unattractive remedy in use throughout
the Middle Ages was that the madman drink fresh blood,
sometimes human.[59] Alternatively, Bartholomeus urges the

58. The physical and psychological treatment of insanity, as of other
diseases, is remarkably constant from Roman times through the Middle
Ages. Compare the recommendations of Caelius Aurelianus, *On Acute
Diseases* 1. 9 (pp. 39–43) and *On Chronic Diseases* 1. 5 (pp. 537–57), and
Celsus, *De medicina*, trans. W. G. Spencer, 3 vols., LCL (London, 1935),
3. 18 (3:295–301), to the suggestions of Bartholomeus (7. 5–7. 7) and Gilbertus Anglicus, cited in note 60. In fact, even religious remedies — exorcism, the use of relics, formulaic prayers — are often similar to Greek
and Roman practices; see Vaughan, *Madness*, pp. 14ff. and 41ff., and
Scarborough, *Roman Medicine*, pp. 18–23, 143–48, and passim.

59. See Celsus, *De medicina* 3. 23 (1:339), and David Riesman, *The Story
of Medicine in the Middle Ages*, corr. ed. (New York: P. B. Hoeber, 1936),
p. 327, who describes several cases in which human blood was fed to ailing
European royalty and even to a pope. Bartholomeus perhaps provides the
rationale for such a remedy in noting that animals eat blood to correct
their disposition and that lack of blood produces the unnatural fear associated with melancholy madness (4. 7).

physical stimulation of the head (7. 5, 7. 7), which would presumably produce a cure by increasing the local supply of blood. All these remedies, incidentally, can imply moral fault at the cause of disease: humoural imbalance often comes from gluttony, laziness, or excessive passion; and the correction of these sins removes the cause of illness and hence the effect.

Physical treatments were often assisted by psychological ones. Thus such influential physicians as Constantinus Africanus and Gilbertus Anglicus (fl. 1250) recommended a combination of fresh air, moderate diet, light wines, exercise, music, and rational discourse for the mad.[60] Reassurance and a sort of occupational therapy are often endorsed.

> Some need to have empty fears relieved, as was done for a wealthy man in dread of starvation, to whom pretended legacies were from time to time announced. . . . In some also untimely laughter has to be put a stop to by reproof and threats; in others, melancholy thoughts are to be dissipated, for which purpose music, cymbals, and noises are of use. More often, however, the patient is to be agreed with rather than opposed, and his mind slowly and imperceptibly is to be turned from irrational talk to something better. At times also his interest should be awakened; as may be done in the case of men fond of literature, to whom a book may be read, correctly when they are pleased by it, or incorrectly if that very thing annoys them; for by making corrections they begin to divert their mind. Moreover, they should be pressed to recite anything they can remember. . . . [The melancholic] should have it pointed out to him now and again how in the very things which trouble him there may be cause of rejoicing rather than of solicitude.[61]

60. For Constantinus, see *Saturn and Melancholy*, p. 85; for Gilbertus, see Talbot, *Medicine in Medieval England*, p. 77.

61. Celsus, *De medicina* 3. 18 (1:295 and 301). As we shall see later, Hoccleve seems to have followed the last suggestion in curing himself of his own melancholy.

Many of these proposed treatments seem to be based purely
on common sense, but others have moral connotations as well.
The suggestion that a man learn to rejoice in his affliction
echoes the Christian view of disease as purgation or test, as a
manifestation of grace leading to a sinner's improvement. And
the almost universal prescription of music as a cure for madness developed strong spiritual overtones in the Middle Ages:
because Saul's possession was cured by David's harping, music
was thought to be particularly efficacious in conquering the
devil and sin-induced diseases. Indeed, music came to symbolize Christ's commandments, the lyre signified the Cross and
its curative power, and the cure of the possessed by music
represented and involved the cure of the sinner through the
agency of Christ and the Church.[62]

As music is both a psychological and a spiritual cure of
madness, so two fairly common treatments — fasting and flogging — have both physiological and spiritual components. Medical historians, viewing such treatment from a purely scientific point of view, are appalled, much as future historians presumably will be at modern shock treatments; thus Benjamin
Lee Gordon notes that madmen were "brutally whipped,
starved, chained, and placed in a dungeon until brought under
control." [63] What is often ignored is that when such treatment
was used, it was intended to benefit rather than to punish the
sufferer. The use of restraint needs little justification: as
Bartholomeus notes, it is sometimes necessary for a frenzied
melancholic to "be bounde that he hurte not hymself and other
men" (7. 6). And most physicians cautioned that restraint,
which should be careful and harmless, ought to be used only
in cases of the utmost necessity, for it may often increase
frenzy.[64] The physiological benefits of fasting in certain cases

62. See, for example, *GO* 2:417–19, esp. the excerpt from Rabanus
Maurus.

63. *Medieval and Renaissance Medicine* (New York: Philosophical Library, 1959), p. 559.

64. See Caelius Aurelianus, *On Acute Diseases* 1. 9 (p. 43) and *On
Chronic Diseases* 1. 5 (p. 543); in discussing Nebuchadnezzar, we shall see
that Nicholas de Lyra knew that the binding of madmen often made them
worse.

of humour-induced madness should be obvious, and even flogging was thought useful to the patient: Hippocrates taught that physical pain alleviates mental disease, and Bartholomeus finds that harsh treatment of the body removes pain from the head and soothes frenzy (5. 1). Flogging might also exhaust a frantic man so that he would no longer be self-destructive.[65]

The spiritual benefits of fasting and flogging, of course, are at least as important. When Christ cast the demon out of the lunatic boy, he commented, "This kind can go out by nothing but by prayer and fasting" (Mark 9:28), and this was interpreted in the Middle Ages to mean that the possessed person as well as the exorcist would benefit from fasting. Moreover, both fasting and flagellation were common methods of doing penance; and, as we have seen, penance was often required as part of a cure. If the madman could not confess, he could at least go through the motions of penance; if we believe contemporary evidence, this course seems to have facilitated many cures.[66]

However, in many cases more overtly spiritual remedies, such as ritual exorcism and the intercession of saints, had to be undertaken. Throughout the Middle Ages exorcism seems

65. Hippocrates, *Aphorisms* 6. 21 and 7. 5, cited by Zilboorg and Henry, *History of Medical Psychology*, p. 47, and Celsus, *De medicina* 3. 18 (1:295). Caelius Aurelianus, on the other hand, disapproved of flogging; *On Chronic Diseases* 1. 5 (p. 557).

66. Two such cures are illustrated in the Trinity Chapel windows (ca. 1220) of Canterbury Cathedral. In one, the maniac Henry of Fordwich approaches the altar; he is dark in color, grinning, his robes are awry, and men beat him with rods. The legend reads, "The madman approaches." In the second panel, the rods lie on the ground, and the kneeling Henry is normal in color and sober in bearing; the legend reads, "He prays and departs healed." Another set of panels tells of the cure of Matilda of Cologne, a mad murderess. In the first panel, her eyes stare wildly, and her limbs are contorted as men beat her with rods. In the next panel, she falls by Becket's tomb as her attendants continue to beat her: "Now she stands gleefully, now she collapses and lies as if dying." In the final panel, she lies prostrate in thanksgiving for her recovered sanity. For references and fuller description, see Bernard Rackham, *The Ancient Glass of Canterbury Cathedral* (London: Lund Humphries for Friends of Canterbury Cathedral, 1949), pp. 90 and 98–99.

to have involved a prayer that the devil be cast out from
whatever was possessed — a house, the water for a trial by
ordeal, incense for the Easter vigil, and, of course, men.[67]
Elaborate forms of exorcism were codified in the Renaissance,
but medieval practice, which varied according to locality, was
probably close to that of the early Church and indeed of
Christ and the apostles. In a typical exorcism, the exorcist,
having prepared himself by fasting and prayer, would place
his hand on the possessed man, praying for him and calling on
the devil to come out in Christ's name.[68] Since demons were
likely to cause a fit upon hearing the Holy Name, the
exorcist might have to wrestle with the devil physically or
engage in a battle of wits and endurance, repeating prayers
and exorcisms many times before achieving success, as was the
case in an exorcism performed by Saint Norbert of Magde-
burg (d. 1134).[69] An attractive young girl harboring an extremely recalcitrant and learned devil was brought to Norbert

67. See s.v. "exorcism" in Rossell Hope Robbins, *Encyclopedia of Witch-
craft and Demonology* (New York: Crown Publishers, 1960); A. Jeffries
Collins, ed., *Manuale ad usum percelebris ecclesia sarisburiensis*, Henry
Bradshaw Society, vol. 91 (Chichester, 1960), p. 21; Karl Zevmer, ed.,
Formulae merowingici et karolini aevi, Monumenta Germaniae Historica,
Legum, sectio V (Hannover, 1886), p. 610. For general comments on medi-
eval exorcism, see Oesterreich, *Possession*, pp. 101–06 and passim; and s.v.
"exorcism" and "exorcist," in *New Catholic Encyclopedia*.

68. Exorcismic formulas are closely related to the baptismal order, in
which the priest performs a triple exorcism over the catechumen, using
such words as "Hear, accursed Satan, adjured by the name of eternal God
and of his Son, our saviour: defeated, depart together with your envy,
groaning and trembling; let there be nothing in common between you
and this servant of God, N. I exorcise you, unclean spirit, in the name of
God the Father, the Son, and the Holy Spirit, that you go out and with-
draw from this servant of God" (*Manuale . . . sarisburiensis*, p. 28). For
other exorcismic formulas, see G. F. Warner, ed., *Stowe Missal*, Henry
Bradshaw Society, vols. 31–32 (London, 1906, 1915), 2:24; and H. A. Wilson,
ed., *Missal of Robert of Jumièges*, Henry Bradshaw Society, vol. 11 (London,
1896), pp. 292–93.

69. *Acta Sanctorum* 21:821–22 (June 6). Oesterreich cites part of the
account but gives a wrong reference; *Possession*, p. 183. The story has the
makings of a fabliau if we see the girl as a nymphomaniac of sorts and the
encounter as a colossal misunderstanding.

for treatment; as usual, he dressed himself in the full regalia of stole and alb for the occasion and then proceeded with the exorcismic ritual, reading the Gospels over the girl. Not at all distressed, the devil noted that he had heard such tunes often and did not intend to depart. When Norbert responded with more exorcisms, the devil countered with Scripture; he recited the Song of Songs from beginning to end, first in Latin, then in French, and finally in German (the possessed girl herself knew nothing but the Psalms). Norbert once again ordered the devil to depart from this servant of God, and the devil agreed to bargain: he would leave provided that he could possess a certain monk. At this, Norbert's saintly patience gave way to an impassioned harangue on the insufferable wickedness of the demon. Eventually he began the ritual once more, only to have the devil inform him that this was wasting everyone's time; moreover, if Norbert did not stop the exorcisms immediately, the demon would call up all his friends to demolish the building. The terrified bystanders fled, but Norbert and a few brothers stood firm. Then the girl put her hand on Norbert's stole in order to clasp his neck, we are told, and Norbert's companions, thinking he was about to be strangled, tried to intervene. Norbert stopped them: "If God has given her the power to strangle me, then let her." Unnerved by this unexpected bravery, the girl let go.

By now it was quite late, so Norbert immersed the girl in holy water and then, "because she was blonde, the priest ordered her hair cut off, for he feared that the devil might keep his power in her by means of her hair." Incensed at this injury, the devil hurled abuse at Norbert, who ordered the girl taken home until the morning. As he began to take off his vestments, the demon clapped his hands, delighted with his temporary victory. He taunted Norbert with having wasted a whole day, at which Norbert, enraged, vowed not to eat until he had cured the girl. The next day the church was filled with spectators as the girl was held at the altar during mass. Again Norbert read the gospels over her, and again the demon mocked Norbert for singing such nice songs. At the elevation of the Host, the demon commented on the "deiculum" (godling) that Norbert held between his hands, and immediately Norbert began to rebuke the demon so strongly that he finally fled in pain, leaving behind a pool of stinking urine.

Given the great strength of some demons and the effort and persistence needed to cast them out, it is not surprising that normal exorcism was not always effective, and often, as in this case, the intervention of a saint was necessary. Perhaps because of the spectacular nature of cures for possession and perhaps because of the apostolic power of exorcism, most saints are reported to have exorcised devils personally.[70] Even the relics of a saint might be sufficient to effect a cure: a notorious madman who spent the night in a church containing Saint Chad's relics was cured, and the ground on which was poured water used to wash Saint Oswald's bones could expel evil spirits.[71] Finally, prayer to saints associated with madness — Dympna, Hubert, Leonard, Hermes, Acarius, and many others[72] — could provide a cure, especially when those prayers were preceded by a pilgrimage to an appropriate shrine.

Such, then, are the religious remedies for madness. Through the constant use of these cures, the spiritual and moral implications of disease and healing, emphasized by Christ in his own miracles, continued to be stressed, especially in literature, where illness is so often seen as a token of sin to be cured by religious and supernatural means. It is, however, important to remember that just as a spiritually significant disease is

70. Examples abound in the *Acta Sanctorum*; see also Bonser, *Medical Background*, pp. 171–77.

71. For Chad, see Bede, *Ecclesiastical History of the English People*, ed. Bertram Colgrave and R. A. B. Mynors (Oxford: Clarendon Press, 1969), 4. 3; for Oswald, ibid., 3. 11. These and numerous other examples are given by Bonser, *Medical Background*, pp. 178–210.

72. See Louis Réau, *Iconographie de l'art chrétien*, 3 vols. in 6 pts. (Paris: Presses Universitaires de France, 1955–59), vol. 3, where the saints are listed alphabetically. John the Baptist is another saint particularly associated with madness. Reasons for John's patronage of the mad are uncertain, but his wild appearance, his association with the mad Herod family in the Bible, the coincidental dates of his festival and Midsummer Day, and the fact that he literally lost his head may all contribute.

also a real physiological disorder, so too a religious remedy may often be paired with a purely medical one; medieval thought tends to see moral and scientific causality and cure as all quite compatible with each other.

A CASE STUDY: CHARLES VI

Perhaps the best way to summarize the complicated medieval attitude toward madness is by considering a fairly detailed case study, the story of Charles VI's recurrent madness as reported by Froissart.[73] In addition to providing a good picture of the symptoms of madness, this case illustrates the medieval fondness for moral interpretations of disease: the king's friends have a marked preference for ascribing his illness to purely natural and morally neutral causes; while his enemies, interpreting Charles's misfortune to suit themselves, favor supernatural and moral causes. According to Froissart, we must understand the circumstances leading up to the king's first bout of madness in order to appreciate its causes. Charles, bent on punishing the Duke of Brittany for alleged treachery, set forth with an army in 1392. At Saint Germain the royal physicians ordered Charles to rest, for he was somewhat ill, but he chose to press on, his illness heightened by his anger at those who had advised the halt. By the time he reached Le Mans, the king had contracted a serious fever, so he had to wait for several weeks. As soon as he had recovered sufficiently, he determined to continue despite unfavorable circumstances and poor health: it was August; the heat was great; the king had been overworked; he suffered constant headaches and fevers; and an earlier attack on his favorite, Olivier de Clisson, had plunged him into a state of melancholy. All conditions for the onset of madness were ripe.

73. I cite from Froissart's *Chronicles*, sel. and trans. Geoffrey Brereton (Harmondsworth: Penguin Books, 1968), pp. 392–401. For the whole account, I follow the translation of John Bourchier, Lord Berners, reprinted from Pynson's edition of 1523 and 1525 (London, 1812), 2:559–764. For additional biographical information, see Auguste Brachet, *Pathologie mentale des rois de France* (Paris: Librairie Hachette, 1903), pp. 593–650.

On the journey, a madman suddenly appeared in the woods, seizing the king's horse and warning of treachery. According to Froissart, this further weakened the king's mind: "His spirits sank and his blood ran cold." But no one else paid any attention to the madman, and the company rode on through heat so intense that even seasoned campaigners suffered greatly. Suddenly disaster struck: a page dropped a lance on another page's helmet, and the clang of armor persuaded Charles that his foes were upon him, just as the madman had warned. Charging back and forth, the king slashed wildly at his own troops, whom he no longer recognized. He started after the Duke of Orleans, and a frenzied chase ensued as the duke tried to escape, the king tried to kill him, and the company tried to catch the king. Finally they confined him within a circle where he attacked first one man and then another; but at last the exertion and heat exhausted him, and he collapsed, his eyes rolling wildly, unable to speak or to recognize his own brothers.

Froissart adds several possible causes for the madness to those he had given before: perhaps astral influence contributed; the king's dress of black velvet was very hot; he should never have been permitted to ride out in the heat of the day in his weakened condition; and his friends should have questioned the madman in the forest to reassure the king that no treachery was afoot. But whatever the cause, all fell as God willed: "In such ways are made manifest God's works and his terrible scourges, greatly to be feared of all creatures." Just so was the great Nebuchadnezzar stricken down to do penance, Froissart notes.

The king's brothers felt sure that the king had been drugged or bewitched into madness, but the royal physicians assured them that the illness had been approaching for some time. As a temporary measure, the king was taken to the castle of Creil, where the good air and pleasant surroundings might bring him to his senses or at least permit him to rest. As for spiritual treatment, envoys were sent to the shrines of Saint Acarius, Saint Hermes, and others able to cure madness; there offerings were made and prayers said for the king's recovery.

Nor was earthly medicine neglected: Guillaume de Harselly, a famous physician, was summoned; he diagnosed the illness as caused by an excessively moist complexion and climate, aggravated by feebleness of the heart and head.[74] Finding the malady theoretically curable, Guillaume tried to reduce the king's fever and restore his appetite; he encouraged rest and sleep, prescribing exercise to dry the king's complexion. Gradually the king's memory and reason returned, but Guillaume warned that the cure was not complete; Charles should not be depressed or excited, he should do little work, and he should exercise and amuse himself as much as possible.

Unfortunately, the cure was only temporary; but before discussing later relapses, we must mention two other interpretations of Charles's disease. Boniface and the Roman cardinals were delighted: "They said that their greatest enemy, the King of France, had been beaten by rods of wrath when God clouded his mind, and that this influence had been rained down from heaven to chastise him; he had inclined too much to the anti-Pope in Avignon, and this bitter scourge had been sent upon him to divide his kingdom." Froissart agrees that the king's madness was a warning of sorts, and he suggests that Clement and the Avignon cardinals might have been prudent to heed it. But their interpretation was quite different: the madness was caused by Charles's youth, his love of hunting, his overwork, and the failure of his counsellors to restrain him. Charles clearly had brought the madness on himself, but Clement felt that it might be a punishment as well: although Charles was amply endowed with reason — as shown by his promise to help Clement destroy Boniface — he had failed to keep that promise, thereby offending God: "As a solemn warning, He has struck him with this scourge of madness, and that, on any reasonable view, supports our case. If he recovers his

---

74. Because the king seems to have been choleric, one might expect his complexion to be dry; probably Guillaume's diagnosis is based on the quenching of natural heat by excess moisture. Foucault notes a later tradition that the English are often mad because of their humid climate (*Madness and Civilization*, p. 13); similar reasoning may be at work in reference to Charles.

sanity, as may well happen, we must send wise and capable
legates to him, who will point out his failure to keep his
promises, so that he shall not be unaware of it through any
neglect of ours."

As we have seen, Charles did indeed recover, but no one
expected his sanity to last.[75] The Duke of Lancaster, who had
planned to bring about peace with Charles, felt that his hopes
were dashed: no one would believe Charles any more. Nevertheless, Lancaster and Gloucester persuaded Charles to join
a council on church unity at Abbeville; but there the excitement sent Charles into his frenzy again. He was sent back to
Creil where he eventually recovered, perhaps because the
queen herself made pilgrimages on his behalf. But by now
everyone felt that it was only a matter of time before another
fit of madness; the king had indulged in all sorts of excess
when young, and as a result his head was weaker than it
should be. Few people were surprised when Charles went mad
permanently upon hearing that his son-in-law, Richard II,
had been imprisoned.

Charles's case is highly representative of medieval attitudes
toward madness. Almost every conceivable cause is considered
except for possession, and the pilgrimages were perhaps intended to take care of that possibility. More important, the
story illustrates the tendency of every man to interpret the
disease as he wishes: to Guillaume it is physiological only; to
the popes it is moral; to the king's brothers it suggests no
weakness on the king's part, coming instead from poison or
from spells cast by political enemies. Both spiritual and physical remedies are employed, but the rather cruel belief "once
mad, always half-mad" may have contributed to further relapses as it almost did with Thomas Hoccleve.

Perhaps some further conclusions about madness in medi-

75. Very shortly after his recovery, Charles participated in the ill-fated
Dance of the Wildmen at court (plate 7), in which the costumes caught
fire and the king was barely saved from the gruesome death that killed
his companions. This disaster, like Charles's madness, was taken as a sign
from heaven that Charles should refrain from "yonge ydell wantonnesse";
Bourchier, 2:591.

eval literature may be drawn from Froissart's account. For one thing, an intelligent man like Froissart seems more familiar with contemporary medical theory than most laymen are now; he demonstrates a highly sophisticated understanding of both medical and moral aspects of disease, and he employs his knowledge with apparent confidence that his readers will understand him. Hence it is certainly possible that many of the writers to be discussed later in this book had as extensive a knowledge of insanity as Froissart. A second and more important point that may be deduced from a study of Froissart is that sin is frequently seen as a major cause of madness in both history and literature. This is hardly surprising, given the difficulty of distinguishing between medieval history and literature on any dimension; but it is nonetheless interesting that "real" contemporary madness is as likely to receive a moral interpretation as madness in the Bible or in classical mythology. A third point is that any case of madness is open to numerous interpretations limited only by the number of theoretical causes of that sort of madness. The simple *fact* of madness is like the fact of a biblical narrative: it is nothing until it is fleshed out with interpretation. And although scientific commentary may be permitted or even encouraged, the favorite glosses are moral ones. Certainly Charles might have gone mad because he disobeyed his doctors and the day was hot, but the two popes and Froissart, although they disagreed among themselves, knew perfectly well that the natural causes were not the most important ones. In literature, madmen are common partly because of their eccentric and colorful behavior, but they are most important in their ability to symbolize the sinner or, occasionally, the saint.

THE IDENTITY OF SIN AND MADNESS

Throughout this chapter we have seen that madness and sin are closely linked in medieval thought; Original Sin was the initial cause of madness, and later actual sin might serve as both moral justification and immediate cause of insanity. Moreover, there is an identity of sorts between sin and mad-

ness: in both, reason is either perverted by passion or completely nonfunctional, and man — whose glory should be his
reason — is reduced to bestiality. This identity of sin and madness, which should be obvious from the many examples already discussed, is nowhere more evident than in a brief look
at common medieval usage of the word *madness* (*wodenes,*
amentia, etc.).[76] In its narrowest sense, of course, the word
refers to a mental and physical disorder, such as frenzy or
mania, with natural causes and consequences and with physiological symptoms; it is in this sense that scientists and encyclo-
pedists like Bartholomeus often use the word. From a more
sociological point of view, madness is lack of reason, and any
unusual behavior will seem mad in comparison to the normal;
thus madness is extended to include holy fools and desert
saints who love God to distraction as well as harmless eccen-
trics and anyone who does not live exactly as the rest of us
do. But when *reason* implies not conformity to a norm but
ideal conduct, unquestioning obedience to God, then madness
encompasses us all, for the just man falls seven times daily,
and even one sin suffices to justify the name of madness. In
closing this chapter, I wish to give a few examples of this most
seemingly metaphorical but, in the eyes of the Church, this
most deadly form of madness.

The first example comes from the *Gesta Romanorum,* where
Saint Peter describes five madmen he has seen:

> The first ate the sand of the sea so greedily, that it
> slipped through his jaws on either side of the mouth.
> Another I observed standing upon a pit full of sulphur
> and pitch, of which the smell was intolerable; yet he
> strove earnestly to inhale it. The third lay upon a burn-
> ing furnace, whose heat was not enough; he endeavoured
> to catch the sparks emitted from the furnace that he
> might eat them. A fourth sat upon a pinnacle of the
> temple, in order to catch the wind. For this purpose

76. For the influential Isidore of Seville (d. 636), sin and madness were
related etymologically: he suggests that *mania* may be derived "from sin,
which the Greeks call 'manie' "; *Etymologiae* 4. 7. 8.

he held his mouth open. The fifth devoured whatsoever of his own members he could get into his own mouth, and laughed incessantly.[77]

Christ then explains to Peter that these are not so much mad as sinful: they represent the covetous, gluttonous, rich, hypocrites, and backbiters. The point seems to be that "normal" human behavior — sin — seems quite mad from a moral perspective, and we all partake of the madness of these five men. The *Ayenbite of Inwyt* makes a similar point in describing one twig of untruth (a branch of pride) as the "wodehede" of refusing to acknowledge that one belongs to God and must account to him for one's use of earthly goods (p. 18).

The madness of sin is also a common theme in the religious drama. In *The Castle of Perseverance,* for instance, Belial boasts, "Al þis werld schal be wood iwys [indeed] as I wene / And to my byddynge bende"; and later in the same play Mankind makes the same equation of sin and madness as he confesses of his former follies, "I was þanne wood and gan to raue." [78] In *Everyman,* Death chastises the hero for his sinful life and his attempts to escape rather than survive judgment:

> Everyman, thou arte made! Thou hast thy wyttes fyue,
> And here on erthe wyll not amende thy lyue;
> For sodeynly I do come.[79]

And the Wakefield Master plays brilliantly with the similarities between sin, madness, and anger in the *Mactacio Abel.* Cain, ever the practical man who defines madness as deviation from the worldly claims of finance and pride, repeatedly accuses Abel and even God of being "woode" and "out of hys wit" — as saints always are from the strictly secular point of view. But from God's point of view it is the wrathful and sinful Cain who is truly mad: "Caym, Caym, thou was

77. Trans. Charles Swan, rev. W. Hooper (London, 1877), no. 164 (pp. 313–14).

78. *Macro Plays,* ll. 229–30 and 1483.

79. Ed. A. C. Cawley (Manchester: Manchester University Press, 1961), ll. 168–70.

wode." [80] A thirteenth-century lyric makes the point most explicitly:

> allas! þat men beit wode,
> bi-holdit an þe rode [cross]
> and silit [sell] — hic li noyt [I do not lie] —
> her souelis in-to sin[81]

A cautionary tale from Mirk's *Festial* provides a suitably macabre ending to this chapter. The man in the story is literally mad, but as the story itself is closer to parable than to history, so is the madness more a grim token of sin and of God's vengeance than a physical disease. No earthly physician could cure such madness.

> Ther was a man, a curset lyuer, þat was an officer to a lord. And as he rode to a maner of þe lordes, he fell wod, and so vnbrydylt his hors þat bare hym into a maner of þe lordes. But when he come yn, anon þe bayly [bailiff] sagh what þe man ayled, and made anon his hynes [servants] bynd hym to a post yn þe berne. Then when þe bayly had ysoupyd, he bade on of his hynes go loke how þys man dyd. And when he come to þe berne, he segh þre grete doggus as blacke as a cole on yche a syde plucke away hys flesche. Þen was þys hyne so sore aferd, þat vnneþe [with difficulty] he huld [held] hys wytte, but ȝode [went] to his bed, and lay seke þer longe aftyr. But, on þe morow, when men comen to þe berne, þay fonden no more of þys man, but his bare bonys and all þe flesche away. Thus who so lyueth a fowle lyfe, he may be sure of a foule ende.[82]

80. *Mactacio Abel*, ll. 148, 159, 173, 300, 350; in *The Wakefield Pageants in the Towneley Cycle*, ed. A. C. Cawley (Manchester: Manchester University Press, 1958).

81. Carleton Brown, ed., *English Lyrics of the XIIIth Century* (Oxford: Clarendon Press, 1932), no. 64, ll. 55–58.

82. John Mirk, *Festial: A Collection of Homilies*, ed. Theodor Erbe, EETS, es 96 (1905), p. 56.

Although it may seem a metaphorical use of the word to us, for the Middle Ages sin was real madness; an unrepentant sinner is more truly mad than the most violent maniac, for he cares not in life that the devil's hounds will possess him horribly in death. And although the rest of this book will deal with clinical as well as religious varieties of madness, it is always the madness of sin that is most important, giving meaning and power to all cases of madness.

2 Nebuchadnezzar and the Conventions of Madness

> And last of all, that which crucifies us most is our own folly,
> madness (whom Jupiter would destroy, he first drives mad;
> and by subtraction of his assisting grace God permits it),
> weakness, want of government, our facility in yielding to
> several lusts, in giving way to every passion and perturbation
> of the mind: by which means we metamorphose ourselves,
> and degenerate into beasts.
>
> Robert Burton, *The Anatomy of Melancholy*

The three purposes for which disease and madness may be inflicted — punishment, purgation, and test — are reflected in three literary conventions of madness. The madness that punishes disobedience and leads to death and damnation is illustrated by the life of the "Mad Sinner," usually a proud pagan king whose disdain for and emulation of the true God and whose persecution of God's people condemn him to the madness of the bestial and unreasonable man, to futile rage, and often to suicide. This figure is the subject of chapter 3. The second form of madness, in which disease is inflicted to purge the sinner, is exemplified by the "Unholy Wild Man." Such a man commits atrocious sins, but for some reason — often because he is graced with excellence in some respect — his sins are at once symbolized, punished, and purged by a period of temporary madness or wildness during which he degenerates into a bestial state of unconscious penance until forgiveness finally brings sanity and restoration. This conventional figure will be considered in chapter 4. The third kind of madness, corresponding loosely to the disease inflicted on saints to test their endurance and virtue, is that of the "Holy

Wild Man." Such a man voluntarily undertakes a life of hardship and penance in the wilderness remarkably similar to the involuntary madness and wildness of the Unholy Wild Man. This ascetic life may be chosen for three reasons. First, it may be penitential if, like Saint John Chrysostom of medieval legend, the Holy Wild Man has committed a sin for which he must atone.[1] Second, if he is guilty of no remarkable sin, he may choose the penitential life in order to be perfected like the desert saints Paul and Anthony. Finally, the life of wildness in exile may be undertaken to atone for Original Sin even as Christ submitted to fleshly exile to work the salvation of Adam, who had been sent into the wilderness from Eden dressed in the skins of the penitential wild man. From a spiritual point of view, the Holy Wild Man is usually sane; but from the worldly point of view, his devotion to God and his sacrifice of worldly values and comforts for a bestial life in the wilderness demonstrate his madness. This figure will be discussed in comparison with the Unholy Wild Man in chapter 4.

Nebuchadnezzar, as he appears in the Bible, in commentaries, and in literature, provides an excellent introduction to all three conventions; in fact, he may be seen as the father of most literary madmen. The pattern of his life — his repeated falls from pride, power, and idolatry into madness and bestiality, followed by the grace of the knowledge of God and eventual restoration — resembles the characteristic life patterns of the three conventions (see table 1). When his pride, his idolatry, his mad rage at the three Hebrew children, and his presumed damnation are stressed, he becomes a prototype of the Mad Sinner. When his madness and sojourn in the wilderness are emphasized, and when this deserved suffering is seen as leading to salvation, he is the father of the Unholy Wild Man. And, perhaps because his penitential wildness is voluntarily imitated by the Holy Wild Man, some commentators see him as a type of the holiest of wild men, Christ. Thus all who fall

1. For John and other examples of what I call the Holy Wild Man, see Charles Allyn Williams's excellent articles, "Hairy Anchorite" 1 and "Hairy Anchorite" 2. My discussion of the life pattern and attributes of the Holy Wild Man is much indebted to these articles.

Table 1
Life Patterns of the Three Conventions

Moral Pattern	Figure/Sin	Madness, Wildness / Punishment, Penance	Cure, Sanity	Voluntary Penance
Mad Sinner	Lucifer /Pride	Fall, deformity, damnation		
	Herod /Pride	Madness, disease, damnation		
	Judas /Avarice, Treachery	Possession, suicide, damnation		
	Pagan Kings /Pride, Idolatry	Madness, death, damnation		
Unholy Wild Man	Nebuchadnezzar /Idolatry	Mad rage (in some commentaries, damnation)	Sight of Christ, conversion	Penance, fasting (in Comestor)
	/Pride	7 years in wilderness, bestial appearance	By grace, restored reason and rule	Missionary work, 30 years in desert
	Mary Magdalene/Lechery	Possession by 7 devils	Cure by Christ, conversion	Penitential life in wilderness
	Merlin /?Excessive grief	Madness in wilderness, bestial appearance	Cure by fountain	Series of good deeds
	Ywain /Pride, oath-breaking	Madness in wilderness	Magic ointment, reform	(Further relapses)
	Charles VI /Sin, physical cause	Madness	Cure by physician, by pilgrimage	?Reform, writing of noble poems
	Hoccleve /Gluttony, Lechery, Avarice	Madness	Cure by grace, ?by pilgrimage	

The Two Adams	Adam	/Pride (Gluttony, Lechery)	Fall, exile, dress of skins, diet of herbs, damnation	Cure through second Adam	
	Christ	/Desire to redeem man*	Incarnation, reduction of divine nature, temptation in wilderness, ?ugliness, suffering	Crucifixion, Harrowing of Hell, Redemption of Adam	Resurrection, Ascension
Holy Wild Man	Saint Anthony / Saint Paul	/Desire for perfection*	Voluntary penance in desert, bestial appearance	Spiritual perfection	
	Hairy Anchorite	/Murder, Lechery	Voluntary penance in desert, bestial appearance	Absolution	Continued penance
	Sir Gowther	/Diabolical nature, deeds	Imposed penance, feigned madness	Absolution	Sanctity as "Gotlak"
	Sir Orfeo	/Desire to redeem wife*	Voluntary exile in wilderness, bestial appearance	Redemption of Heurodis	Return to earth, eventual salvation

NOTE: All figures are discussed in the text, though not necessarily in connection with the conventions. Adam's life pattern resembles all three patterns; Christ's is that of the Holy Wild Man.

* In these cases I have suggested the figure's motivation, for there is no actual sin.

through sin may see Nebuchadnezzar, like Lucifer and Adam, as their distant ancestor; all who fall into madness only to rise again through grace and virtue are his children. Not surprisingly, Nebuchadnezzar was a popular figure in literature, and the symptoms of his wildness seem to have had great influence on later depictions of madness. In this chapter I shall consider him as the prototype of later literary madmen and especially of the three conventions; treatments of Nebuchadnezzar in the Bible, the commentaries, and other literature will all be considered as an aid to understanding this most important madman.

Any study of Nebuchadnezzar is necessarily complicated: the Nebuchadnezzar of Daniel, that of Judith and Tobias, the biblical prince of Tyre, the king of Assyria, and the Lucifer of Isaiah are all part of the Nebuchadnezzar legend in the Middle Ages. The Nebuchadnezzar of Daniel dominates the legend and is most important for this chapter, but his other aspects should also be considered briefly.[2] Both biblical descriptions

2. The historical Nebuchadnezzar II (ca. 605–562 b.c.), who conquered most of the Middle East and ruled long and successfully, has very little to do with the biblical and medieval legend; as the *New Catholic Encyclopedia* notes, there seems to be no historical evidence for the Nebuchadnezzar of either Judith or Daniel. As for the king's madness, it seems that the author of Daniel confused Nebuchadnezzar with Nabonidus, his son-in-law and the father of Belshazzar. For some reason, Nabonidus left the throne he had inherited and went to live at Têmâ, an oasis in the desert. Perhaps Nabonidus was considered mad for the same reason that many Holy Wild Men were: Why would any sane man leave the pleasures of Babylon and the powers of royalty to live in the desert miles from civilization? On this subject, see Raymond P. Dougherty, *Nabonidus and Belshazzar: A Study of the Closing Events of the Neo-Babylonian Empire,* Yale Oriental Series, Researches, vol. 15 (New Haven: Yale University Press, 1929). There is also a rather tantalizing possibility that Nabonidus may have suffered a punitive disease: the Dead Sea Scrolls include the prayer of Nabunai, king of Babylon, telling of his seven years' suffering from an ulcer before a Jewish exorcist cured him by forgiving his sins; see Geza Vermes, trans., *The Dead Sea Scrolls in English,* rev. ed. (Harmondsworth: Pelican Books, 1965), p. 229.

Major sources of the legend in the Middle Ages include the following

and commentaries on Nebuchadnezzar are inconsistent and in places contradictory, but literature is the richer for the confusion; it is largely because of these inconsistencies that Nebuchadnezzar is representative of all three conventions and thus presumably so extremely influential.

From the many non-Danielic references to Nebuchadnezzar, two major viewpoints arise, the first having little relevance to the king's madness but the second being quite important for Nebuchadnezzar's role as Mad Sinner. On one hand, Nebuchadnezzar is seen by Isaias, Ezechiel, and Jeremias as a just conqueror ordained by God to punish the sinful pride and disobedience of Tyre, of Egypt, and especially of Jerusalem. The prophets warn the Jews that Nebuchadnezzar's cause is just: "Because you have not heard my words: Behold I will send . . . Nabuchodonosor the king of Babylon my servant . . . against this land, and against the inhabitants thereof" (Jer. 25:8–9). This view is shared much later by Wyclif, Lydgate, and the *Cleanness*-poet.[3]

Yet even as God's executioner, Nebuchadnezzar is sometimes seen as wicked. According to Jeremias and other prophets, Babylon will fall: "Israel is a scattered flock, the lions have driven him away: first the king of Assyria [Sennacherib] devoured him: and last this Nabuchodonosor king of Babylon hath broken his bones. Therefore thus saith the Lord of hosts

---

books of the Bible: 4 Kings, 2 Paralipomenon, Esdras, Nehemias, Tobias, Judith, Esther, Isaias, Jeremias, Baruch, Ezechiel, and Daniel. At least as important are such early sources as a history of the Chaldeans by Berosus, and *JA;* later influential commentaries include Hippolytus, *Fragments from his Commentaries* (ca. 204), trans. S. D. F. Salmond, ANCL, vol. 6 (Edinburgh, 1868); Jerome, *Commentaria in Danielem* (fifth century), *PL* 25; Richard of Saint Victor, *De eruditione hominis interioris* (twelfth century), *PL* 196; Peter Comestor, *Historia scholastica* (twelfth century), *PL* 198; Albert the Great, *Commentaria in librum Danielis* (thirteenth century), in *Opera omnia,* vol. 18; Nicholas de Lyra's commentary (early fourteenth century) and the *Glossa ordinaria,* in *GO* 4.

3. The *Cleanness*-poet will be discussed later. For Wyclif, see *Tractatus de civili dominio,* ed. R. L. Poole and J. Loserth, Wyclif Society, no. 2, 4 vols. (London: Trübner, 1885–1904), 2:50–51; for Lydgate, see *Fall of Princes,* ed. Henry Bergen, EETS, es 121–24 (1924–27), 2, ll. 2815–940.

the God of Israel: Behold I will visit the king of Babylon and
his land, as I have visited the king of Assyria" (Jer. 50:17–18).
The fall of Babylon should, of course, be associated with Belshazzar, but such quotations as this also implicate Nebuchadnezzar, who first brought about the captivity of the Jews. Because Nebuchadnezzar gloried in his triumph over Jerusalem
even though it deserved to fall, "because you rejoice and speak
great things, pillaging my inheritance: because you are spread
abroad as calves upon the grass, and have bellowed as bulls"
(Jer. 50:11), the king must fall, and the man who bellowed as
a bull must become "as an ox" (Dan. 4:22) in fitting punishment.

This interpretation of Nebuchadnezzar as an evil conqueror,
a precursor of the Mad Sinner, was reinforced by the attribution to him of other men's deeds. Judith makes him the Assyrian king who ordered Holofernes to destroy the Israelites
and whose pride was astounding: "There is no God, but Nabuchodonosor. . . . And thou shalt find that Nabuchodonosor is
lord of the whole earth" (Jth. 6:2, 4). According to R. H.
Charles, this Nebuchadnezzar is completely unhistorical, and
this reference to him illustrates the tendency of the Jews (and
certainly of many later commentators) to make him a symbolic archenemy, diabolical in function and inclination.[4] At
least as important for the blackening of Nebuchadnezzar's character is the common misinterpretation of these three prophetic
passages erroneously taken to refer to Nebuchadnezzar:

> [1.] And the word of the Lord came to me, saying: Son of
> man, say to the prince of Tyre: Thus saith the Lord God:
> Because thy heart is lifted up, and thou hast said: I am
> God, and I sit in the chair of God in the heart of the sea:
> whereas thou art a man, and not God: and hast set thy
> heart as if it were the heart of God. . . . Thou wast per-
> fect in thy ways from the day of thy creation, until iniquity
> was found in thee. . . . And thy heart was lifted up with

4. *Apocrypha and Pseudepigrapha of the Old Testament in English*, 2
vols. (Oxford: Clarendon Press, 1913), 1:246.

thy beauty: thou hast lost thy wisdom in thy beauty, I
have cast thee to the ground: I have set thee before the
face of kings, that they might behold thee. [Ezech. 28:1–2,
15, 17]

[2.] Behold, the Assyrian was like a cedar in Libanus,
with fair branches, and full of leaves, of a high stature,
and his top was elevated among the thick boughs. . . .
And when he had spread forth his shadow, all the fowls
of the air made their nests in his boughs, and all the beasts
of the forest brought forth their young under his branches,
and the assembly of many nations dwelt under his shadow.
And he was most beautiful for his greatness, and for the
spreading of his branches: for his root was near great
waters. The cedars in the paradise of God were not higher
than he, the fir trees did not equal his top, neither were
the plane trees to be compared with him for branches:
no tree in the paradise of God was like him in his beauty.
. . . Therefore thus saith the Lord God: Because he was
exalted in height, and shot up his top green and thick,
and his heart was lifted up in his height: I have delivered
him into the hands of the mighty one of the nations, he
shall deal with him: I have cast him out according to his
wickedness. And strangers, and the most cruel of the nations shall cut him down, and cast him away upon the
mountains, and his boughs shall fall in every valley, and
his branches shall be broken on every rock of the country:
and all the people of the earth shall depart from his
shadow, and leave him. All the fowls of the air dwelt upon
his ruins, and all the beasts of the field were among his
branches. [Ezech. 31:2–3, 6–8, 10–13]

[3.] And it shall come to pass in that day, that when God
shall give thee rest from thy labour, and from thy vexation,
and from the hard bondage, wherewith thou didst serve
before, Thou shalt take up this parable against the king
of Babylon, and shalt say: How is the oppressor come to
nothing, the tribute hath ceased? The Lord hath broken
the staff of the wicked, the rod of the rulers. . . . Hell be-

low was in an uproar to meet thee at thy coming, it stirred
up the giants for thee. . . . Thy pride is brought down to
hell, thy carcass is fallen down: under thee shall the moth
be strewed, and worms shall be thy covering. How art
thou fallen from heaven, O Lucifer, who didst rise in the
morning? how art thou fallen to the earth, that didst
wound the nations? And thou saidst in thy heart: I will
ascend unto heaven, I will exalt my throne above the stars
of God, I will sit in the mountain of the covenant, in the
sides of the north. I will ascend above the height of the
clouds, I will be like the most High. But yet thou shalt
be brought down to hell, into the depth of the pit. . . .
But thou art cast out of thy grave, as an unprofitable
branch defiled. [Isa. 14:3-5, 9, 11-15, 19]

Despite their apparent appropriateness, none of the passages
in fact refers to Nebuchadnezzar: the first warns that the prince
of Tyre will fall to Nebuchadnezzar; the second tells of Senna-
cherib, king of Assyria; the third concerns Belshazzar's fall to
Darius. Yet Albert the Great, commenting on Nebuchadnezzar's madness, refers to passage 1 to illustrate the punishment
of pride, without noting that Nebuchadnezzar and the prince
of Tyre are different, and this erroneous identification is common.[5] Passage 2 is more easily applied to Nebuchadnezzar,
partly because the image of the huge tree cut down at God's
command is used to predict Nebuchadnezzar's fall in Daniel 4
and partly because Nebuchadnezzar is often confused with the
king of Assyria.[6] Passage 3, which does at least refer to a king
of Babylon, is most commonly applied to Nebuchadnezzar,
"the most powerful of the Babylonian kings," according to
Nicholas de Lyra.[7]

5. *Commentaria in librum Danielis*, p. 532.
6. This mistake is made in Judith and, as we shall see, in the *Eclogue
of Theodulus* and in Froissart's *Chronicles*.
7. *GO* 4:32. Nicholas himself does not make the mistake he notes, however; in the following column he states that the application of passage 3
to Nebuchadnezzar does not mean that the king was really a devil or that
he went to hell, and he cites Gregory's *Decretals* to prove that it was Belshazzar who went to hell.

The issue becomes still more complicated and more damning to Nebuchadnezzar, however. All three passages are sometimes taken to describe Antichrist, and the first and third may refer to the fall of Lucifer-Satan.[8] The identification of Nebuchadnezzar with the devil is made explicit in the *Glossa ordinaria,* where references to Lucifer are glossed "Nebuchadnezzar, or the devil" (*GO* 4:32–33). And Nicholas de Lyra, who explains that passage 3 refers primarily to the devil and to Belshazzar, "who was the devil's member literally," notes that since Nebuchadnezzar was the devil's member temporarily, he too in a sense is Lucifer (*GO* 4:32). As Lucifer fell, so fall all those possessed by him, whether totally and finally possessed like Belshazzar or only temporarily possessed like Nebuchadnezzar. Even Jerome, who vehemently denies that Nebuchadnezzar is the devil, contributes to the confusion by linking passage 1 with the falls of Nebuchadnezzar and Lucifer, who proudly thought themselves gods and whose boasts of power were "not so much the words of men as of raving demons." [9] Thus the commentaries link Nebuchadnezzar's pride with madness and possession, and they associate his fall with the falls of other proud men and angels, implying that all falls conform to the same pattern and carry the same warning. To this way of thinking, it is unimportant to make petty distinctions between one fall and another if the moral lesson of all falls is thereby obscured; the similarities between Lucifer-Satan, Nebuchadnezzar, Belshazzar, and the rest are far more important than the differences. It matters little whether this passage refers to this man and that to another; what matters is that men learn to avoid pride and its punishment. That each passage applies to all fallen princes simply proves the power and universality of God's laws against pride.

In the non-Danielic accounts and commentaries, then, Nebuchadnezzar is usually seen as a sinful tyrant rather than as a just pagan; and despite protestations to the contrary by the

---

8. See *GO* 4:33 and 255; for the identification of Lucifer with Satan, see J. M. Evans, *Paradise Lost and the Genesis Tradition* (Oxford: Clarendon Press, 1968), pp. 27–29, 34, and 87.

9. *Commentaria in Ezechias, PL* 25:266.

influential Jerome, he is often seen as a devil or the instrument
of the devil.[10] In turning to Daniel, we find some additional
support for this view of the king as a black and demonic prototype of the Mad Sinner, the proud tyrant who scorns God and
is punished with madness. Nebuchadnezzar's pride, already
suggested by the three prophecies just cited and by his claim to
divinity in Judith, is further developed in Daniel 2–3. The
king's dream of the statue with the head of gold is there interpreted by Daniel as proof of Nebuchadnezzar's great excellence, the basis for his pride: "Thou art a king of kings: and
the God of heaven hath given thee a kingdom, and strength,
and power, and glory: And all places wherein the children
of men, and the beasts of the field do dwell: he hath also given
the birds of the air into thy hand, and hath put all things
under thy power: thou therefore art the head of gold" (Dan.
2:37–38). Suitably impressed by Daniel's skill, Nebuchadnezzar
worshiped Daniel's God for a while. But then he grew proud
in the knowledge that he was the best earthly king; according
to Hippolytus, "The king, being puffed up with this address,
and elated in heart, made a copy of this image, in order that
he might be worshipped by all as God." [11] This novel and un-
biblical explanation of the golden statue explains Nebuchadnezzar's apostasy and his intense rage when the three Hebrews
(Shadrach, Meshach, and Abednego) refused to worship the
statue: "filled with fury" (*repletus furore;* Dan. 3:19), he condemned them to the fiery furnace. This fury or frenzy, largely
a result of his hurt pride, is typical of tyrants and of the Mad
Sinner in particular, for it is not only a sin but literally a
form of madness, as Richard of Saint Victor makes clear in a
passage with important implications for all Mad Sinners. He
finds that the Latin *furor* (here translated "fury" or "frenzy")
is quite distinct from *ira* or "wrath," which is not necessarily
a form of madness:

10. See, for example, Origen, *Homiliae in Ezechielem*, trans. Jerome, *PL*
25:772–74; Isidore of Seville, *Allegoriae quaedam sacrae scripturae, PL*
83:116; and Rupert of Deutz, *Commentarium in Danielem, PL* 167:1500.

11. *Fragments*, p. 469.

Furor is the mental disturbance that is wholly without reason. *Ira* is a great disturbance of the mind, but not thoroughly divorced from reason. We are moved . . . as if by frenzy when, without any regard for reason, we throw ourselves headlong into what we ought not to do. Often when we are wrathful we understand what we ought to do, though our wrath cannot be restrained if it is great. And so in the first impulse of our passion we often do not even consider reason; presently we see reason but cannot follow it; and finally we both consider and follow it. [*PL* 196:1241]

Although *furor* may become the milder *ira* with the passing of time, there is an important qualitative difference between the two: *furor* is a kind of madness, but *ira* need not be (although, of course, wrath may be madness in that the wrathful man voluntarily ignores his reason and thereby sins). Jerome would agree with Richard that Nebuchadnezzar is truly mad here, or very close to it: the king ordered the furnace heated seven times hotter than necessary (Dan. 3:19) because "frenzy and the wrath that is close to madness cannot observe due measure" (*PL* 25:508).

Nebuchadnezzar, then, appears as a triple sinner in Daniel 3: first, his pride leads him to emulate God; second, his wrath leads him to madness; third, that madness leads him to persecute the faithful. Up to this point in his story, he is close to the Mad Sinner: he is an omnipotent tyrant of overreaching pride; he falls into insane rage when that pride is challenged; he insists on the worship due to God; and he persecutes those who refuse that worship. It is hardly surprising that many commentators assume he must have been damned, for his presumption should have led to as great a catastrophe as that which befell Lucifer or Herod. If Nebuchadnezzar's fury had led directly to his seven years' madness, and if his madness had then ended in death, he would be a true picture of the Mad Sinner.

Although Nebuchadnezzar is akin to Lucifer and Herod in his pride, Daniel and many later writers stress his role as an

example of pride humbled and redeemed rather than of pride
fallen and damned; thus for Wyclif, Nebuchadnezzar represents godliness that falls through pride only to be saved by
penance and restoration to grace.[12] It is this Nebuchadnezzar,
prototype of the Unholy Wild Man, similar in some respects
to the Holy Wild Man, that was most popular in the medieval
period. His life gives force to the Christian precept that even
the most sinful man may be saved by God's grace, and not once
only but repeatedly.

This more optimistic view of Nebuchadnezzar is based on his
life after the episode of the fiery furnace; where the typical life
pattern of the Mad Sinner would end, Nebuchadnezzar begins
anew through grace. This grace took the form of a vision of
Christ in the furnace with the three Hebrews: "Behold I see
four men loose, and walking in the midst of the fire, and there
is no hurt in them, and the form of the fourth is like the Son
of God" (Dan. 3:92). Through the vision's healing power, the
king lost his fury and madness, both literal and metaphorical,
and again he acknowledged Daniel's God. This testimony of
Nebuchadnezzar, taken up in the *Ordo prophetarum*,[13] contributed greatly to the medieval tendency to view him favor-
ably. The drama typically portrays Nebuchadnezzar as a proud
monarch who learned humility at the sight of Christ. Perhaps
it is this reverence at the moment of confrontation with God
that distinguishes those who can be saved — Nebuchadnezzar,
the Unholy Wild Man — from the damned — Herod, the Mad
Sinner par excellence.

But, as had happened before, Nebuchadnezzar's pride soon
got the better of his humility and devotion, and he was warned
of his coming fall: "I Nabuchodonosor was at rest in my house,
and flourishing in my palace: I saw a dream that affrighted me"
(Dan. 4:1–2). Significantly, the chapter about the king's fall
and penance is told in the first person, a sort of public confession in which he testifies to God's power and mercy and

12. *Tractatus de civili dominio,* 1:161.
13. See Karl Young, *The Drama of the Medieval Church,* 2 vols. (Oxford: Clarendon Press, 1933), 2:125–71.

proves himself worthy of salvation. Although the story he tells is familiar, it is worth considering in some detail because of its importance for the medieval view of madness and particularly for an understanding of the Unholy Wild Man. Nebuchadnezzar's dream is of an enormous tree:

> The tree was great, and strong: and the height thereof reached unto heaven: the sight thereof was even to the ends of all the earth. Its leaves were most beautiful, and its fruit exceeding much: and in it was food for all: under it dwelt cattle, and beasts, and in the branches thereof the fowls of the air had their abode: and all flesh did eat of it. I saw in the vision of my head upon my bed, and behold a watcher, and a holy one came down from heaven. He cried aloud, and said thus: Cut down the tree, and chop off the branches thereof: shake off its leaves, and scatter its fruits: let the beasts fly away that are under it, and the birds from its branches. Nevertheless leave the stump of its roots in the earth, and let it be tied with a band of iron, and of brass, among the grass, that is without, and let it be wet with the dew of heaven, and let its portion be with the wild beasts in the grass of the earth. Let his heart be changed from a man's, and let a beast's heart be given him; and let seven times pass over him. This is the decree by the sentence of the watchers, and the word and demand of the holy ones; till the living know that the most High ruleth in the kingdom of men; and he will give it to whomsoever it shall please him, and he will appoint the basest man over it. [Dan. 4:7–14]

According to Daniel, the tree was Nebuchadnezzar, whose greatness touched heaven and whose power extended throughout the earth. The watcher angel pronounced the sentence of God:

> They shall cast thee out from among men, and thy dwelling shall be with cattle and with wild beasts, and thou shalt eat grass as an ox, and shalt be wet with the dew of heaven: and seven times shall pass over thee, till thou

know that the most High ruleth over the kingdom of men, and giveth it to whomsoever he will. But whereas he commanded, that the stump of the roots thereof, that is, of the tree, should be left: thy kingdom shall remain to thee after thou shalt have known that power is from heaven. [Dan. 4:22–23]

But Daniel felt that the dream might be monitory rather than inevitable, that reform might forestall disaster: "Wherefore, O king, let my counsel be acceptable to thee, and redeem thou thy sins with alms, and thy iniquities with works of mercy to the poor: perhaps he will forgive thy offences" (Dan. 4:24). Apparently Nebuchadnezzar took Daniel's advice, but eventually his pride returned: one day in the halls of Babylon he asked, "Is not this the great Babylon, which I have built to be the seat of the kingdom, by the strength of my power, and in the glory of my excellence?" (Dan. 4:27). Immediately the sentence was enforced: "The same hour the word was fulfilled upon Nabuchodonosor, and he was driven away from among men, and did eat grass like an ox, and his body was wet with the dew of heaven: till his hairs grew like the feathers of eagles, and his nails like birds' claws" (Dan. 4:30). But exile and trial eventually led to the return of sanity:

> Now at the end of my days, I Nabuchodonosor lifted up my eyes to heaven, and my sense was restored to me: and I blessed the most High, and I praised and glorified him. . . . At the same time my sense returned to me, and I came to the glory and honour of my kingdom: and my shape returned to me: and my nobles, and my magistrates sought for me, and I was restored to my kingdom: and greater majesty was added to me. Therefore I Nabuchodonosor do now praise and magnify and glorify the King of heaven: because all his works are true, and his ways judgments, and them that walk in pride he is able to abase. [Dan. 4:31, 33–34]

Several points in the story repay closer attention, for they are prominent in later literary treatments. First, although

Daniel does not explicitly blame Nebuchadnezzar's fall on his pride, medieval writers are unanimous in doing so. For Jerome, the tree in the king's dream shadows all creation, not because Nebuchadnezzar really was that powerful, as Daniel implies, but because the king thought himself omnipotent; and Albert claims that the tree touched heaven because Nebuchadnezzar thought himself God's equal.[14] Richard of Saint Victor takes a slightly kinder view: the tree's beauty signifies Nebuchadnezzar's perfect virtue, and its fall is caused by the king's tendency to take pride in that virtue, as so many good people do. But even the fall is a sign of grace: "Many fall according to God's plan, so that they may rise again the stronger." [15] This view of the king's excellence and his fall through pride recurs in many literary versions to be considered shortly.

Another point often noted is the appropriateness of Nebuchadnezzar's punishment. His bestiality and madness are taken as examples of what happens to a man, figuratively at least, when he sins. Sometimes Nebuchadnezzar is seen as a type of Adam, whose pride and aspirations to be a god led to exile from Eden, exposure to harsh nature, loss of control over his own bestial elements, and the beastlike clothing of skins.[16] Morally, Nebuchadnezzar represents any sinner who destroys reason, the image of God, and thereby becomes bestial, mad, and an outcast; and he particularly represents the proud man and the tyrant:

> As much as you exalted yourself above other men in your arrogance, so far will you be cast down below other men because of your guilt, and your habitation shall be with beasts and wild animals. He is cast out from men and descends to live with beasts and animals who, forsaking the way of reason, lives henceforth irrationally, so that, living bestially and behaving like a wild animal, he is

14. Jerome, *Commentaria in Danielem, PL* 25:514–15; and Albert, *Commentaria in librum Danielis*, p. 513.

15. *PL* 196:1321, 1346.

16. For Nebuchadnezzar as a type of Adam, see Richard, *De eruditione, PL* 196:1318ff.; and *Miroure of Mans Saluacionne*, p. 128.

abandoned to complete carnality in the company of those who live bestially, and he is unrestrainedly given over to all kinds of cruelty in the company of those who live like wild animals.[17]

Such interpretations have two important implications that are picked up in literary versions of the story: first, the presumptuous Nebuchadnezzar had to be made like a beast so that he could know what it was to be truly human; second, Nebuchadnezzar's external appearance and habitation are often taken as projections of the moral deformity and wilderness inside him. This second implication is strengthened by the fact that, according to Daniel, Nebuchadnezzar became "*like* an ox," his hair "*like* the feathers of eagles," his nails "*like* birds' claws" (italics mine). Although his appearance, habits, and dwelling place were bestial, he did not actually turn into a beast; instead he merely thought himself one: "He suffered not a physical transformation but insanity, and he lost the use of his tongue for speaking, and grass was given as food for [to restore?] human nature. And it seemed to him that he was an ox in front and a lion behind." [18] Thus the once-proud king simply underwent physical degeneration and delusions; he was granted neither the dignity nor the anonymity of a real transformation, although some later writers like Gower choose the more romantic alternative of metamorphosis.

Just as Nebuchadnezzar's bestiality is at once moralized and scientifically rationalized, so too his madness, which is universally interpreted as having symbolic and moral connotations, is simultaneously explained as fully as possible in scientific or commonsense terms, an interpretative tendency that clearly operated not only in later treatments of Nebuchadnezzar but also in such cases as that of Charles VI. Thus Jerome and the literal-minded Nicholas de Lyra, for example, acknowl-

---

17. Richard, *De eruditione*, PL 196:1339; Richard consistently advances a moral reading of Nebuchadnezzar's life, and the moral interpretation printed in *GO* 4:305, seems to be derived from Richard's.

18. Comestor, *Historia scholastica*, PL 198:1452. I follow A. G. Rigg's suggestion in reading *anterioribus* for *interioribus* in the Latin text.

edge that it is surprising for a king to be allowed to run wild, eat hay, and live among beasts unhurt. But Jerome notes that many madmen live in the wilderness like beasts, and Nicholas comments that madmen have strange tastes in food.[19] As for companionship with animals, Nicholas explains that madmen, being themselves without reason, befriend wild animals freely, and the animals do them no harm. After all, he claims, "the fiercest dogs naturally refrain from hurting fools and madmen." He offers an equally good explanation for why the king was not bound: "These expedients would have aggravated his malady, for it is quite obvious that when madmen are fettered, they grow worse." As for why he was allowed to run free like a common madman, the answer is that God predicted it and ensured his eventual restoration, so the courtiers permitted God's will to stand. The mixture of scientific detail and didactic moralism found in such accounts of Nebuchadnezzar's madness is characteristic of most late medieval stories of madness.

Other aspects of Nebuchadnezzar's madness fascinate commentators and influence the direction of literary interpretations. One of these aspects is the length of his madness, "seven times shall pass over thee" (Dan. 4:29). Usually this is interpreted as seven years, though there is some disagreement on the subject.[20] The number, however, is what is most significant: Richard, using reasoning like Lancelot's in his trance at Corbenic, thinks that seven years' madness properly punished the king's submission to the seven deadly sins; Albert links the number to seven parts of the sacrament of penance, thereby marking the penitential nature of Nebuchadnezzar's madness.[21] The implication is that with Nebuchadnezzar, as with other

19. *PL* 25:513; and *GO* 4:304.

20. Jerome (*Commentaria in Danielem, PL* 25:513) assumes the time is seven years; Peter Comestor (*Historia scholastica, PL* 198:1452) holds for seven months, the initial period of seven years having been reduced at Daniel's request. Nicholas de Lyra objects vehemently to Peter's suggestion; *GO* 4:304.

21. Richard, *De eruditione, PL* 196:1327–28; Albert, *Commentaria in librum Danielis,* p. 515.

Unholy Wild Men, madness in the wilderness can be an effective penance even if the suffering is inflicted rather than undertaken voluntarily.

A similar interpretation is sometimes made of the grass or hay that the mad king eats. In Daniel 1, the prophet and his three friends refused to eat food from the king's table, preferring pulse and water. Hippolytus comments, "These, though captives in a strange land, were not seduced by delicate meats, nor were they slaves to the pleasures of wine. . . . They teach that it is not earthly meats that give to men their beauty and strength, but the grace of God." [22] Nebuchadnezzar's diet may be related to this notion. According to Peter Comestor, "herba data est naturae cibus humanae"; the sentence is ambiguous, and it may mean that Nebuchadnezzar thought that normal human food was grass. It is more likely, however, that the grass was necessary to restore the king's human nature, that penance and fasting restore sanity. This latter interpretation is supported by Peter's later emphasis on the king's voluntary penance after an initial seven months of intermittent madness: "For twelve years he did penance, refusing to eat bread and meat or to drink wine. He ate pulse and grass, according to Daniel's advice" (PL 198:1452). This diet is clearly penitential, and it is similar to Daniel's in Daniel 1; it is also the diet followed by countless wild men, holy or unholy, as will be seen later.

The process by which Nebuchadnezzar recovers his sanity also has penitential and moral connotations often expanded by later writers such as Gower. For instance, the dew which falls on him is almost universally interpreted as God's grace, a preparation for restoration. As for the fact that Nebuchadnezzar "lifted up my eyes to heaven, and my sense was restored to me" (Dan. 4:31), Jerome notes that turning toward God brings sanity (PL 25:517), and Richard comments that Nebuchadnezzar is finally able to contemplate eternal truths, thereby regaining his moral sense (PL 196:1341–42). The return of the king's "shape" (Dan. 4:33) signifies not his trans-

22. *Fragments,* p. 464.

formation from beast to man but his taking on the appearance and habits proper to a religious man.[23] Nebuchadnezzar's return to his senses, then, is the result of his recognition of God's power and his own insufficiency. In the desert of his madness, he learns how mad he had been in his former earthly glory; and his return to reason, to human appearance, and to his kingdom follows his long penance, his acknowledgment of God, and his persistence in virtue and humility. This moral interpretation dominates almost all later uses of the legend.

I have suggested that Nebuchadnezzar in the wilderness is the prototype of two conventions, the Unholy and the Holy Wild Man (see table 1); after this discussion of the biblical Nebuchadnezzar, we are in a better position to understand how this is so. Both Nebuchadnezzar and the Unholy Wild Man share the same life pattern and symptoms. They live initially in sin and spiritual blindness, and as a result they fall suddenly from glory to a madness that is at once punitive, symbolic of sin, and penitential. In their madness, they run wild in forest or desert, eating grass, berries, and occasionally wild animals; their appearance is bestial, for they run on all fours, they are naked, and their hair and nails grow long. They suffer terribly from the harshness of nature, but when their sins have been suitably, though unconsciously, atoned for, they are restored to sanity by grace rather than by merit or natural cure. This grace usually comes directly from God or indirectly through the prayers and generosity of others. Return to sanity is usually followed by a life of virtue, which may be active, as with Ywain; contemplative, as with Merlin; or a mixture of the two, as with Sir Gowther.

Since Nebuchadnezzar is an undoubted sinner, and since his sojourn in the wilderness is linked with madness in both the spiritual and the worldly sense, his similarity to the Holy Wild Man is less marked. There are, nevertheless, some notable parallels. First, portions of the two figures' life patterns are

23. Richard, *De eruditione*, PL 196:1345–46. For a more realistic interpretation involving Nebuchadnezzar's return to a shaven, clothed state, see Albert, *Commentaria in librum Danielis*, pp. 521–22; and Nicholas, GO 4:305.

alike: the Holy Wild Man often goes into the wilderness to atone for sin, his own or someone else's. And after a long time in the wilderness he too is given a sign of grace, though this grace is not likely to be the restoration of literal sanity or the return to worldly splendor. Second, the wilderness carries the same meanings for both Holy and Unholy Wild Men: it is a place of hardship, exile, purgation and perfection, and ideally of solitude with the ultimate realities — the soul, the devil, and God. It is where a man comes to know what he really is. Third, the Unholy and Holy Wild Men both share Nebuchadnezzar's wild appearance and bestial mode of life; as a result, both conventional figures, like Nebuchadnezzar himself, are often mistaken for demons or animals.

The crucial distinction between the Unholy and the Holy Wild Man is that the former is mad in every sense, and his penitential life is forced on him; the latter, mad to the world but sane in relation to God, voluntarily undertakes the life of the wilderness so that he may be purged and perfected like the saints.[24] In essence, the Unholy Wild Man must live like a beast so that he may truly be a man; the Holy Wild Man chooses the external life of a beast so that he may remember that he is a man and God's subject, and this life elevates him from common humanity to saintliness. It is hard to say how far or exactly in what ways Nebuchadnezzar influenced these two conventions and how much of the similarity is coincidental; but a study of Nebuchadnezzar remains an essential part of any study of medieval attitudes toward madness and its conventions.

To turn now to medieval art and literature, we find that although Nebuchadnezzar occasionally appears as a just con-

---

24. An Unholy Wild Man may, upon regaining his sanity, choose to continue to live in the wilderness as a Holy Wild Man, as Merlin does (see chapter 4). In Peter Comestor's version, Nebuchadnezzar's continued penance for twelve years after regaining his sanity may indicate a similar choice; *Historia scholastica, PL* 198:1452.

queror or a prophet,[25] most frequently he is a proud king who falls into bestiality to be saved eventually by penance and grace. According to Richard, "Nebuchadnezzar serves as an example that, whenever and however he pleases, God can humble those who walk in pride" (*PL* 196:1348); and throughout the Middle Ages, writers and artists agree that the Babylonian king is a forceful argument for humility. The reasons for Nebuchadnezzar's popularity with didactic authors are easy to deduce: the details of his story are colorful and rich in symbolic import; the pattern of his fall, penance, and restoration resembles the fall and redemption in Christ of Adam and each sinner; and stories of the falls of princes, particularly of those originally blessed with great beauty and power, exercise a perpetual appeal for the less fortunate.

A lesser but still important reason for Nebuchadnezzar's popularity may be found in artistic tradition: richly illuminated manuscripts of Jerome's commentary on Daniel circulated widely in France and Spain, and many of them include an illustration of Nebuchadnezzar's Dream, showing the king on all fours as a beast, with long hair on his head and often on his body, with great nails and wild expression. These manuscripts influenced Romanesque sculpture along the pilgrimage route to Compostela, thereby indirectly affecting later sculpture throughout much of Europe. Thus Nebuchadnezzar appears as a beast on a cloister capital at Moissac, in the transept at Saint-Benoît-sur-Loire, at Saint-Gaudens, and on the west portal at Bourg-Argental; in the last example, he seems to hold a scepter in one paw as token of his former glory.[26] Of course

25. E.g. Nebuchadnezzar appears as a prophet in the company of Moses, Isaiah, Jeremiah, and Daniel on the facade of Notre-Dame-la-Grande in Poitiers: see Émile Mâle, *L'art réligieux du XIIᵉ siècle en France* (Paris: Librairie Armand Colin, 1928), p. 144. Presumably the iconography derives from the *Ordo prophetarum.*

26. For the Beatus MSS including Jerome's commentary, see Mâle, *L'art réligieux*, pp. 4–17; for the sculpture, see ibid., and A. Kingsley Porter, *Romanesque Sculpture of the Pilgrimage Roads*, 10 vols. (Boston: Marshall Jones, 1923), vol. 8, pl. 1152.

there are numerous other artistic representations of Nebuchadnezzar: he appears as a wild man in Bibles and books of hours,[27] and there are two particularly good illuminations in a commentary by Nicholas de Lyra (plate 8) and in a manuscript of the *Concordia caritatis* (plate 9). The latter shows the rare subject of Nebuchadnezzar's cure: the hairy but crowned king is raised to his feet by angels, and the instrument of his cure is apparently the dew of grace, for the event is grouped with the cure of the paralytic at the pool of Bethesda (John 5), with the duck's use of water to escape the hunter, and with the ibis's hatching of her eggs under water. Still more numerous are illustrations in the highly popular *Speculum humanae salvationis,* where the king's dream — typologically equated with the Crucifixion — is pictured.[28] Such illustrations surely added to the familiarity and popularity of the legend; and it is even possible that sometimes the ubiquitous figure of the wild man in all varieties of art might have been interpreted as Nebuchadnezzar.

Despite the many appearances of Nebuchadnezzar in art, his literary popularity is derived chiefly from the intrinsic merits of the story and from its moral significance as elucidated by the numerous and excellent commentaries on Daniel. Another contributing factor may be the story's inclusion in the *Eclogue of Theodulus* (ca. tenth century), a well-known school text.[29] The poem is structured as a singing contest between Pseustis (Falsehood), who praises the heroes and gods of classical mythology, and Alithea (Truth), who counters with biblical lore. The stories are paired so that each pagan legend is seen as the deceiving fiction of which the Christian tale is the corresponding truth; the poem as a whole is an example of the Christian exegesis of classical mythology. In this work Nebuchadnezzar is compared to Salmoneus, whose emulation of Jupiter led to

27. E.g. the Roda Bible (Paris, Bibl. nat. lat. 6), 3, fol. 65v; and Hours of the Duc de Berry (Paris, Bibl. nat. lat. 18014), fol. 9v.

28. E.g. B.M. MS Harley 4996, fol. 25r.

29. Joannes Osternacher, ed., *Theoduli Ecloga* (Urfahr-Linz, 1902), ll. 237–44.

his death. Nebuchadnezzar, equally proud, also set himself up as a rival to God, but God was more forbearing than Jupiter, instructing rather than killing the usurper:

> Not aware that there was a god except himself,
>   the Assyrian king
> Endured dew and rain for seven seasons,
> A man turned beast. Through him all are urged
> To learn to be happy with natural powers.

This version follows Daniel quite closely, although some predictable changes are made, perhaps through the influence of Judith: Nebuchadnezzar is Assyrian rather than Babylonian, and his sin is the emulation of God. The poet's elliptical style produces an interesting ambiguity in the first line: "inscius esse Deum nisi se" should probably be read as indicating the *cause* of Nebuchadnezzar's transformation — his false pride; but it also may be read as describing his state in the wilderness — a madman, ignorant of God, cured only by the eventual knowledge that there *is* a god beyond himself. This fruitful ambiguity emphasizes that Nebuchadnezzar's punishment is symbolic of his sin: voluntary denial of God becomes involuntary inability to acknowledge him, and metaphorical folly becomes literal madness. "The fool hath said in his heart: There is no God" (Ps. 13:1); such a fool was Nebuchadnezzar, and the *Eclogue* makes the point economically. The four lines quoted here contain the central points of the medieval legend: Nebuchadnezzar's pride, his transformation, and the lesson that men must learn they are only men lest they become irrational beasts.

Other medieval Latin literature also emphasizes Nebuchadnezzar's pride: for instance, the thirteenth-century Laon *Ordo prophetarum* describes him as "proud in bearing" even as a prophet.[30] The Beauvais Daniel play of the previous century follows Daniel 5 in having Daniel warn Belshazzar that he should have profited by his father's fall:

30. Young, *Drama of the Medieval Church*, 2:145.

Your father, once powerful
Above all powerful men,
Swollen with excessive pride,
Was cast down from his glory.

For he would not walk with God
But pretended to be a god himself;
He plundered the vessels of the temple
And had them for his own use.

But after many mad acts,
At last losing his riches,
Stripped of human shape,
He ate grass for food.[31]

Here, as in the *Eclogue* and the commentaries, Nebuchadnezzar's pride and his emulation of God are stressed more than in Daniel, and the king's mad behavior while he is still nominally sane is clearly related to his punishment.

Nebuchadnezzar exemplifies both pride and the strength of tyranny in the late fourteenth-century lyric "The Bird with Four Feathers": in telling how she lost her third valuable feather, strength, by abusing it in pride, the bird describes Nebuchadnezzar's similar abuse and loss. After conquering Jerusalem, apparently with undue brutality,

Him thought þer schold no þing withstonde,
His herte was set so heigh In Pryde:
Till þe king of myghtes most
Browght him þere þat lowest was,
And caught him from his real [royal] oost,
And drof him to a wildirnesse;
And there he lyued with erbe & rote,
Walkyng euer on foot & on honde,
Till god of mercy dede him bote [remedy],
And his prison out of bonde:

31. Ibid., 2:294, ll. 151–62. Historically, of course, Belshazzar was Nebuchadnezzar's grandson, but most medieval accounts follow Dan. 5:2 in making Belshazzar the son.

Thanne seide þis kyng thise wordes, Iwis:
"Al thing be, lord, at thi powste [power],
Mercy I crie; I haue do mys [amiss] —
Parce michi domine [Have mercy on me, Lord]!" [32]

Froissart appropriately uses Nebuchadnezzar's fall as an
analogy to Charles VI's madness, but he diplomatically refrains
from mentioning Nebuchadnezzar's idolatry, tyranny, and
pride as possible causes of his fall. Rather, he and Charles are
shown to be alike in their great power and sudden downfall,
even though Charles's degradation is not so complete as Nebuchadnezzar's:

> Was there not Nebuchadnezzar, King of Assyria, who
> reigned for a time in such might that there was no whisper
> of another higher than him? And suddenly, at the height
> of his power and glory, the King of Kings, God, Lord of
> Heaven and earth and maker and disposer of all things, so
> visited him that he lost his reason and his kingdom, and
> remained in that state for seven years. He lived on acorns
> and crab-apples, with the tastes and appetite of a swine.
> And when he had done penance, God restored his memory
> to him and he said to the prophet Daniel that above the
> God of Israel there is no other God.[33]

Like most late medieval retellers of Nebuchadnezzar's story,
Froissart assumes that the king was not transformed into an
animal. Rather, he emphasizes the penitential aspect of the
punishment and adds touches of realism: a real wild man running about the woods in France might subsist on acorns and
crab–apples, but the biblical grass is harder to credit. Such
additions facilitate comparison between the two mad kings:
the more believable Nebuchadnezzar's madness, the more
likely it would be that his case and Charles's could be similar
in all respects; if Nebuchadnezzar's quite real madness had
clear moral connotations, then so might Charles's insanity.

---

32. Carleton Brown, ed., *Religious Lyrics of the XIVth Century*, 2d ed.,
rev. G. V. Smithers (Oxford: Clarendon Press, 1957), no. 121, ll. 151–64.

33. *Chronicles*, trans. Brereton, pp. 393–94.

Chaucer's pretentious Monk provides a pedestrian and highly traditional account of Nebuchadnezzar (*CT* 7. 2143–82, 2210–22). He seems to have followed the Vulgate closely even though there are several factual errors (e.g. that Daniel was a eunuch and that he was cast into the fiery furnace), for his Nebuchadnezzar ate hay, lay in the rain, had hair like eagles' feathers and nails like birds' claws, lived with asses (Dan. 5:21), and was granted the return of "resoun" (*sensus*) and "figure" (*figura*). There are also clear echoes of the commentators in the account: Chaucer stresses Nebuchadnezzar's pride, changing the emphasis from pride in Babylon to the emulation of God:

> This kyng of kynges proud was and elaat;
> He wende that God, that sit in magestee,
> Ne myghte hym nat bireve of his estaat.
>
> [ll. 2167–69]

He notes that Nebuchadnezzar was not really an ox but only thought that he was: "And lyk a beest hym semed for to bee" (l. 2171). He seems to have been aware of the controversy over the length of time that Nebuchadnezzar actually was mad, for he does not commit himself: the madness lasted a vague "certein tyme" (l. 2174). Chaucer's statement that "God relessed hym a certeyn yeres" (l. 2177), although it may mean only that after some years God released him, may also refer to the abridgment of Nebuchadnezzar's punishment at Daniel's request, a belief held, so far as I know, chiefly by Peter Comestor and his followers.[34] The emphasis on Nebuchadnezzar's penitential bearing until his death (ll. 2180–84) may also derive from Comestor. Chaucer's account, then, is largely dependent on the Vulgate and probably on either the *Historia scholastica* or a commentary derived from it.[35] It typifies the medieval

34. *Historia scholastica, PL* 198:1452 (and see n. 20 above).

35. Comestor quotes large portions of the Vulgate text, which Chaucer follows closely; Chaucer's errors might have come from his having mistranslated or misunderstood certain ambiguities in the *Historia*, and this might also explain Chaucer's vagueness about the duration of Nebuchadnezzar's insanity, his possible reference to the abridgment of that punish-

tendency to emphasize Nebuchadnezzar's pride, his emulation of God, and his penitence, but it is in the scholastic rather than the literary tradition in its strict adherence to the biblical details of the king's madness. This version's dullness and conservatism are pardonable only if they are seen as an attempt to fit tale to teller.

At least two of Chaucer's contemporaries — the *Cleanness*-poet and Gower — wrote elaborate, realistic, and moving accounts of Nebuchadnezzar's reign and fall. *Cleanness* contains two separate uses of the story: first it describes Nebuchadnezzar's capture of Jerusalem and the holy vessels and his illustrious reign; later, at Belshazzar's feast, Daniel reminds Belshazzar of the more unfortunate aspects of his father's career.[36] Both accounts praise Nebuchadnezzar highly, but in very different ways. In the first account the poet presents Nebuchadnezzar as a just conqueror, the punisher of idolatry; the king is commended for his reverence for the temple vessels and for God:

---

ment, and his assurance of the king's continuing penitence. Pauline Aiken believes that Chaucer followed Vincent's considerably abridged summary of the *Historia* ("Vincent of Beauvais and Chaucer's *Monk's Tale*," *Speculum* 17 [1942]:56–68), but I think it more likely that Chaucer had a full text of the *Historia*. For instance, Aiken derives Chaucer's notion that Daniel was a eunuch from Vincent's "He was so chaste that his compatriots thought him a eunuch"; but Comestor's full text provides a better source: "When Nebuchadnezzar had brought the more noble Judaean boys, some of them of royal blood, into Babylon, he castrated the more beautiful and clever of them"; cf. Chaucer's "The faireste children of the blood roial / Of Israel he leet do gelde anoon" (ll. 2151–52). Dudley R. Johnson argues that Chaucer follows Desmoulins's *Bible Historiale*, a French commentary that follows Comestor closely; "The Biblical Characters of Chaucer's Monk," *PMLA* 66 (1951):827–43. Not having seen a MS of the *Bible*, I cannot say whether it includes all the relevant parts of the *Historia scholastica*.

36. I follow Israel Gollancz's edition, *Select Early English Poems* (London: Oxford University Press, 1921), vol. 7; I have also used Robert J. Menner, ed., *Purity*, Yale Studies in English, vol. 61 (New Haven: Yale University Press, 1920; reprinted Hamden, Conn.: Archon Books, 1970). The author of *Cleanness* is, of course, generally assumed to have written *Patience*, *Pearl*, and *Sir Gawain and the Green Knight* as well; since his dialect is notoriously difficult, I have appended my translations in the text.

He sesed hem wyth solemnete, þe souerayn he praysed,
þat watȝ aþel ouer alle, Israel dryȝten. . . .

[ll. 1313–14]

[He took them ceremoniously, he praised the Sovereign,
the noblest of all, the Lord of Israel.]

Because the poet is concerned to set up Nebuchadnezzar's virtue in contrast to Belshazzar's villainy, he makes some curious
changes in emphasis in the story. Nebuchadnezzar's career is
described in wholly favorable terms, and his excellence and
piety are stressed. His occasional backslidings are almost completely ignored: there is no mention of the fiery furnace, and
the only possible indication of pride is the comment "als þe
god of þe grounde watȝ grauen his name" ("his name was
engraved as god of the land"; l. 1324), which may well refer
to the king's virtue and popularity rather than to any emulation of God. Most astonishing is the omission of any clear
reference to the king's fall into bestiality. We find this transformation only if we look for it very hard, and only in these
lines: Nebuchadnezzar reigned long and well,

& al þurȝ dome of Daniel, fro he deuised hade
þat alle goudes com of God, & gef hit hym bi samples,
þat he ful clanly bi-cnv his carp bi þe laste,
& ofte hit mekned his mynde, his maysterful werkkes.

[ll. 1325–28]

[and all through Daniel's advice, for he had explained
that all goods come from God, and he gave examples, so
that he wholly acknowledged those words at last, and
God's lordly works often meekened his mind.]

If the "samples" include the interpretation of the dream of the
tree, then there may be a reference to the madness that certainly "mekned his mynde"; but there is no indisputable mention of this crucial event in Nebuchadnezzar's life until the
second account in the poem, where Daniel uses Nebuchadnezzar as an example to chastise Belshazzar's blasphemous corruption of the holy vessels. But in the first account, instead of the

fall into madness, that darker fall which we all must share is presented:

> Bot al drawes to dyȝe wyth doel vpon ende;
> Bi a haþel neuer so hyȝe he heldes to grounde;
> & so Nabugo de Noȝar, as he nedes moste,
> For alle his empire so hiȝe in erþe is he grauen.
>
> [ll. 1329–32]

[But all draws toward death, with grief at the end; be a hero never so great, he falls to the ground; and so Nebuchadnezzar, as he needs must, for all his empire so high is buried in the earth.]

It is the simple Fall of Princes story that the poet tells here. All men must die; even the good and mighty Nebuchadnezzar, whose name "als þe god of þe grounde watȝ grauen," is finally "grauen in erþe." This use of the legend, almost as moving in its way as the full account of bestiality and restoration, is unique in the versions I have studied, and it testifies to the poet's inventiveness.

The poem then describes Belshazzar's many crimes, centering on his double perversion of the holy vessels and of himself. As in the Bible, Daniel interprets the writing on the wall which has further maddened the already witless king. He begins with a homily on the lessons to be learned from Nebuchadnezzar's life. First he notes that Nebuchadnezzar was beloved by God, who "fylsened euer þy fader & vpon folde cheryched" ("ever aided your father and cherished him on earth"; l. 1644). So long as he honored God, there was none on earth so powerful. But then he grew proud, forgetting God:

> þenne blynnes he not of blasfemy on to blame þe
>   dryȝtyn,
> His myȝt mete to Goddes he made wyth his wordes:
> "I am god of þe grounde, to gye as my lykes,
> As he þat hyȝe is in heuen his aungeles þat weldes.
>
> If he hatȝ formed þe folde & folk þer vpone,
> I haf bigged Babiloyne, burȝ alþer-rychest,

Stabled þer-inne vche a ston in strenkþe of myn armes,
Moȝt neuer myȝt bot myn make such anoþer."

[ll. 1661–68]

[Then he ceased not to blame and blaspheme the Lord;
he judged his own might equal to God's in these words:
"I am god of this earth, to guide it as I please, just as the
high one in heaven rules his angels. If he made earth and
the people thereon, I have built Babylon, richest of cities,
establishing each stone in it by the strength of my arms;
no might but mine could make such another.]

As in the Bible, a voice from heaven condemns the proud king,
but the terms of his punishment have been anglicized:

& þou, remued fro monnes sunes, on mor most abide,
& in wasturne walk, & wyth þe wylde dowelle,
As best, byte on þe bent of braken & erbes,
Wyth wroþe wolfes to won & wyth wylde asses.

[ll. 1673–76]

[And, removed from men's sons, you must live on the moor
and walk in the wilderness, and dwell with wild creatures;
like a beast, eat bracken and herbs in the fields, live with
fierce wolves and with wild asses.]

The punishment is inflicted immediately. The poet has omitted
any reference to the king's prophetic dream, perhaps because
the story is strange enough without it; and the year's delay is
also ignored, since vengeance must follow directly upon the
one sin mentioned in this account.

In-mydde þe poynt of his pryde de-parted he þere
Fro þe soly of his solempnete, his solace he leues,
& carfully is out-kast to contre vnknawen,
Fer in-to a fyr fryth þer frekes neuer comen.

His hert heldet vnhole, he hoped non oþer
Bot a best þat he be, a bol oþer an oxe;
He fares forth on alle faure, fogge watȝ his mete,
& ete ay as a horce when erbes were fallen.

þus he countes hym a kow, þat watȝ a kyng ryche,
Quyle seuen syþeȝ were ouer-seyed, someres I trawe,
By þat mony þik theȝe þryȝt vmbe his lyre,
þat alle watȝ dubbed & dyȝt in þe dew of heuen.

Faxed fyltered & felt flosed hym vmbe,
þat schad fro his sculderes to his schere-wykes,
& twenty-folde twynande hit to his tos raȝt,
þer mony clyuy as clyde hit clyȝt to-geder.

His berde i-brad alle his brest to þe bare vrþe,
His browes bresed as breres aboute his brode chekes,
Holȝe were his yȝen & vnder campe hores,
& al watȝ gray as þe glede, wyth ful grymme clawres,

þat were croked & kene as þe kyte pauue,
Erne-hwed he watȝ, & al ouer brawden,
Til he wyst ful wel who wroȝt alle myȝtes,
& cowþe vche kyndam tokerue & keuer when hym lyked.

[ll. 1677–1700]

[In the midst of his pride, he left his solemn throne; he left his solace and was cast out, full of care, to an unknown country, deep in a far forest where men never came. His heart grew mad; he thought nothing but that he was a beast, a bull or an ox; he fared forth on all fours, grass was his food, and he ate hay like a horse when the herbs were dead. Thus, once a rich king, he considered himself a cow until seven times had passed, seven summers, I trust. By then many thick muscles crowded his flesh, that was clothed and dressed in heaven's dew. His hair grew tangled, covering him in shaggy mats, falling from his shoulders to his groin, and, entwining twenty-fold, it reached to his toes, where burrs, like plaster, held it together. His beard spread over his breast down to the bare earth; his brows bristled like briars about his broad cheeks; his eyes were hollow under bristly hairs; and he was grey as a kite, with grim claws crooked and keen as a kite's talons. Eagle-hued he was, and covered all over, till he

knew full well who wrought all great works and who could
divide kingdoms and restore them when he chose.]

The place of exile, vague in the Vulgate, becomes a remote
and deserted English forest with wolves and wild asses; and
Nebuchadnezzar, like other wild men in art and literature,
runs on all fours and eats what he finds. His long matted hair,
his beard, his bristly brows, his hollow eyes, his grey color, and
his long claws seem to be derived at least as much from the traditional figure of the wild man as from Daniel or the commentaries.[37] The picture is at once more realistic and more
conventional than in the commentaries; the *Cleanness*-poet's
Nebuchadnezzar is more akin to Froissart's than to Chaucer's.
Nebuchadnezzar may well have helped to initiate the wild
man tradition in medieval literature, but that tradition, once
started, grew beyond the biblical account to combine with
traditions of the desert saints, of Christian hermits, of real
madmen in the forests, and of the wild man of popular lore;
the Nebuchadnezzar of *Cleanness* is closer to these figures than
to his biblical original, represented in the *Monk's Tale*.

Gower's version of the tale is more concerned with the pathos
of Nebuchadnezzar's transformation than with his role as a
just prince overthrown by one vice; his Nebuchadnezzar is less
dignified than the *Cleanness*-poet's, but the king's agony in
the wilderness is more thoroughly described and presented
from a more subjective point of view.[38] The *Cleanness*-poet

37. The tradition of the wild man will be discussed in chapter 4; see also
Bernheimer, *Wild Men*, pp. 1–48; and Larry D. Benson, *Art and Tradition
in Sir Gawain and the Green Knight* (New Brunswick, N.J.: Rutgers University Press, 1965), pp. 67–83. The remarkably perceptive eye for detail
and the tendency to anglicize biblical events, so typical of the *Cleanness*-
poet, are discussed more fully in A. C. Spearing, *The Gawain-poet: A Critical Study* (Cambridge: Cambridge University Press, 1970), pp. 55–65.

38. Nebuchadnezzar's fall is discussed in *Confessio Amantis*, in *The
English Works of John Gower*, ed. G. C. Macaulay, EETS, es 81, 82 (1900,
1901), 1. 2772–3042. For a discussion of "pointing," or detailed description,
as a characteristic technique of Gower and other Ricardian poets, see
Burrow, *Ricardian Poetry*, pp. 69–78. Certainly much of the charm of
Gower's version of the Nebuchadnezzar story comes from this technique.

rearranges the biblical story to suit his purposes, delaying the
story of Nebuchadnezzar's bestiality until his habitual virtue
has been established, completely omitting the story of the
prophetic dream, and subordinating Daniel's role as counsellor,
all in order to magnify Nebuchadnezzar's essential goodness
and close relationship to God. Gower's version is closer to
Daniel and the commentaries in its preliminaries, including
an emphasis on Nebuchadnezzar's habitual pride, a detailed
presentation of the dream and of Daniel's interpretation, and
the injunction by Daniel to reform and to perform deeds
of mercy to forestall the punishment.

The description of Nebuchadnezzar's real transformation
into a beast — for so Gower takes it — calls forth Gower's
greatest talents, making the tale one of the most moving in
the *Confessio Amantis.* Nebuchadnezzar is Genius's first example against vainglory. Having prepared the way for the king's
real loss of memory by stating that

> He was so full of veine gloire,
> That he ne hadde no memoire
> That ther was eny good bot he . . . ,
>
> [1. 2799–801]

Genius tells of the dream, the interpretation, and Daniel's
warning that reformation might bring forgiveness. Nebuchadnezzar, however, was so proud that he refused to believe any
dream, let alone Daniel's advice, and persisted in boasting of
Babylon. God immediately punished him, removing him on
the instant from man's sight. This sudden vanishing is found
explicitly only in Gower, and it contributes to the romance-
like quality of the tale from this point on. The next lines play
upon the contrast between Nebuchadnezzar's royal state and
his life as a beast.

> And thus was he from his kingdom
> Into the wilde Forest drawe,
> Wher that the myhti goddes lawe
> Thurgh his pouer dede him transforme
> Fro man into a bestes formes;

And lich an Oxe under the fot
He graseth, as he nedes mot,
To geten him his lives fode.
Tho thoghte him colde grases goode,
That whilom [once] eet the hote spices,
Thus was he torned fro delices:
The wyn which he was wont to drinke
He tok thanne of the welles brinke
Or of the pet [pit] or of the slowh,
It thoghte him thanne good ynowh:
In stede of chambres wel arraied
He was thanne of a buissh wel paied [pleased],
The harde ground he lay upon,
For othre pilwes hath he non;
The stormes and the Reines falle,
The wyndes blowe upon him alle,
He was tormented day and nyht.

[1. 2968–89]

The contrast between the royal and outcast states is pathetic, growing even more so when Nebuchadnezzar begins to regain his senses. First he becomes aware of his own beastlike appearance.

Upon himself tho gan he loke;
In stede of mete gras and stres [straw],
In stede of handes longe cles [claws],
In stede of man a bestes lyke
He syh; and thanne he gan to syke [sigh]
For cloth of gold and for perrie [jewelry],
Which him was wont to magnefie.
When he behield his Cote of heres,
He wept and with fulwoful teres
Up to the hevene he caste his chiere [face]
Wepende, and thoghte in this manere;
Thogh he no wordes myhte winne,
Thus seide his herte and spak withinne:
"O mihti godd, that al hast wroght
And al myht bringe ayein to noght,

Now knowe I wel, bot al of thee,
This world hath no prosperite."

[1. 2992–3008]

Gower has admirably filled out the concise biblical account.
Each thought, each feeling of the king in his gradual return to
sanity is fully and brilliantly conceived, from his initial yearn-
ing for finery to improve his appearance to his realization —
perhaps brought about by the sight of his unorthodox but
penitential "Cote of heres" — that prayer is the only hope.
Where the biblical Nebuchadnezzar merely acknowledged
God's power and praised him, Gower's conducts himself in
more specifically Christian fashion, confessing his sin, asking
mercy, and pledging amendment (1. 3013–21). His next actions,
in which his still bestial body is contrasted with his newly
human mind, are a stroke of genius on Gower's part. The picture of the miserable but engaging beast raising its hooves and
braying its appeal to God is charming.

And so thenkende he gan doun bowe,
And thogh him lacke vois and speche,
He gan up with his feet areche,
And wailende in his bestly stevene [voice]
He made his pleignte unto the hevene.
He kneleth in his wise and braieth,
To seche merci and assaieth
His god, which made him nothing strange,
Whan that he sih his pride change.
Anon as he was humble and tame,
He fond toward his god the same,
And in a twinklinge of a lok
His mannes forme ayein he tok.

[1. 3022–34]

Nebuchadnezzar's unusual plight has clearly captured Gower's
sympathy and imagination, and the result is splendid. The tale
is closer to romance than to the Bible — that Nebuchadnezzar
really becomes a beast is indicative — and his madness is sub-
ordinated to his bestiality. But that bestiality is still symbolic

of madness and sin, and with the return of some measure of
sanity the penitential nature of the punishment becomes clear.
Gower's Nebuchadnezzar in his madness is closer to Ywain than
to Macarius, whose one brief lapse into the sin of anger led
him to spend six months in conscious penance, naked in the
wilderness, returning "tobittyn and skrattyd with thornys and
breers" (*AT* 771), but all are members of the same family: sinners who become wild men so that their guilt may be forgiven.
The pattern and the symptoms will appear again in chapter 4.

Three other interesting adaptations of the legend are worth
mention. The first is in the *Miroure of Mans Saluacionne*.
One reference to the king there is quite traditional: the falls
of Lucifer, Adam, and Nebuchadnezzar, all caused by pride, are
equated typologically (p. 128). But another reference is quite
peculiar: Nebuchadnezzar's vision of the tree and his subsequent fall are compared to Christ's life, Resurrection, and
Crucifixion.[39] The tree signifies both Nebuchadnezzar and
Christ, whose power reaches heaven and spreads over the whole
earth. The creatures under the tree are those nourished by
Christ's grace. The cutting down of the tree is the Crucifixion;
the cutting of branches, the scattering of the disciples; the
shaking off of the leaves, the Jews' scorn for Christ's teachings.
The fruit is scattered because the Jews refused to believe
Christ's miracles; birds and beasts disperse because neither
angels nor men could help Christ in his agony; the root remaining in the ground is the promise of Resurrection; the
binding of the tree with iron and steel signifies the nailing of
Christ to the Cross.

He [the watcher angel] saide with dewe of heven / shuld alle
    be wette the kinge
ffor verraly fro amanges men / he shuld haf his dwelling

39. Pp. 85–87. This comparison is aptly illustrated in at least one MS of
the *Speculum humanae salvationis*, where Nebuchadnezzar is shown dream-
ing of a tree with several animals in it, including the pelican rending her
breast, a standard symbol of Christ's sacrifice; see B.M. MS Harley 4996,
fol. 25r.

With hevens dewe wette that is / with his blude ouer ronnen
　bene
And with the same blude wet alle / fro thraldome qwhitte fulle
　clene
He saide that als a beeste / was to be fedde this kinge
ffor crist of Ayselle [vinegar] and galle / to drynk shuld haf
　offring
He addid that the kinges hert / shuld haf fro manhed chaung-
　ing
And therfore taken hym an hert / beestisshe als of feling
ffor the Jewes crist als a man / shuld noght treet nor addmitte
Bot als a wilde beest or a worme / hym crucify and bespitte
Or els that the Jewes to crist / shuld noght like men thaym bere
But grynne on hym like beestes / the cruwelest that evre were
He saide that seven tymes / shuld be chaunged on the king
So hadde seuen houres canonyke / crists passionne pro-
　loignyng.

Finally, both Nebuchadnezzar and Christ bear witness to God's
great power. This curious interpretation, equating the madness
of Nebuchadnezzar with the passion of the incarnate God,
seems to play on the following identifications: man become
beast is analogous to God become man; the wilderness is symbolic of the Cross, both places of atonement; man's suffering
for his own sins represents Christ's suffering for the sins of
others. Both Christ and Nebuchadnezzar are essentially wild
men, one holy and the other unholy, working out salvation,
voluntarily or involuntarily, in the place of exile. The rami-
fications of this comparison will become more apparent in
chapter 4.

Another story related to the Nebuchadnezzar legend in plot
and moral, even though the king's name and many details
have been changed, may be found in the *Gesta Romanorum*
(pp. 75–87). Jovinian, a proud Roman emperor, audaciously
wonders "whethir þere be any god without me?" One day he
goes hunting, and a cloud arises to separate him from his company. Wandering alone, he finds a pool in which he bathes;

meanwhile a man who looks exactly like him steals his clothes and returns to Rome, claiming to be the emperor. The real emperor, naked, tries to find someone to shelter him, but no one will do so, for everyone thinks he is a mad liar when he claims to be the emperor, whom everyone believes to be in his palace. The poor man is beaten and scourged for his presumption. At last he "bygan to thenk, what haue I do, or what haue I grevid god, þat I am thus put oute of the Empire, and þat no man knowith me?" He suddenly recalls his earlier pride and goes to a hermit to confess and do penance. After his confession the hermit recognizes him: "but as long as þou duelledist in synne, I coude not know the." Jovinian borrows humble clothes from the hermit and returns to the palace, where everyone recognizes him again. The false emperor appears to explain: " 'Hit happid þat this man bygan to be so hy in hert, & so proudely, and therfor god put him oute of his empier, tyll þat he had made amendis; and in thys tyme I was commaunded by god to occupie his stede, þat the Empire shuld not perissh; and I am his aungell, that haue I-be in the gouernaile and keping, as ye know, vnto þe tyme that he were reconsiled to god." Jovinian, humbled and cured, lives a devout life thereafter.

The general outline of the story is similar to that in Daniel: a proud king is punished for thinking that there is no other God; in punishment, he is cast out of his kingdom naked, to wander about unaided and unrecognized; upon the recognition and confession of his sin, he is restored to his kingdom. Even the presence of the false emperor-angel has a precedent in commentaries on Daniel: many commentators wondered what might happen to so powerful a realm as Babylon during the king's absence, but Jerome dismisses such concerns with the assurance that God provided for Babylon (*PL* 25:513), and Peter Comestor assumes that Daniel and seven judges ruled (*PL* 198:1452).

There are also similarities between the moral interpretations of the *Gesta* story and of Daniel. The *Gesta* forest, like Nebuchadnezzar's grass, represents "worldly vanytes"; the cloud is demonic temptation, which Richard suggests was implicated in Nebuchadnezzar's fall as well (*PL* 196:1319–21, 1339–40). The clothes are virtues in the *Gesta* version, and they have implicitly the same meaning in Daniel; in both cases, nudity is a token of sinfulness. The pool in which Jovinian bathes may correspond to Nebuchadnezzar's dew; the first is interpreted as fleshly affections, and the second as earthly pleasures suggested by the devil, according to Richard.[40] Whether or not the Nebuchadnezzar legend directly influenced the *Gesta* story, it seems likely that the second derives ultimately from the first. Both Nebuchadnezzar and Jovinian belong to the same family of sinners exiled and stripped for their pride, which was eventually forgiven because of their penance in the wild and their confession and amendment.

The charming and popular homiletic romance *Robert of Sicily* is clearly a version of the *Gesta* story, and it makes explicit the similarity of its plot to the Nebuchadnezzar legend.[41] The proud King Robert, listening to the Magnificat one evening in church, decides that the *deposuit potentes* verse (Luke 1:52) could never apply to him. As a result of this presumption, an angel assumes Robert's appearance and place; and Robert, unrecognized, is mocked and humiliated when he claims to be king himself. Eventually he is made the new king's fool. The biblical Nebuchadnezzar's madness is here represented by everyone's conviction that Robert must be mad to think himself king; the moral madness of his pride is so clear that the poet presumably felt it unnecessary to show Robert as literally mad. Nebuchadnezzar's bestiality is suggested humorously and ingeniously: the angel-king dresses Robert and an ape in the same clothes, and this comic doubling ensures that no one will

---

40. *De eruditione, PL* 196:1325. More usually the dew is interpreted as grace; see Albert, *Commentaria in librum Danielis*, p. 515.

41. I follow the text in Walter Hoyt French and Charles Brockway Hale, eds., *Middle English Metrical Romances*, 2 vols. (New York, 1930; reprinted New York: Russell & Russell, 1964), 2:933–46. Lillian H. Hornstein notes that the English version of the story is the only one with the Nebuchadnezzar interpolation; she also describes numerous analogues to *Robert* and to the *Gesta* story; "King Robert of Sicily: Analogues and Origins," *PMLA* 79 (1964):13–21.

take Robert's ravings seriously. Finally, Robert remembers Nebuchadnezzar's similar plight; although he thinks his own state even worse, he resolves to follow Nebuchadnezzar's example of prayer and humility. Reciting a formal confession with the refrain "Lord, on þi fool þou haue pite," he realizes that he really is what his dress indicates: a fool. He stops protesting against what he had formerly considered his maltreatment, and after some time the angel-king questions him: "Fool, art þow kyng?" (l. 387). He responds humbly that he is merely a fool, "And more þen fol, ʒif hit may be" (l. 391). Such humility is rewarded: having learned what he is before God, he is restored to his kingdom; and, like Nebuchadnezzar, he orders his story to be written so that all might learn of God's power and mercy. This delightful romance helps illustrate the importance of the Nebuchadnezzar legend — of the general plot of the fall from power and pride into madness or patent folly as well as of the specific details of the biblical version. It matters little whether a story like the *Gesta* version was intended as an adaptation of Daniel; *Robert of Sicily* shows that this sort of plot might easily be associated with Nebuchadnezzar and that inventive poets as well as fallen kings might see the many possible uses to which the legend might be put.

The pattern of Nebuchadnezzar's life, as examined in this chapter and as illustrated in table 1, is extremely important in Christian literature. It is shared by many famous saints and sinners, most of whom also manifest his mental derangement or his outward appearance. Such figures and the conventions they represent — the Mad Sinner, the Holy and the Unholy Wild Man — will be the subject of the rest of this study; and it will become increasingly clear how all of them are related, if not indebted, to Nebuchadnezzar, father of them all.

3 The Mad Sinner: Herod and the Pagan Kings

And again the madman, the deranged man, attempts and expects to rule over not only men but gods.

Plato, *The Republic* 573C

For when a soul is wicked and incurable, it yields to no medicine granted by God.

Saint John Chrysostom, *Homily on Matthew 2:16*

There are few greater villains in medieval literature than Herod the Great, first foreign king of Judea and wrathful persecutor of the infant Christ. And there are no better examples of the conventional Mad Sinner, that proud and cruel pagan tyrant who thinks himself a god, who falls into that rage which is both clinical and symbolic madness when his pretensions to grandeur are threatened, who persecutes the just, and whose myriad sins against God and his fellow men are finally punished by madness, death, and damnation.

Of course, this view of Herod as Mad Sinner is largely a creation of the Christian Middle Ages. The historical Herod was an able monarch somewhat given to pride, cruelty, and ambition. An Arab by birth, he murdered several members of the royal Hasmonean family to obtain the Judean crown, and his rage was easily aroused by the plots of his rebellious wives and children, a fair number of whom he killed.[1] He

---

1. Major sources for the historical Herod are *JW* 1 and 2, and *JA* 15–19. For a modern history, see Stewart Perowne, *The Life and Times of Herod the Great* (London: Hodder & Stoughton, 1956).

95

took religious matters less seriously than he might have done. According to Josephus, he earned God's wrath by rifling the tombs of David and Solomon to find money for building projects, and he broke Jewish law by placing the image of a Roman eagle in the temple. When the Pharisees, Jewish nationalists, tried to pull down the eagle, Herod summarily tried them and burned them alive. The result of such blasphemy was a punitive and fatal disease involving gangrene, general inflammation, mild fever, foul breath, and extreme pain. In his final agony, he tried to ensure general mourning at his death by ordering a young man from each Jewish family to be slain, but the massacre was never carried out. Shortly after a fit of depression in which he unsuccessfully tried to kill himself with a fruit knife, Herod died, lamented by few: most Jews seem to have shared Josephus's assessment of him as "a man who was cruel to all alike and one who easily gave in to anger and was contemptuous of justice" (*JA* 17. 191).

But such a man — and I have purposely selected some of the most damning details — is hardly a Mad Sinner, cruel and tyrannical though he might be. The particularly vicious and absurd madman who enlivens the medieval drama is the product of centuries of Christian vilification, distortion, and fabrication. Some real traits and deeds are distorted beyond recognition: Herod's occasional anger becomes full-blown madness, and his proposed massacre of the young Jews after his death is probably the source of the unhistorical Slaughter of the Innocents (Matt. 2:1–18). Other damning details, such as his burning of the Jewish genealogies so that no one would know he was not a true Jewish king,[2] are unsupported by even the flimsiest fact. Still another technique of blackening Herod's soul was to attribute to him deeds performed by other members of the Herod family: his son Herod Antipas ordered the execution of John the Baptist and mocked Christ, according to the Bible (see Matt. 14:1–11; Luke 13:31–32 and 23:8–12); while his

2. This act is first mentioned by Eusebius, *Ecclesiastical History* (early fourth century), trans. Roy J. DeFerrari, Fathers of the Church, vols. 19 and 29 (Washington, D.C.: Catholic University of America Press, 1953, 1955), bk. 1, ch. 7.

grandson Agrippa killed Saint James Major, imprisoned Saint Peter, and died of a miraculous disease inflicted by an angel while Agrippa was sitting in splendid robes accepting the worship due to God.[3] By such misinterpretation and even invention of fact, Christian writers created a moral madman capable of emulating and even of trying to murder God, a powerful and colorful tyrant who makes an ideal foil for the humility and gentleness of the Christ-child, the true king of the Jews.

Before turning to the brilliant portraits of Herod the Great as a Mad Sinner in late medieval literature, I would like to sketch the outlines of the tradition developed by commentators and preachers from Eusebius (early fourth century) through the author of the *Stanzaic Life of Christ* (early fourteenth century).[4] Although no single commentator presents all the

---

3. For Herod Agrippa, see Acts 12:1–23, and *JA* 19. 344–47. For examples of Herod as a composite figure, see the Letter of Herod to Pilate, in *The Apocryphal New Testament*, trans. M. R. James, corr. ed. (Oxford: Clarendon Press, 1913), pp. 155–56; Bede, *Super Acta Apostolorum Expositio*, PL 92:971–72 (ostensibly on Herod Agrippa); and the *Book of the Knight of La Tour-Landry*, p. 105, where all three biblical Herods are fused. For examples of possible conflation of the Herods in English drama, see S. S. Hussey, "How Many Herods in the English Drama," *Neophil* 48 (1964):252–59.

4. Important commentaries from which I draw material are the following: Eusebius, *Ecclesiastical History*; John Chrysostom (d. 407), *Commentaria in Sanctum Matthaeum 7–9*, in *Opera*, ed. D. A. B. Caillau and D. M. N. S. Guillon (Paris, 1835), vol. 5; Isidore of Seville (d. 636), *Etymologiae* 7. 10. 6, and *Allegoriae quaedam sacrae scripturae*, PL 83:118; Bede (d. 735), *Expositio in Evangelium Sancti Matthaei*, *Expositio in Evangelium Sancti Lucae*, and *Super Acta Apostolorum Expositio*, all in PL 92; Remigius of Auxerre (ninth century), Homilia 6 on Matt. 2:19, PL 131:895–99 (Remigius is responsible for the late medieval belief that Herod actually did massacre the Jews at his death and that he succeeded in committing suicide); Peter Comestor, *Historia scholastica*, PL 198:1541–689 (following Bede, Josephus, and Eusebius closely); and three works depending largely on Comestor: Peter Riga's highly influential versified Bible (Ca. 1200), the *Aurora* (*Evangelium*, 11. 425–890), ed. Paul E. Beichner, Notre Dame Publications in Medieval Studies, no. 19, 2 vols. (South Bend, Ind.: University of Notre Dame Press, 1965); Jacobus de Voragine's *Legenda aurea* (late thirteenth century), ed. Th. Graesse, 3d ed. (Leipzig, 1890; reprinted

characteristics of the Mad Sinner of medieval drama, the available material was easily combined and shaped by the dramatists to create or embody that convention.

First, Herod is shown as extremely proud. Josephus had hinted that the historical Herod perhaps dyed his hair, but later his personal vanity becomes excessive: the *Stanzaic Life of Christ* notes that he was concerned with seeming young and handsome (ll. 3491–93), and common etymologies of his name include "glorying in bodily appearance" and "vainglorious." [5] The theme of Herod's preoccupation with his own surpassing beauty, however, is not fully developed until the medieval drama, where it is a major device of characterization. Similarly, Herod is "gloriosus," boastful, according to Isidore of Seville;[6] and his resemblance to the miles gloriosus is often evident in the plays.

Herod's pride is naturally accompanied by the desire for fame and power at any cost, a desire that leads him into variously evil and absurd acts. Early described by Chrysostom as a tyrant,[7] Herod shows the tyrant's ruthlessness in killing everyone who might prevent his gaining and keeping the throne. His cruel treatment of his own sons is often stressed: accounts of their trials are common, and a rather grim joke attributed to Caesar Augustus — "I'd rather be Herod's pig than Herod's son" — is often repeated.[8] But it is most common to show

---

Osnabrück: Otto Zeller Verlag, 1969), pp. 62–66; and Foster, *Stanzaic Life*, ll. 3165–612. Some critical assessment of the contribution of the commentaries to the Herod of the Latin and English drama may also be found in Hussey, "How Many Herods in the English Drama," and in Rosemary Woolf, *The English Mystery Plays* (Berkeley and Los Angeles: University of California Press, 1972), pp. 202–11. Woolf's valuable work, which in some cases suggests similar interpretations to my own, came to hand too late for me to do more than make occasional references to it in the notes.

5. See D. W. Robertson, Jr., *Preface to Chaucer: Studies in Medieval Perspectives* (Princeton: Princeton University Press, 1962), p. 385.

6. *Etymologiae* 7. 10. 6.

7. *Commentaria in . . . Matthaeum* 8. 1.

8. The source of the joke seems to be Macrobius (early fifth century), *Saturnalia*, trans. Percival Vaughan Davies (New York: Columbia University Press, 1969), 2. 4. 11; cf. *Legenda aurea*, p. 65, and *Stanzaic Life*,

Herod as a usurper who seized the Jewish throne by foul means and who then attempted to legitimize his rule by burning the Jewish genealogies and prophecies that proved him ignoble and predicted Christ's birth as a true Jewish king. Indeed, the *Stanzaic Life* makes Herod look even more ridiculous by claiming that he burned the books so that no one would know there had ever been another king; he thought this would increase his own fame immensely.[9] This alteration heightens our sense of Herod's mad pride and demonstrates the almost pathetic futility of his ambition; the *Stanzaic Life* is careful to note that of course the Jews had many other copies of the burned books. Herod's pride and mania for power also lead him into blasphemy and the emulation of God, traits much emphasized in the drama; the commentaries, however, generally limit themselves to using Herod as a type of the heretic, the devil, and others who strive against God.[10]

One of Herod's most outstanding characteristics is his violent and sudden rage, noted by almost all the commentators and deriving in part from Josephus and in part from the Bible's description of him as "exceeding angry" upon hearing of the Magi's escape (Matt. 2:16). Sometimes incidents are made up to illustrate this rage. For instance, Peter Comestor and his followers tell that while Herod was on his way to Rome to answer charges made by his sons,[11] he stopped by Tarsus to

---

ll. 3519-20. Macrobius notes the occasion for this remark as the news that one of Herod's sons had been killed in Herod's alleged massacre of Syrian children, but later writers assume the comment applies to Herod's general habit of killing his sons. Macrobius is, however, responsible for the widespread idea that part of Herod's temporal punishment was the accidental death of his son in the Slaughter of the Innocents.

9. *Stanzaic Life*, ll. 3597-612; cf. *Legenda aurea*, p. 585.

10. See Chrysostom, *Commentaria in . . . Matthaeum* 7. 5; Bede, *Expositio in Evangelium Sancti Matthaei*, PL 92:13-14; Isidore, *Allegoriae*, PL 83:118; Garnier de Rochefort, *Allegoriae in universam sacram scripturam*, PL 112:961; and Orm's *Ormulum* (ca. 1200), ed. Robert Holt and R. M. White, 2 vols. (Oxford, 1878), l. 8027 and passim.

11. Thus these commentators blacken Herod's reputation: historically he charged his sons with crimes and had them executed, but here they are made to accuse him, implying that he was a terrible king.

destroy the ships that had carried the Magi safely from Judea.
Thus he fulfilled the prophecy in Ps. 47:8, translated in the
Stanzaic Life as "with wode spirit he con destry / the shippes
of Tarse in foule maner" (ll. 3363–64). Such vindictiveness is
of course natural in a proud tyrant who feels that his power is
threatened; indeed, the destruction of ships is rather mild for
the man who would massacre all the infants of Bethlehem or
even, as the story is developed, all the infants of Judea.[12]

But there are other more interesting ways to use or interpret
Herod's anger. Sometimes it is viewed simultaneously as a sin
and as a passion with clear physiological effects that eventually
cause Herod's punitive disease. Thus the *Historia scholastica*
and related commentaries, all of which assume that Herod's
death was punishment for his slaying of the Innocents, include
one important detail in their description of his disease: Josephus noted that a light fever accompanied Herod's more
serious symptoms, but these commentaries describe the cause
of death as "a strong feuer," "non mediocris," "valida." [13] The
reason for this change is easy to deduce from medieval medical theory. Herod's habitual wrath would suggest that he was
of a choleric temperament, hot and dry. Each access of rage
would further dry and heat the body, in turn producing more
choler and more wrathfulness.[14] In Herod's last days, his anger
would feed on itself as he raged at the Magi, at Christ, at the
ships of Tarsus, at his own wicked sons, at the Pharisees who
removed the eagle from the temple, and at the Jews he expected to rejoice at his death. In addition to being sinful, all
this anger would produce an extraordinary fever. Josephus
must, therefore, have been quite wrong: Herod must have died
of one of the most virulent fevers known to man, and this idea
is perpetuated in the English drama.[15]

12. See Bede, *Expositio in Evangelium Sancti Matthaei, PL* 92:13–14.
13. *JA* 17. 168; *Stanzaic Life*, l. 3529; Comestor, *PL* 198:1546; *Legenda aurea*, p. 66.
14. For the physiological effects of passion, see Mirfeld, *Florarium*, p. 155.
15. For the somewhat oversimplified view that Herod's symptoms and
death in the English drama are indebted to the details of Herod Agrippa's
dealth in Acts 12, see Hussey, "How Many Herods in the English Drama?"

The idea that Herod suffered from extreme choler is suggested by Isidore and confirmed by Peter Riga's graphic account of his last illness: "Fever oppressed him, swelling, [an
excess of] humour, sickness and constricted breathing; a yellow
color and a pain in the groin, wasting testicles, streaming eyes,
gooseflesh, terror on his face, a savage mind always loving evil,
the foulness of stench, rapid panting through the mouth — all
this, by God's agency, was the penalty for this guilty man." [16]
Notable here, in addition to the implication that Herod's persistence in evil aggravated his disease, is the fact that he suffers from "humour" and has a "yellow color." The humour
referred to must be choler, for passion and fever would stimulate no other; and the color clinches the matter, for according
to the well-known *Flos medicine* the choleric man is yellowish
in complexion.[17] Herod's wrathful behavior, then, led to a new
description of his disease which is consonant with both the
doctrine of humours and the notion that passion so alters the
body that it brings about its own physical punishment. Hence-
forth Herod's wrath, his character as the choleric man, and
his self-produced punitive disease are emphasized in almost all
literary treatments.

But Herod's wrath can be interpreted in another and more
important way — as a form of madness. As we saw in chapter
1, anger and madness are related psychologically, morally, and
physiologically. Psychologically, anger is a kind of madness in

16. *Evangelium*, ll. 831–36, in *Aurora*.
17. The full description of the choleric man is interesting in relation
to Herod:

> The choleric humour accords with impetuous men;
> This kind of man wants to surpass everyone;
> He learns easily, eats much, grows quickly;
> He is generous, liberal, seeking the highest things.
> Hairy, deceitful, irascible, prodigal, bold,
> Clever, slender, dry, and yellowish in complexion.
>
> [*Flos medicine* 4. 1704–09]

Oddly, Isidore gives *pellicius* ("made of skins") as an etymology for Herod
(*Etymologiae* 7. 10. 6); perhaps the word is synonymous with the *Flos
hirsutus* ("hairy"), and Isidore helped further the view of Herod as choleric.

that it deprives a man of reason; and when anger becomes a
way of life rather than a temporary aberration, the angry man
is permanently and clinically mad. Morally, unjust wrath is a
sin that leads to further sins of violence and to the loss of
reason, the image of God; Aquinas habitually uses anger as
an example of voluntary and therefore sinful madness.[18] Physiologically, repeated fits of anger produce far more than fever
and physical disease. As Bartholomeus notes (7. 5), passion and
excessive choler lead to frenzy, the first clinical category of
madness and that kind of insanity often inflicted by God on
the disobedient. So long as the causes of frenzy persist, the
disease cannot be cured; and the medieval Herod was hardly
inclined to follow the advice of both spiritual and medical
healers, that to remedy his frenzy he would have to control
his temper. To continue with the prognosis as Bartholomeus
would have it, Herod's choleric madness, with its moral and
physiological components, would be aggravated by his dread
of Christ and by his busy schemes to prevent usurpation; this
fear and this activity would create a secondary complication
of melancholia, involving paranoia, violent attacks on others,
and even attempted suicide, all of which are present in many
versions of Herod's story.[19] Further symptoms of Herod's madness, both physiological and psychological, appear in the
drama; for the present it suffices to note that Herod's behavior
is precisely the kind that normally produces and characterizes
madness, that such madness both causes and is aggravated by
additional mad acts, and that Herod would probably be recognized as a madman even when his madness is not explicitly
spelled out. For the Middle Ages, habitual wrath like Herod's
is madness in every sense.

18. E.g. *ST* 1–2. Q. 77, A. 2, 7 (2:634, 641).

19. For Herod's successful suicide, see Mirk's *Festial,* p. 37; Roscoe E.
Parker, ed., *Life of St. Anne,* EETS, os 174 (1928), MS Minnesota Z 822, N.
81, ll. 1435–37; and BM MS Add. 47682, fol. 17r (printed in the *Holkham
Bible Picture Book,* ed. W. O. Hassall [London: Dropmore Press, 1954]).
It is of course appropriate on other grounds that the wrathful Herod take
his own life: the allegorical figure Ira traditionally kills herself in frustration; see Prudentius, *Psychomachia,* ll. 131–61.

The idea that Herod was mad occurs at various points in the sources and commentaries. Josephus claims that Herod's love for his second wife, Mariamne, was close to madness and that after ordering her execution he suffered a brief but intense fit of grief-madness (*JA* 15. 240–46); but Chrysostom is chiefly responsible for pointing out Herod's moral insanity in his strivings against Christ: "Wishing to kill the boy was an act not only of anger [*furor*] but of the utmost insanity [*dementiae*]." [20] Perhaps Herod was possessed: Chrysostom notes that Herod was as irrational "as if aroused by some demon of wrath and envy"; in any case, his "extreme madness" led to his well-deserved suffering and punishment.[21] The commentaries of Comestor's group, recognizing the importance of Herod's choleric nature, also betray an awareness of his madness, although they do not develop the theme as fully as the plays. Comestor notes that Herod Antipas contested his father's last will, advocating acceptance of an earlier one "that his father had written when he was of sound mind" (*PL* 198:1548), and the *Stanzaic Life* suggests that Herod was mad in destroying the ships of Tarsus (l. 3363), adding that Herod's son Alexander wished to kill his father "that al his lif hade ben so wode" (l. 3496). Peter Riga claims that Herod was mad when he heard of the Magi's deception: "He became angry, raved in his mind, he roared in frenzy" (ll. 473–74). Herod's madness, then, is recognized in these influential commentaries; even though it is not a major part of his punitive final illness as it will be in other versions, it is clearly sinful, producing both deeds that damn him and the physiological disease that kills him.

Herod's madness is treated more thoroughly in two non-dramatic Middle English works which rely heavily on the commentaries but at the same time shape their material so that Herod emerges more clearly as a Mad Sinner. The early fourteenth-century *Cursor mundi* provides an inventive and colorful version of the story. After acknowledging Herod's tend-

20. *Commentaria in . . . Matthaeum* 7. 2–3.
21. Ibid., 9. 1.

encies to choleric madness — when the Magi fail to return, "wrooþ he was as he wolde wede" [22] — the poet gives an exuberantly gruesome account of the consequences of Herod's wrath and of God's anger at the Massacre of the Innocents:

> þe palesy smoot his oon side
> þat dud him faste abate pride
> On his heed þere wex a scalle
> þe scabbe ouergooþ his body alle . . .
> þe ȝicche toke him sikerly
> þe fester smoot þourȝe his body
> þe goute potagre euel to bete
> hit fel doun into his fete
> Ouer al was he mesel [leper] pleyne
> þerwiþ he hadde þe feuer quarteyne
> þe dropesy so to gider him prest
> þat he wende his body wolde brest
> þe fallyng euel had he to melle [as well]
> his teeþ out of his heed felle . . .
> Maþes [moths] cruled in him þore
>
> [ll. 11817–36]

If sin brings disease, then the author seems determined to have so evil a man suffer every conceivable ailment. Some of the diseases have precedent in Josephus — the itch and the fever, for instance. But generally the author chooses his diseases for their moral connotations; thus palsy explicitly punishes pride, and most of the other afflictions are traditionally associated with sin in the Bible and in commentaries.[23] The addition of

22. Richard Morris, ed., *Cursor mundi*, EETS, os 57, 59, 62, 66, 68, 99, 101 (1874–93), l. 11548 (TCC MS R. 3. 8, which I follow generally). Herod's story is told in ll. 11435–906.

23. E.g. the *Templum Domini* (fifteenth century) associates dropsy with pride, palsy with sloth, fever with envy, and leprosy with gluttony; see Morton W. Bloomfield, *The Seven Deadly Sins: An Introduction to the History of a Religious Concept, with Special Reference to Medieval English Literature* (East Lansing: Michigan State University Press, 1952), p. 233. Similarly, Rabanus Maurus equates fever with carnality, leprosy with heresy and blasphemy, and scabs with lechery: *De universo, PL* 111:501–03.

epilepsy, the falling evil, is particularly interesting, however. This disease, considered a form of madness, was sometimes compared to pride.[24] But, more important, John the Baptist was invoked for its cure: commenting on Herod Antipas's murder of John, the Cotton MS of the *Cursor mundi* notes that all of Herod's descendants grow mad and may be cured only by John's intercession (ll. 13185–91). The association of the Herod family with madness and particularly with epilepsy may explain why this disease, so appropriate a reflection of Herod's moral state, was added to his other woes.

But the poet's originality, fondness for the grotesque, and sense of poetic justice do not end here: his account of Herod's death is superb. Not surprisingly, no doctor could cure the miserable Herod; so, enraged, he murdered them all in a characteristic act of mass slaughter (ll. 11837–42). After this, his ambitious son Archelaus managed to convince the barons that Herod was completely mad:

> "wod is he þus in þis debate
> he is in a sorweful state
> For wo he is out of his wit"
>
> [ll. 11863–65]

Archelaus then planned his father's assassination: a brimstone and pitch bath was prepared as a cure of sorts.[25] Herod was somewhat suspicious of the endeavor, but he and his protests were summarily drowned and carted off to hell (ll. 11866–904). Thus was Herod — mad, sinful, proud, rotten with disease inflicted as a punishment — fittingly murdered; the killer of sons was killed by a son, the insanely attempted execution of Christ was punished by insanity and disease inflicted by God. The author of the *Cursor mundi* saw the didactic possibilities of the story and presented them energetically and effectively. Here Herod is the Mad Sinner. The proud tyrant, wrathfully

24. See *Middle English Sermons*, p. 69.

25. In Josephus, Herod was vainly given a hot oil bath as a cure; *JA* 17. 172. Here, the historical oil bath has become appropriately diabolical in significance and sinister in purpose.

and madly seeking to destroy God, is reduced to abject madness and disease, stinking so foully that no one comes near
him (ll. 11843–48). His humiliation in death is extended beyond the grave, where he is placed with Satan and Judas.

Lydgate's version of Herod's fall from deserved youthful
glory to madness and damnation is characterized by a particularly fortuitous selection and adaptation of incident and detail
and by an unusual emphasis on his insanity.[26] Unlike most
biographers, Lydgate at first arouses our sympathy for the
young man whose "hih prudence" and "notable knihtli excellence" (ll. 83–84) promised a brilliant future. But then disaster
struck — his beloved wife Mariamne was accused of adultery
— and Lydgate replaces her historical trial and execution
with Herod's first act of insane violence: "With rigerous suerd
he slouh hir furiousli" (l. 101). This rash deed caused Herod's
insanity, initially presented so that it almost arouses our sympathy:

>   . . . he for thouhte fill into anoye
> Of hertli sorwe & malencolie.
>
> Reste hadde he non novther day nor niht,
> Troublid with furye that he wex frentik,
> With dremys vexid & many an vnkouth siht;
> Of cheer nor colour to no man he was lik,
> And eueri moneth onys lunatik.
>
>   [ll. 111–17]

But this madness, caused by crime, soon becomes overtly crimi-
nal as Lydgate traces its development to show how one sin led
to another. Because of his outrageous desire for fame, "This
same Herodes in his malencolie" (l. 159) slaughtered two Hasmonean high priests, unhistorically murdering one by his own
hand at his own table. Then he killed his children, "causeles,
as fadir most vnkynde" (l. 175). Clearly, anyone this irrational
and wicked would be capable of anything, so it was not surprising that he should be enraged at the Magi's quest for

26. *Fall of Princes,* pp. 777–81.

Christ, and, "Lik a tiraunt of venymous outrage" (l. 193), vow
to kill both the Magi and the Innocents. In the execution of
his plan, one of his own sons was killed, apparently by accident,
but Lydgate thinks otherwise:

> I trowe it was vengaunce.
> Ech tiraunt gladli eendith with myschaunce,
> And so must he that wex ageyn Crist wood,
> Which for his sake shadde innocentes blood.
>
> [ll. 200–03]

Anyone mad enough to fight Christ must expect due punishment, and Herod is no exception:

> Fro that day forth, as maad is mencioun,
> He fill in many vnkouth malladie;
> His flessh gan turne to corrupcioun,
> Fret with wermys upon ech partie,
> Which hym assailed bi gret tormentrie:
> His leggis suelle, corbid [crooked] blak gan shyne;
> Where vengaunce werkith, a-dieu al medecyne.
>
> Of his seeknesse the stench was so horrible,
> Tawaite on hym no man myhte abide,
>
> .   .   .   .
>
> Of greuous constreynt he sodenli wex wood.
>
> [ll. 211–19, 224]

Shortly the proud and guilty man died in pain and madness,
for, as Chrysostom too had noted, no earthly medicine can help
the sinner whose very soul is diseased.[27] Herod's fall into madness and disease from pride and glory was as inevitable as the
fall of Lucifer, for as Lucifer was the first enemy of God, so
was Herod

> The firste tiraunt (ye may the Bible reede)
> Which ageyn Crist gan frowardli maligne.
>
> [ll. 252–53]

27. *Commentaria in . . . Matthaeum* 9. 1.

Like Lucifer, Herod was created with great potential merit,
and much of the originality of Lydgate's treatment of the story
lies in his recognition of Herod's great worth and the consequent tragedy of his perversion by sin and madness. For once
in medieval literature Herod is almost a hero and a man of
dignity; but Lydgate fails to fulfill the promise of his early
stanzas, and his Herod eventually degenerates into the comical
villain and madman of the drama. But perhaps that is precisely
the point that Lydgate was trying to make in this exemplum,
which develops so thoroughly the madness and absurdity of sin.

A brief discussion of the traditional iconography of Herod
may be helpful before the investigation of the Herod plays, for
as M. D. Anderson has pointed out, there may well have been
considerable mutual influence of drama and art.[28] One aspect
of Herod's conventional representation has been mentioned:
he is frequently shown with a demon whispering in his ear or
dancing above his head in the standard iconography of possession (plate 3). Herod is shown in this manner as early as the
fifth century and at least as late as the sixteenth.[29] Since this
iconography precedes the religious drama, perhaps art and
the commentaries combined to encourage Herod's madness in
the drama; and the iconographic tradition may also have inspired dramatists to assume that Herod and the devil, his counsellor in the massacre, were good friends.

A related common attribute of Herod in art is his cross-
legged and often contorted pose. The early fourteenth-century
Queen Mary's Psalter shows Herod ordering the massacre with
legs crossed, robes awry, and a demon over his head (plate 3).
A boss (ca. 1509) in the north transept of Norwich Cathedral

28. *The Imagery of British Churches* (London: John Murray, 1955), p. 30,
and *Drama and Imagery in English Medieval Churches* (Cambridge: Cambridge University Press, 1963), pp. 1–3 and passim.

29. See Réau, *Iconographie*, 2. 2. 245 and 269–72; and Anderson, *Drama
and Imagery*, pp. 89–98 and 163. Anderson's discussion of the Herod bosses
in Norwich Cathedral as possibly based on lost plays is fascinating if not
wholly convincing.

pictures Herod's reaction to the Magi's escape: cross-legged, contorted, with what may be a devil over his crown, he pulls on his beard as two advisers try to restrain him (plate 10). Herod is often shown thus, and in a sense there is historical precedent for such violent poses: Josephus notes that the king suffered from convulsions in his last illness. But there is also an interesting artistic convention at work: as Meyer Schapiro has shown, the cross-legged pose is characteristic of such pagan rulers as Pharaoh and Herod, where it "may transmit something of the wilfulness of the despot," [30] sometimes even serving as a marker of pride. I have found the posture to be associated particularly with extreme rage and madness, or at least with mad acts of violence — the mad Saul, Saul slaying Abimelech, Pharaoh ordering the murder of the newborn Hebrew boys, Nebuchadnezzar ordering the execution of Zedekiah's sons, and Henry II's vindictive acts against Becket are all similarly depicted.[31] Of course this does not mean that all cross-legged figures are mad or enraged; Schapiro shows that the posture may be merely a royal attribute, and there are many cross-legged kings in Tree of Jesse illustrations and in pictures of harpists. But I would suggest that the cross-legged position, especially when it is violent, indicates extreme wrath or madness as well as pride. Both artist and dramatist thus show Herod's anger as violent and convulsive, and the gesticulations of Herod on the stage, if they bear any relation to his representation in art, were probably unrestrained, spectacular, and either terrifying or very funny depending on one's point of view.

The iconographic tradition makes one other contribution to the theme of the Mad Herod: the influential *Biblia pauperum* (ca. 1300) twice uses the mad Saul as a type of Herod; David's

30. "An Illuminated English Psalter of the Early Thirteenth Century," *Journal of the Warburg and Cortauld Institutes* 23 (1960): 179–89.

31. See plate 1 and the following illuminations: Saul and Abimelech, BM MS Royal 2 B. vii, fol. 52r; Pharaoh, BM MS Royal 2 B. vii, fol. 22v; Nebuchadnezzar, MS Bodley 270b, fol. 184r; Henry, MS Royal 2 B. vii, fol. 291v.

flight from Saul prefigures Christ's flight into Egypt, and Saul's
slaying of Abimelech and his sons (1 Kings 22) anticipates the
Slaughter of the Innocents.[32] It is impossible to say whether the
typological equivalence of the possessed Saul and Herod had
any direct influence on the English drama, but it seems likely
that the compiler of the *Biblia pauperum* and some of its readers recognized the mental states of the two kings to be as similar
as their actions.

It is in the medieval drama that the many themes associated
with Herod as Mad Sinner receive their fullest treatment. His
tyranny, pride, and wrath reach monumental proportions,
particularly in contrast to the humility and grace of the infant
Jesus and to the obedient and worshipful demeanor of the
Magi. His incorporation of all that is opposed to Christ —
the law, Jewry, Mohammedanism, temporal power — is emphasized; his diseased and imperfect nature and his rejection of
Christ's spiritual medicine are developed quite extensively in
several plays; and the spiritual madness of those who reject
Christ is juxtaposed with the madness of Christianity as seen
by the worldly wise. The better plays are astonishingly successful in developing the contrast between reality and appearance,
between the gentle and omnipotent child-God and the blustery
megalomaniac whose pretensions to the Godhead lead to apparent disaster for the Innocents and to utter catastrophe for
himself. Paradox lies at the very heart of Christianity — the
paradox of the child-God, of the Holy Fool, of true power —
and many Nativity sequences demonstrate their authors' appreciation of the dramatic and thematic possibilities of this
central fact.

The dramatic and symbolic potentialities of the conflict between Herod and God were not fully realized in the Latin
liturgical drama, but the Herod of these early plays has much
in common with the English Herod, who may well be indebted

32. J. P. Berjeau, ed. (London: John Russell Smith, 1859), pp. 26–27
(pls. 5 and 7). Anderson describes this as one of the most important books
for medieval iconography; *Imagery of British Churches*, p. 76.

to the Latin drama as well as to the commentaries and vernacular sermons for his characterization and prominence.[33] I will not consider here the problems of dating, development, and mutual influence of the Latin plays, nor of their general relationship to the vernacular drama; I could add nothing to the discussions of Chambers, Young, Craig, Wickham, Hardison, and Woolf.[34] I shall merely draw from the plays themselves what seems relevant; although a given Latin play may not have influenced any English dramatist or commentator, the presence of similar elements in both Latin and English certainly indicates the potentialities of the received Herod figure himself. That the figure was developed similarly by both Latin and English dramatists may indicate a widespread tendency to see his role in the eternal Christian drama as important and well-defined. I would argue that the Latin drama moves tentatively toward a concept of Herod which is enunciated much more fully in the English drama: that Herod is a proud, wrathful, paranoid tyrant, Christ's first enemy, a man both terrifyingly powerful and foolishly, even comically, subject to human limitations and to his own passions; that he bears witness to the doctrine that with sin and without Christ nothing really important is possible; that he represents the Mad Sinner, who, setting himself up as God and attempting to destroy the truest image of God, Christ, destroys instead only his own right to be called a man.

33. In a review (*Speculum* 9 [1934]:114) of Young's *Drama of the Medieval Church*, George R. Coffman suggests that the English drama's Herod is at least as much indebted to the Latin plays as to vernacular sermons, a source stressed by G. R. Owst, *Literature and Pulpit in Medieval England*, 2d ed. (Oxford: Basil Blackwell, 1961), p. 493. Roscoe E. Parker, in "The Reputation of Herod in Early English Literature," *Speculum* 8 (1933):59–67, discusses Herod's indebtedness to all three traditions.

34. E. K. Chambers, *The Medieval Stage*, 2 vols. (Oxford: Clarendon Press, 1903); Young, *Drama of the Medieval Church*; Hardin Craig, *English Religious Drama* (Oxford: Clarendon Press, 1955); Glynne Wickham, *Early English Stages 1300 to 1600* (London: Routledge and Kegan Paul, 1959), vol. 1; O. B. Hardison, *Christian Rite and Christian Drama in the Middle Ages* (Baltimore: Johns Hopkins Press, 1965), and Woolf, *English Mystery Plays*.

Young notes that in the Latin drama Herod's role expands as the plays develop, and the expansions seem designed to enhance the characterization of Herod as *iratus*.[35] As early as the eleventh-century Compiègne *Officium stellae*, "Herod . . . begins to disclose those traits of pomposity, impetuousness, and violence which promise well both for dramatic conflict and for comedy," [36] and these attributes of the Mad Sinner continue to appear in later plays. Sometimes Herod's pomposity and pride are such that he madly claims to rule all earth or even all creation: in the twelfth-century Bilsen *Ordo stelle*, Herod blasphemously mounts his throne to the Advent antiphon "Super solium David" (above David's throne and kingdom he shall reign eternally, alleluia), and later, Herod's messenger describes him as "the king . . . who possesses and rules the whole world." [37] The late thirteenth-century Benediktbeuern Herod, furious that the Magi seek another king, introduces himself with claims more accurate for Christ to make: "I am Herod, able to subjugate all that is contained in the world, heaven, earth, or sea." [38] The Latin Herod, like the English, is *gloriosus*, proud, tyrannical, and, whether he knows it or not, setting himself up in opposition to Christ as ruler. Sedulius's famous hymn, "Hostis Herodes," could not have reassured the Benediktbeuern Herod with these lines:

> Herod, impious enemy,
> Why do you fear Christ's coming?
> He who confers celestial kingdoms
> Does not steal earthly ones.[39]

Herod would prefer to confer celestial kingdoms himself. Herod and Christ did not have to be rivals, but Herod's delu-

---

35. Young, *Drama of the Medieval Church*, 2:29–196 passim. For the view that the Latin plays did not develop consistently in the direction of greater complexity of characterization, see Woolf, *English Mystery Plays*, chapter 1.

36. Young, 2:58.

37. Ibid., 2:75–78.

38. Ibid., 2:ll. 394–97 (text on pp. 172–90).

39. Ibid., 2:447.

sions of grandeur and pretensions to divine power forced the issue; there could be no question of the outcome after that. If one reason for Herod's importance in all Nativity literature is to show the conflict between Christ and Herod — between spiritual and temporal power — we should expect Herod to challenge Christ on his own ground. In the Benediktbeuern play, and in most of the English plays, Herod does just that in his foolish boasts of omnipotence and even divinity. Such pride and blasphemy were as mad in the Middle Ages as similar boasts would be now.

Herod's violence, characteristic of frenzy and rage, is manifested most directly in the Slaughter of the Innocents itself. But there are other instances too: in some plays, as in many illuminations, he brandishes a sword; in the eleventh-century Freising *Officium stellae* he jumps up and down.[40] In his rage he often throws to the ground the books from which the prophecies of Christ are read; in the Fleury *Ordo ad representandum Herodem*, he does this "seized by frenzy."[41] Perhaps this act is simply a colorful bit of violence, but it may be that the dramatist was inspired by the apocryphal story of Herod's burning of the books. In any case, the Fleury *Ordo Rachelis* adapts another Herodian legend to the dramatic context. When Herod hears of the Magi's deceit, he seizes a sword and tries to kill himself.[42] He is persuaded to kill the innocents instead, but his abortive suicide, which recalls the historical Herod's similar attempt, serves as a clear indication of his insanity and exemplifies that self-destructive violence so characteristic of frenzied madmen in general and of the dramatic Herod in particular.

Herod's abundant and exuberant wrathfulness, also a token and cause of his insanity, is fully developed in the Latin plays, and examples may be found on almost any page. I will mention here only one outstanding case, the Padovan *Representatio Herodis in nocte epyphanie*.[43] After the eighth lesson, Herod

40. See Rouen (ibid., 2:72), Fleury (2:111) and Freising (2:96–97) plays.
41. Young, 2:87; for more book-throwing, see pp. 71 and 95.
42. Ibid., 2:111.
43. Ibid., 2:99–100.

and his ministers burst forth from the sacristy in disarray; "with the greatest frenzy," Herod hurls a spear at the choir and proceeds to read the ninth lesson "with so much fury," while his companions beat the clergy with inflated bladders. After finishing the lesson, Herod joins the uproar "with the above-mentioned frenzy" until subdued by a deacon so that an antiphon, a gospel reading, and the *Te Deum* may proceed. Then, clearly tamed, Herod presents the gospel to be kissed by the bishop and canons. This ritual is not a fully developed play, but it does indicate how Herod's rage, violence, and antagonism to Christianity had come to dominate his characterization. The Padovan *Representatio* is also an emblem of Herod's essential function in the Nativity story; despite his rage and frustration, despite his brief and comparatively harmless foray into the ranks of the faithful, the mad Herod must do God's will — read the lesson and honor the gospel which bears witness to his own humiliation. Just so must Herod fear and persecute Christ, his efforts ending in futility, his own destruction, and the greater glory of God.

Herod's madness is seldom mentioned by name in the Latin plays, but many of his words and deeds would have clearly indicated both his moral and his actual insanity to a medieval audience. His wild anger, his attempted suicide, and probably his gestures and appearance would have convinced viewers that he was much more seriously mad than the town idiot, whose irrationality was involuntary and therefore not blameworthy. Two plays — the Fleury *Ordo Rachelis* and the Benediktbeuern play — show the inevitable fruits of Herod's madness and persistence in evil: his death. In the latter play, Herod dies right after the Slaughter of the Innocents, and the stage direction suggests the horror of the death of such a man: "Let Herod be consumed by worms, and, leaving his chair as a dead man, let him be received by devils with great rejoicing." [44] Although most of the Latin plays stress Herod's pride, anger-madness, and damnable opposition to God's kingdom, these two plays which physically represent divine vengeance over-

44. Ibid., 2:189.

taking Herod are the stronger dramatically in that they carry Herod's actions to their logical conclusion. Of course the medieval audience would know that a tyrant who emulated God, who insulted the reverent Magi, whose rage so crippled his reason that he could not accept the inevitability of divine prophecy, and whose desire to kill Christ led to the murder of innocent children, would suffer dire punishment in death if not in life. But those Latin and English plays treating Herod's life as a morality play or as a medieval tragedy satisfy aesthetic demands as more fragmentary plays cannot. The unrepentant sinner should ideally bear witness to his ultimate subjection to God by losing control of external events and of himself in his madness, in disease, or in death. The Mad Sinner must be visibly punished.

The English Herod plays, richer and more complex than the Latin drama, show the same tendency to make Herod titanically proud, arrogant, and wrathful. So extreme is this characterization that, as V. A. Kolve has noted, Herod is almost a caricature of the sins *Ira* and *Superbia*.[45] The historical Herod was remarkable for these qualities, of course; but they were increasingly emphasized in the commentaries and the drama, probably so that Herod would present a sharper contrast to the humble and meek Christ-child. According to the *Legenda aurea*, Christ was born to give an example of humility to the proud, and he was born as a child so men would love his gentleness as they could not immediately love the Godhead appearing in omnipotence and righteous wrath.[46] In the English plays Herod becomes everything that Christ is not; the madness of worldly wisdom is contrasted with the spiritual sanity of the Holy Fool, and the false god Herod is contrasted with the true one. Many details of Herod's characterization are justified by this opposition between true and apparent godliness and wisdom.

45. *The Play Called Corpus Christi* (Stanford: Stanford University Press, 1966), pp. 222–23.

46. *Legenda aurea*, pp. 46–47, which follows in part Bernard's *Sermo 1*, *In nativitate Domini*, PL 183:116.

A few important general comments about the English plays' treatment of this contrast should perhaps be made before any plays are discussed individually. Herod is made to mimic God as closely as possible: he claims to rule all creation, to have defeated the devil, to move the planets and bring thunder. His anger and threatened destruction of all opponents recall the avenging God of the Old Testament; he insists on maintaining the Law; he speaks eloquently of his own beauty. Like Christ, he proclaims his kinship to God.[47] Many of these similarities are implicit, relying on the audience's knowledge of God's true attributes — perhaps gained from earlier plays in the cycles — to show how short Herod falls of the standard set by God in majesty. But Herod's claims are juxtaposed with the reality of God made man in Christ; and this contrast not only points out the absurdity and the madness of Herod's pretension in comparison with Christ's quiet presence but also shows how limited is Herod's concept of God: he sees only the power and the glory, not the suffering and responsibility. Finally, most plays show the punishment meted out to false gods and bad kings: Herod suffers excruciating disease in four plays, and in three he dies horribly. The coming of Christ the physician cures all disease, but those who will not be cured are themselves diseases to be destroyed.

Herod's role as Mad Sinner and archenemy of Christ is skillfully developed in the Chester cycle.[48] Herod's traditional characteristics — his pride, blasphemies, anger, violence — are presented as evidence of his madness, which leads him to ever greater sins and to excessive wrath which physiologically de-

47. Woolf reaches similar conclusions on Herod's pretensions to divinity; she also provides interesting comments on Herod's similarities to Lucifer and on the dramatic importance of Herod's grotesque death in several of the plays, especially in the Ludus Coventriae *Innocents* play; *English Mystery Plays*, pp. 202–11.

48. Hermann Deimling and J. Matthews, eds., *The Chester Plays*, EETS, es 62, 115 (1892, 1916). Textual references are to the lines of each play; I use these abbreviations: Pageant 6, *The Nativity* — Nativity; Pageant 8, *Adoration of the Magi* — Magi; Pageant 10, *Slaying of the Innocents* — *Innocents*.

stroys him. The plays forcefully dramatize the contrast between
the mad, diseased Herod and Christ, the physician who would
have cured both Herod's moral and physical ills had his aid
only been sought. The first symptom of Herod's insanity is his
blasphemous pride; when the Magi tell him that they seek
"Roy de Caelli et Terrae" (*Magi*, 1. 152), the outraged Herod
proclaims his own supremacy as "king of kinges" (*Magi*, 1. 161):

> For I am king of all mankinde,
> I byd, I beat, I loose, I bynde,
> I maister the Moone; take this in mynde
> that I am most of mighte.
>
> I am the greatest aboue degree,
> that is or was or euer shall be.
> the Sonne it dare not shyne on me
> if I byd hym goe downe.
>
> [*Magi*, ll. 169–76]

With the hyperbolic language characteristic also of Lucifer,[49]
Herod works himself into a frenzy, threatening all who disobey
him with violent death. But sin and frenzy begin to take their
toll; he suffers the first twinge of the punitive disease which
further rage and sin will increase to fatal proportions: "All for
wrath see how I sweate. / my hart is not at ease" (*Magi*, ll.
187–88). After hurling his sword at the Magi and dismissing
the prophetic books, Herod continues to rage against the up-
start Christ until he loses control:

> Out alas! what the Deuil is this?
> for shame almost I fare amisse,
> for was I neuer so woe, I wis,
> for wrath I am nere wood.
>
> [*Magi*, ll. 374–77]

Wrath is, of course, the immediate cause of Herod's madness
here, but the motive for his wrath (pride) and its object (Christ)
augment the seriousness of his offense. His madness is ulti-

49. See Pageant 1, *Fall of Lucifer*, ll. 161–72.

mately the result of his way of life, his conception of himself, rather than of the passion that can make any man temporarily "wood." But Herod is superbly unmindful of his moral state; he continues to threaten Christ and to invoke Mahound's aid in humbling the child's alleged pride. And once again his wrath has physiological as well as moral consequences:

> This bost dothe me so great anoy
> that I wax dull and pure drye;
> haue done and fill the wyne in hye!
> I dye but I haue drinke.
>
> [*Magi*, ll. 406–09]

The playwright knows his physiology: an angry man would be thirsty because the heat of passion would dry his bodily fluids; such a man would be "dull" because his powers of perception — his mind, his animal spirits, for instance — would be considerably impaired. Thus Herod's choleric madness leads him to call for drink; but ironically the drink he wants would do him no good, for wine would heat the body even more and further increase wrath and frenzy. Only one drink could cure Herod: the blood of Christ, which he seeks rather to spill than to treasure. The wrathful king might have profited by the lesson of the hart in the bestiaries:

> Ofte we brennen [burn] in mod [mind]
> and wurþen [become] so we weren wod;
> þanne we þus brennen
> bihoueþ us to rennen
> to cristes quike well
> þat we ne gon to hel.[50]

This cycle stresses the importance of Christ as humble healer of sin and disease in direct contrast to Herod's role as proud and diseased madman. The theme appears early: in *Balaam and Balak*, Christ is man's "ioy and heale" (l. 250) who comes to "wyn againe mankindes heale" (l. 399). In the *Nativity*

---

50. Richard Morris, ed., *An Old English Miscellany*, EETS, os 49 (1872), p. 11.

pageant Christ's first miracle — the healing of the skeptical
Salome's withered hand — is shown, and the Expositor's moralization foreshadows Herod's death by rotting:

> her hand roted, as you have seene,
> wherby you may take good teene
> that unbeleefe is a foule synne.
> [*Nativity*, ll. 733-35]

The same theme of man's need for a healer appears in the
Adoration of the Shepherds,[51] where the First Shepherd seeks
herbs to cure his sheep of rot and cough, while the Third Shepherd looks for ingredients for a salve for his sheep. What they
find that night in the fields is a physician for more metaphorical sheep: "a 'Deo' / me thought that healed my hart" (ll. 441–
42). And early in the first play in which Herod appears the
theme is also stressed: the Second King describes Balaak as
"wood" (*Magi*, l. 19) for ordering Balaam to curse Israel, an
action similar to Herod's desire to kill Christ; but instead of
succeeding in this attempt, Balaam was blessed "to prophesie
mankindes heale" (*Magi*, l. 24). Thus the futility and madness
of striving against God is asserted, and the absurdity of the
conflict is implied to lie in the fact that God has sent men a
healer, not a usurper or a rival or a judge. The health that
Christ brings is, of course, *salus*, the double health of spirit and
body, and not even Herod can have the latter without the
former.

Normally, sick men strive for health, but Herod's diseased
mind struggles against it. Like Bartholomeus's frenzied man,
Herod "hath moost peryllous sykenesse, but he knoweth not
that he is seke" (7. 5). Conscious of no offense, he will not be
cured in spirit, and it is hardly surprising that the contagion of
pride and wrath should spread to his body. His downfall begins
in the *Adoration of the Magi*; his decay, in every sense, is completed in the *Slaying of the Innocents*. As the pageant opens,

---

51. For a more complete treatment of the theme of Christ the physician
in the Chester cycle, and especially in the *Adoration of the Shepherds*, see
Kolve, *Play Called Corpus Christi*, pp. 152–54.

Herod once more rages against the Magi and "that misbegotten marmoset (l. 15), Christ; thanks to Him, all the children will die. As Herod orders the execution, his anger masters him and increases his already dangerous heat:

> but yet I burne as doth the fyre,
> what for wroth, what for ire,
> till this be brought to ende.
>
> [*Innocents,* ll. 134–36]

In the ensuing slaughter Herod's own son is killed; Herod rages against the woman responsible, but his anger is cut short by its physiological and moral consequences:

> My legges rotten and my armes;
> I haue done so many harmes,
> that now I see of feendes swarmes
> from hell cominge for me.
>
> [*Innocents,* ll. 421–24]

A demon leads the dead king off to hell to be burned with all other false believers who do not repent as Salome did.

The Chester Herod is truly a Mad Sinner. Much like Nebuchadnezzar in his refusal to acknowledge any power but himself, he succumbs to pride and wrath, both of which lead to madness as their fitting deformity. His wrathful insanity, ever increasing and feeding upon itself, causes both his disease (through the physical effects of passion) and his damnation. The *Nativity* pageant includes a paraphrase of the *Magnificat* with its significant lines, "He hath scattered the proud in the conceit of their heart. He hath put down the mighty from their seat, and hath exalted the humble" (Luke 1:51–52).[52] Thus are the proud punished by madness and loss of power; but the cycle shows that fatal consequences are not inevitable: just as Nebuchadnezzar was saved by acknowledging God, so too the *Nativ-*

---

52. For the thematic importance of these lines, see Kolve, *Play Called Corpus Christi,* pp. 156–58. Incidentally, this passage was the occasion for Robert of Sicily's hubris and punishment, as described in chapter 2.

ity pageant shows another boastful king, Octavian, in strong contrast to Herod — by refusing deification and revering Christ when he hears of the birth, he wins honor and keeps his power and life.

That Herod is mad and that his sins provoke physical illness are also important ideas in the Towneley Herod plays.[53] But whereas in the Chester plays Herod's disease was contrasted with Christ's healing powers, here a major aspect of Herod's madness is his insistence on the powers of Mahound and himself; and this false faith is set against the true faith, which seems mad to Herod. One of the ways the *deposuit potentes* theme figures in these plays is stated in 1 Corinthians 1:20, 27: "Hath not God made foolish the wisdom of this world? . . . But the foolish things of the world hath God chosen, that he may confound the wise." Herod's confidence in Mahound, his wrath at Christ, his pride in his own power and beauty are all part of the worldly wisdom that is madness in God's sight.

Once again, Herod's pride is the first token of his madness. Boasting that he rules the world, he threatens death to misbelievers and mocks the Magi because they proclaim Christ's power: "When thare wytt in a starne [star] shuld be, / I hold thaym mad" (*Magi*, ll. 293–94). But Herod is nonetheless disturbed at their news: "ffor wo my wytt is all away" (*Magi*, l. 299). His refusal to believe renders him as witless as he thinks the Magi are, and his madness is compounded by a long harangue against Christ. He demands to know quickly where the child is, "or I go wode" (*Magi*, l. 440), and he plots to destroy both the Magi and Christ.

The second and better Herod play develops the themes of the first, also adding physiological symptoms of Herod's choleric madness. After being announced by a messenger who orders everyone to worship Herod and his cousin Mahowne, Herod lashes himself into a frenzy at the thought of Christ's presumption:

53. For the *Offering of the Magi* (abbreviated as *Magi*), I follow George England and Alfred W. Pollard, eds., *The Towneley Plays*, EETS, es 71 (1897); for *Magnus Herodes*, I follow Cawley, *Wakefield Pageants*.

My myrthes ar turned to teyn [grief], my mekenes into ire,
And all for oone, I weyn, within I fare as fyre.

.   .   .   .

I anger:
I wote not what dewill me alys.

[*Magnus Herodes*, ll. 100–01, 113–14]

When he learns that the Magi have deceived him, his frenzy
increases:

Why, and ar thay past me by? We! outt! for teyn I brast!

.   .   .   .

I wote I yelde my gast, so sore my hart it grefys,

[*Magnus Herodes*, ll. 148, 155]

A soldier tells him to stop gnashing his teeth and beating his
men, but Herod still rushes about frantically; and when his
counsellors confirm Christ's birth from prophecy, Herod's
anger knows no bounds:

Fy! the dewill the spede, and me, bot I drynk onys!

.   .   .   .

Fy! dottypols [blockheads], with youre bookys —
Go kast tham in the brookys!
With sich wylys and crokys
My wytt away rafys.

[*Magnus Herodes*, ll. 226, 231–34]

Cawley finds Herod's need to drink "an intrusive comic
touch," [54] which may well be true; but it also suggests Herod's
dangerously dry physiological state thanks to his raving. Since
he cannot or will not calm his passions, drink will do little
good, as he seems to realize: "Bot I kyll hym and his, I wote
I brast my gall" (*Magnus Herodes*, l. 301). Again physiology
appears in the drama: Herod knows that his gall bladder, the
home of choler, is swollen to bursting, and he finds temporary
relief from the physical consequences of his anger only by
ordering the violence that ironically damns him.

54. *Wakefield Pageants*, p. 117n.226.

The soldiers carry out the massacre, accusing the mothers of being "woode" for not giving in graciously (*Magnus Herodes,* l. 340). And Herod, delighted with the slaughter, attains physical relief: "So light is my saull / That all of sugar is my gall!" *(Magnus Herodes,* ll. 474–75). His belief that Christ's blood has been let has cured him physically as Christ's real sacrifice might have done spiritually, and his bitter gall has grown sweet with the passing of passion. His moral madness, of course, remains, and he concludes by accusing Christ himself of insanity:

> Thus shall I tech knauys ensampyll to take,
> In thare wyttys that raues, sich mastré to make.
> [*Magnus Herodes,* ll. 496–97]

Throughout, Herod sees himself as a glorious and powerful lord, the faithful as mad, and Christ as a knave; but we see that the opposite is true, that real madness lies in Herod's attempt to master Christ.

The *Ludus Coventriae* treatment of the story is more somber than most and adapted to the Fall of Princes form.[55] There is less raging and less overt emphasis on Herod's madness here, but it is rather because Herod's insanity is demonstrated by his conduct, his disease, and his death than because he is in fact any saner than in other plays. The *Adoration of the Magi* begins with Herod's boasts:

> Of bewte and of boldnes I bere ever-more þe belle
> Of mayn and of myght I master every man
> I dynge with my dowtynes þe devyl down to helle
> Ffor bothe of hevyn and of herth I am kyng sertayn.
> [*Magi,* ll. 5–8]

After having exhibited himself to the audience in a handsome set of golden robes, Herod leaves to change into still more mag-

---

55. I follow K. S. Block, ed., *Ludus Coventriae,* EETS, es 120 (1922); I use these abbreviations: *Adoration of the Magi, Magi; Massacre of the Innocents, Innocents.*

nificent ones.[56] While he is offstage, the Magi speak of their
mission, departing as Herod returns to comment on his new
clothes and to threaten everyone who would challenge him or
Mahound. Hearing of the Magi's search, he warns that heresy,
or madness, will be punished by death:

> Iff they raue
> or waxyn wood
> I xal hem reve [plunder]
> here wyttys deve [stupefy]
> here hedys cleve
> And schedyn here blood.
>
> [*Magi*, ll. 145–50]

If it is mad to strive against true omnipotence and divinity, as
Herod here implies, then his own insanity is evident in his actions and words; the penalty for blasphemy which he invokes
against the "mad" Magi is fitly visited upon himself.

Plotting to undo Christ, Herod sends the Magi off to seek
their "lech" (*Magi*, ll. 184, 204, 230). But eventually news of
their treachery reaches Herod, who warns Mahound that a
rival threatens them both and then orders the execution of the
children. Herod is delighted at its success, and he orders a banquet to celebrate his position as king "both of hevyn and of
erth and of helle cost" (*Innocents*, l. 131). As the banquet progresses, Mors enters. He has heard "a page make preysyng of
pride" (*Innocents*, l. 168), blaspheming against the true King of
Kings. In words that echo and correct Herod's earlier boasts,
Mors describes his function:

> I am sent fro god deth is my name
> All thynge þat is on grownd I welde at my wylle
> both man and beste and byrdys wylde and tame
> Whan þat I come them to with deth I do them kylle
>
> [*Innocents*, ll. 181–84]

---

56. The emphasis on Herod's rich clothes and divinity seems to be indebted in part to the biblical story of Herod Agrippa, who also set himself
up as God in rich silver robes at the Caesarean feasts (Acts 12). As Herod
Agrippa was stricken with disease by God's messenger coming unasked to
the feast, so too is Herod the Great here afflicted by Mors.

Coment dauid fust mainde venenir a saul p̄ confail de ses gentz a li conforter oue la harpe q̄nt il estoit trauaille de li mal espirats.

Plate 1. David playing to the possessed Saul. Queen Mary's Psalter. London. British Museum. MS Royal 2 B. vii, fol. 51v. English, early fourteenth century.

Plate 2. The miracle of the Gadarene swine. Holkham Bible Picture Book. London. British Museum. MS Add. 47682, fol. 24r. English, early fourteenth century.

Plate 3. Herod, urged on by a devil, orders the Slaughter of the Innocents. Queen Mary's Psalter London. British Museum. MS Royal 2 B. vii, fol. 132r. English, early fourteenth century.

osui oii meo aistodiam: aim cō
sisterer pcōr aduersum me
bmutui et humiliatus sum. et su
ui a bonis: et dolor meus renouatus est.

Plate 4. The devil instigating lechery. *Der Seelentrost.* Augsburg: Anthoni Sorgen, 1478. London. British Museum. IB 5874, fol. 126r.

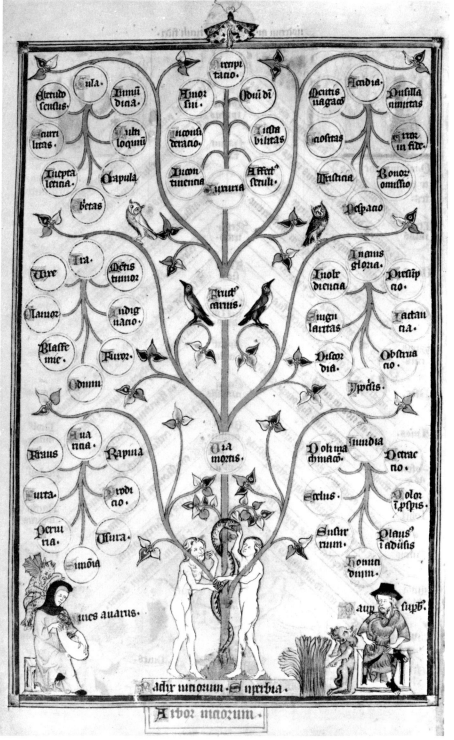

Plate 5. The Tree of Vices. Arundel Psalter. London. British Museum. MS Arundel 83, fol. 128v. English, early fourteenth century.

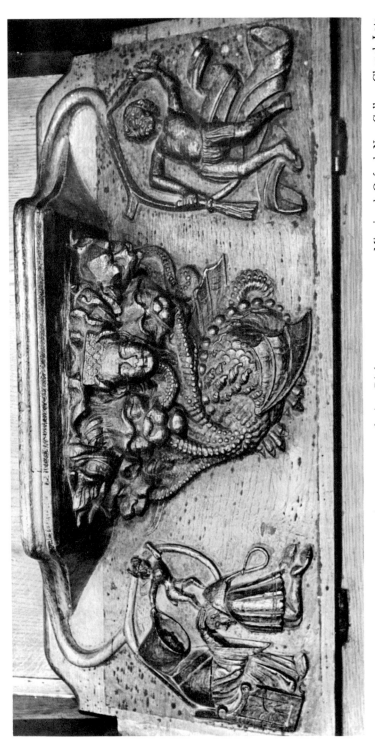

Plate 6. Beast of the Seven Deadly Sins. Left supporter: confession. Right supporter: penance. Misericord. Oxford. New College Chapel. Late fourteenth century. (Photo: National Monuments Record, London)

Plate 7. Dance of the Wodwoses at the court of Charles VI. Froissart, *Chronicles*. London. British Museum. MS

Plate 8. The mad Nebuchadnezzar. Nicholas de Lyra, *Postilla to Daniel*. Basel. Oeffentliche Bibliothek der Universität Basel. MS A II 5, fol. 86v. Freiburg i. Br. 1393. Ca. 1400. (Photo: Reprophoto Marcel Jenni, Offentliche Bibliothek der Universität Basel)

Plate 9. Nebuchadnezzar's Cure. Ulrich von Lilienfeld, *Concordantia caritatis*. Stiftsbibliothek Lilienfeld. MS 151, fol. 40r. After 1351. (Photo: Wagner Lilienfeld)

Plate 10. The enraged King Herod. Roof boss, north transept. Norwich Cathedral. Ca. 1509. (Photo: National Monuments Record, London)

Plate 12. Wild Man in garden. Bedford Book of Hours. London. British Museum. MS Add. 18850, fol. 9v. French, early fourteenth century.

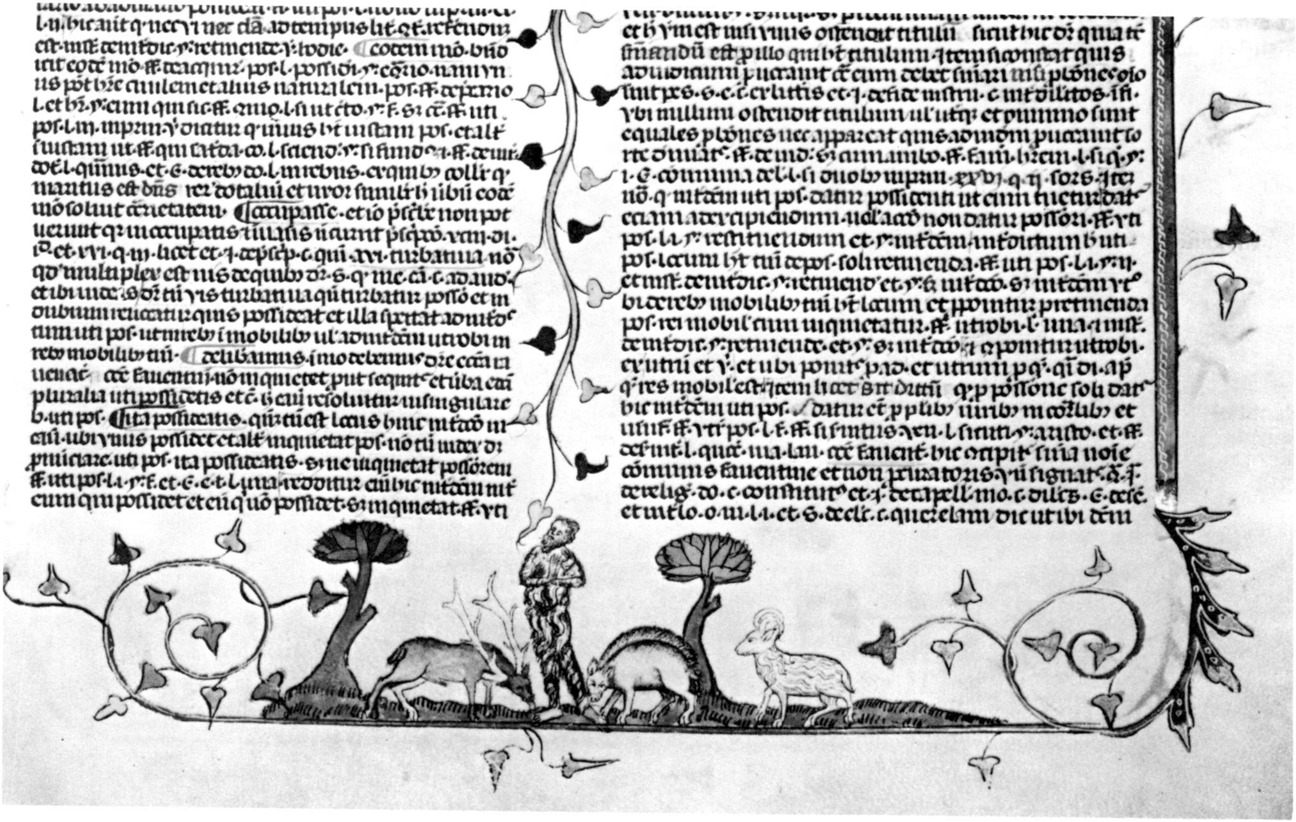

Plate 13. Hairy Anchorite with animals. Smithfield Decretals. London. British Museum. MS Royal 10 E. iv, fol. 116r. English, early fourteenth century.

Plate 14. Hairy Anchorite crawling into cave. Smithfield Decretals. London. British Museum. MS Royal 10 E. iv, fol. 117v. English, early fourteenth century.

Plate 15. Saint Mary of Egypt buried by friendly lions. Smithfield Decretals. London. British Museum. MS Royal 10 E. iv, fol. 287r. English, early fourteenth century.

Plate 16. Adam and Eve in their coats of skin. Roof boss, south aisle. Winchester Cathedral. Ca. 1400 (Photo: National Monuments Record, London)

Since Herod will not accept the *salus* given to those who acknowledge Christ as lord, he receives disease and Death's mastery instead:

> Ow se how prowdely ʒon kaytyff sytt at mete
> of deth hath he no dowte he wenyth to leve evyr-more
> to hym wyl I go and ʒeve hym such An hete
> þat all þe lechis of þe londe his lyf xul nevyr restore
>
> . . . .
>
> All þe blood of his body I xal hym owt swete
> Ffor now I go to sle hym with strokys sad and sore
>
> . . . .
>
> and so cast down his pride
>
> [*Innocents,* ll. 194–97, 200–01, 206]

The fever symbolic of rage and frenzy that first came to prominence in the commentaries is here inflicted on Herod as token and punishment of his sin; there is no hope of cure, for the only physician has been driven to Egypt. But Herod still has a few moments' respite which he uses to boast:

> aboue me is no kinge . on growend nere on gerth
> merthis þerfore make ʒe and be ryght no thynge sadde
>
> . . . .
>
> ffor now my ffo is dede.
>
> [*Innocents,* ll. 212–13, 219]

Herod's appalling madness is nowhere clearer than in these lines, spoken as Mors stalks toward him; suddenly Herod is dead in the midst of the revelry, and Diabolus carries him off to the mirth of hell where the "mery fytt" of the carnal feast becomes the singing of "welawey" (*Innocents,* ll. 232, 245) in the charnel house. Mors speaks the moral: all proud men will fall as low as Herod, who now feeds worms. The Mad Sinner's career can end only in death and damnation.

Two other Herod plays — the Digby *Killing of the Children* and the Coventry *Shearmen and Taylors' Pageant*[57] — are

---

57. I follow F. J. Furnivall, ed., *The Digby Plays*, EETS, es 70 (1896), and Hardin Craig, ed., *Two Coventry Corpus Christi Plays*, 2d ed., EETS, es 87 (1957). The York plays are not discussed here because they are not directly relevant to the view of Herod as Mad Sinner.

probably later than the plays already mentioned, and their
literary and dramatic merit is less. But both plays are interesting in a study of Herod as Mad Sinner because they stress the
ranting that made Herod a byword in Elizabethan drama.[58]
The Poeta introduces the Digby Herod "like as a wod man,"
who orders the massacre "in his furious wynde" (ll. 39, 45), and
the play proper opens with the traditional boasts illustrating
the madness of pride and blasphemy. If Nebuchadnezzar deserved seven years' madness for his pride in Babylon, this
Herod clearly merits damnation. After threatening death to all
who will not worship his gods and himself, Herod orders the
killing of the children, which is carried out after a great deal of
scene-stealing by Watkyn, a cowardly page who wants to be a
knight. The soldiers then tell Herod of their success; and
Watkyn reports that one mother called for Herod's death,
while another cursed him with damnation. Immediately vengeance comes; instead of being pleased at his success or angry at
the curses, Herod simply goes mad:

> Oute, I am madde . my wyttes be ner goon,
> I am wo for the wrokyng of this werke wylde,
>
> .   .   .   .
>
> Alas, I am so sorowfull and sett out of Sadnes;
> I Chille and Chever for this Orrible chaunce.
>
> [ll. 365–66, 373–74]

Shortly he dies in frenzy:

> What out, out, allas! I wene I shall dey þis day;
> my hert tremelith and quakith for ffeer,
> my Robys I rende a to for I am in a fray
> that my hert will brest a-sunder evyn heer.
>
> [ll. 381–84]

The play is not very coherent. Watkyn is a charming miles
gloriosus whose absurdities might have been used to point up
the folly of that other miles gloriosus, Herod; but the playwright saw only his farcical possibilities, and Watkyn usurps
too much of the action without contributing much to the play's

58. See *Hamlet* 3. 2 for Hamlet's famous instructions to the players.

doctrinal content. Herod's rage is not as impressive as the Poeta leads us to expect, and the king's madness and fever at the end seem to be produced miraculously, not by the rage that causes fever and death in other plays. Herod's illness in the Chester, Towneley, and *Ludus Coventriae* plays is no less a consequence of vengeance, but that vengeance is implemented scientifically through physiological and psychological means so that it is clear that Herod causes his own destruction. The Digby author seems to have known that Herod must rage, go mad, and die of fever, but he did not understand how the three steps are related. The moral and physiological logic behind the convention of the Mad Sinner is missing, and Herod's madness maintains its flamboyance at the expense of its deepest significance.

The Coventry *Shearmen and Taylors' Pageant* presents a delightfully mad Herod reminiscent of the Padovan Herod who attacks clergy and congregation. The play opens with the events preceding and including the birth of the "Makar of mon" (l. 284), after which Herod's messenger announces his own all-powerful king. Herod struts in, bragging exuberantly:

> For I am evyn he thatt made bothe hevin and hell,
> And of my myghte powar holdith vp this world rownd.
>
> .   .   .   .
>
> I am the cawse of this grett lyght and thunder;
> Ytt ys throgh my fure that the soche noyse dothe make.
>
> > [ll. 487–88, 493–94]

We are reminded of Bartholomeus's melancholic madman who also believes he holds up the world (4. 11) and of Salmoneus, whose attempt to imitate Jupiter's thunder and lightning was fatal. But Herod is even greater: he causes earthquakes, rules hell, and is so beautiful that anyone who beholds him needs neither food nor drink; he rules all princes, for he is God's cousin.[59] The contrast between this Herod and the infant

59. Here Herod parodies the idea that those who look on God need no food; cf. York *Creation*, ll. 75–76: "Ay with stedefaste steuen lat vs stande styll, / Lorde! to be fede with þe fode of thi fayre-face" (Lucy Toulmin Smith, ed., *York Mystery Plays* [Oxford, 1885; reprinted New York: Russell & Russell, 1963]).

Christ, already presented, must have been vastly amusing; indeed, the Coventry Herod is so engaging that his evil nature may have been quite forgotten. When the Magi are brought before him, he graciously commands them to have no fear of his "bryght ble [complexion]" (l. 643); when he has heard their errand, he sends them off with a passport and an invitation to dinner (perhaps a purely visual one?) on their return.

Eventually news comes of their defection, and Herod runs mad in one of the funniest scenes in medieval drama:

> A-nothur wey? out! owt! owtt!
> Hath those fawls traytvrs done me this ded?
> I stampe! I stare! I loke all abowtt!
> Myght I them take, I schuld them bren at a glede!
> I rent! I rawe! and now run I wode!
> A! thatt these velen trayturs hath mard this my mode!
> The schalbe hangid yf I ma cum them to!
>
> *Here Erode ragis in the pagond and in the strete also.*
>
> [ll. 777–83]

That Herod's pride is so great that even his madness is thus self-centered — I do this, I do that, as though his every action needed glossing for mere mortals — must have seemed thoroughly ludicrous to the audience. At the same time his childishness and impotent fury must have brought to mind the great contrast between Herod and Christ: Herod the childish king madly shouting vain threats, Christ the humble child and true king; Herod the mad and sinful, Christ the healer of madness and sin. In his madness, Herod decides to kill the children, and when his soldiers note the possible disadvantages of a massacre, Herod rages again until his tantrum forces them to agree. But his triumph is short-lived: he learns that Christ has escaped, and he rides off to Egypt to conquer Christ.

Despite the pathos of the Slaughter of the Innocents scene, the play's tone is triumphant. The vicelike Herod has been baited and routed even if he has not been tamed like the Padovan Herod or crippled and killed like the Herod of other English plays. He may return from Egypt to plague the Church, but so do all vices, and the Coventry Herod is much closer to the vice of the moralities than to the damned king of Chester and the *Ludus Coventriae*. The Mad Sinner is still a sinner, but he is also a Lord of Misrule who would be perfectly at home in the Feast of Fools.[60] The theme of inversion which is central to the Nativity sequence — God born as a child, a child the King of Kings, a madman claiming to be God — may be treated as a serious and profound theological paradox, as it is in many of the cycles and as it probably was in the celebration of the Boy Bishop; but it may also be handled with boisterous exuberance, as in the Feast of Fools, the Padovan *Representatio Herodis,* and the Coventry pageant. Although it may have been subject to abuse, such exuberance is not in itself irreligious; in the Coventry play especially, Herod's monomaniacal rantings against the Christ-child contribute fitly to the celebratory atmosphere of the feast.[61]

Chrysostom claimed that Herod's attack on Christ in the spirit of wrathful pride was mad, and he suggested that such willful madness could never be cured; the English plays reflect the same idea. For medieval science and theology, Herod's biblical anger, a sin in any context, becomes real madness leading to further sin, to loss of control over body and mind, to disease, death, and damnation. This madness grows out of and punishes pride and blasphemy: setting himself up as God, Herod is too proud to acknowledge any authority but his own or, at best, Mahound's. Herod's presumption and insanity are far greater than Nebuchadnezzar's, and his story shows the absurdity, stupidity, and madness of refusing the grace of God and Christ's healing power. Through Herod's example, the medieval audi-

60. For the possible relationship of the Feast of Fools to Herod plays, see Chambers, *Medieval Stage,* 2:56–57; the celebrations of the Feast of Fools and of the Boy Bishop are described in the same work, 1:274–371. For a warning against confusing the feasts and for a discussion of the extent and manner of their observance, see Kolve, *Play Called Corpus Christi,* pp. 135–37.

61. I have argued throughout the didactic and aesthetic utility of Herod's mad rantings. Anderson, however, finds them examples of the abuse of religious drama's purpose; see *Drama and Imagery,* p. 36.

ence is enjoined to forget petty considerations of pomp, position, and idolatry — the placing of anything, not only Mahound, before God — and to forsake the madness of sin for the
health of Christ.

The life pattern of the Mad Sinner, so well exemplified by
Herod, is also typical of other proud, wrathful pagan tyrants
who delight in persecuting Christians. I should like to end this
chapter with a few examples to show how widespread was the
association of madness with heresy and heathenism in general
and with pagan kings in particular. The Bible and commentaries endorse this association: for instance, Zacharias notes
that foes of the holy city Jerusalem will be punished with madness (Zach. 12:4), and commentaries interpret the possessed
man in the miracle of the Gadarene swine as one who lacks
faith in and persecutes Christ and the Church. Similarly, those
stricken with madness in Deuteronomy 28:28 are those who
deny the divinity of Christ.[62] The Christian view that pagan
gods were really devils probably contributed to the notion that
pagans, and especially pagan priests, were possessed,[63] while
heresy within the Church could also be considered madness; in
his *Glossary of Later Latin,* Souter gives a meaning of *furor* as
"false doctrine, heretical error." As for the Jews, those who
persecuted Christ, Stephen, and Paul are often called mad in
Middle English literature.[64]

Frequently madness punishes those who persecute the saints.
Saint Longinus was tortured by having all his teeth pulled out
by the Prince of Cappadocia; Longinus responded by chopping

62. *Glossa ordinaria, PL* 114:275; and *PL* 113:485.

63. E.g., Minucius Felix, *Octavius,* trans. Rudolph Arbesmann, Fathers
of the Church, no. 10 (Washington, D.C.: Catholic University of America
Press, 1950), 27. 1–2.

64. See *Miroure of Mans Saluacionne,* p. 83; the legend of Mary Magdalene, in *Legendae Catholicae,* ed. W. B. D. D. Turnbull (Edinburgh, 1840),
p. 218; Carleton Brown, ed., *Religious Lyrics of the XVth Century* (Oxford:
Clarendon Press, 1939), no. 76, ll. 9–10, and no. 109, l. 146; *Cursor mundi,*
ll. 19451 and 20968; for the same topic in the drama, see Kolve, *Play
Called Corpus Christi,* p. 197.

up the prince's idols, from which devils poured out to possess the prince and his men:

Somme become blinde anon and some gidie & wode
And todrowe [rent] al hore lymes wyþ oþer sorwe ynowe
þe prynce was boþe blind & wod & al is lymes tognowe
[gnawed] 65

Longinus told the prince that he would be cured if he would kill the suffering saint and become a Christian; the king agreed and was immediately cured and baptized. Another evil king, Astriages, crucified Bartholomew after that saint had converted the king's brother. But as Astriages proceeded in triumph to Bartholomew's tomb, he and all his followers were driven mad:

þe deuel þat hore maister was tormented hom anon
For wrecche of þe holymon hi bicome gidie echon66

Andrew's tormentor Egeas fared similarly: angry that Andrew had converted his wife, he "wax wod wroth" and killed the saint. "þus, when Egeas segh þat he was ded, he ʒeode homward. þen aftyr þe way he waxet wod, and sone aftyr, among all men, he stervet yn þe way." 67

The madness of Nero, a medieval commonplace, was often associated with his refusal to believe in Christ. *The South English Legendary* notes that Paul appeared to Nero as a ghost, telling the king he would be damned for his paganism:

þo þe emperor hurde þis witles he was and wod
Wod he bileuede al is lif and to deþe he let do
Fader and moder and is breþeren and is sostren also
So wod was þe ssrewe bicome. . . .68

According to Mirk, Nero had both Peter and Paul as instructors in Christianity: "But for he sett noght by hor lore, God

65. Charlotte D'Evelyn and Anna J. Mill, eds., *The South English Legendary*, EETS, os 235, 236, 244 (1956, 1959), 1:85.
66. Ibid., 2:382.
67. Mirk, *Festial*, p. 9.
68. D'Evelyn and Mill, 1:273.

suffryd Symon Magus to betraylon hym and encharme hym, þat
he lost hys kynd wytte þat God ȝaf hym, and ȝaf hym all to
foly aftyr, and laft hit neuer til he wer vndon." Stricken with
madness for his denial of Christianity, Nero killed himself as
so many madmen do: "Then þe Romayns seen how þys man
was all yn a fransy, and huntet hym out of þe cyte, and woldyn
hauen slayne hym. And he þen fond a staf, and wyth his teþe
he gnow hit scharpe, and so rowude [thrust] hym þeron." [69]
Mirk goes on to note the similar ends in madness and suicide
of other pagans: Herod, Simon Magus, Pilate.

The madness of pagan persecutors of the Church also figures
in romances. Almost everyone in the extravagant English
Charlemagne romances goes mad at some point for love, sorrow, wrath, or diversion; but the Saracen king is mad more
often than anyone. His insanity is usually linked with his refusal to become a Christian even though that would save his
life and with his abuse of Mahound when things go badly —
the implication is that even a pagan ought to revere his own
gods. For instance, in the *Sowdone of Babylone*[70] Laban chastises his gods "nere wode for tene" (l. 2104) during a siege; and
later, when his daughter scatters his treasure to distract his
men from their attack on the French, he grows mad and smites
Mahound's image to the ground (ll. 2487–510). In *Sir Ferum-
bras*[71] the "ameral" Balan is mad with anger when Charles
offers to spare his life if he will be baptized; his gestures are
worthy of Herod:

Wanne þe Ameral hym vnderstod, A clew ys heued, & riȝte ys
     hod,
  & starede with ys eȝene wronge,
& prauncede & blew as he were wod, & miȝt noȝt speke for his
     heȝe mod,
  or was after longe.

                                                    [ll. 5339–42]

69. *Festial*, pp. 192–94.
70. Emil Hausknecht, ed., EETS, es 38 (1881).
71. Sidney J. Herrtage, ed., EETS, es 34 (1879).

The same thing happens shortly thereafter when Charles repeats the request (ll. 5620–25). After his defeat, Balan agrees to baptism, but during the service he breaks the baptismal font and bashes in the priest's teeth, claiming that he would be mad to leave Mahound (ll. 5799–800). Clearly Balan's madness is quite perverse: he feels himself mad to trust his gods and mad to forsake them. Although he is not mad as Nero, nevertheless his periodic bouts of insanity join with the illogic of his attitude toward both Mahound and Christ to show how foolish it is to be pagan. His madness is funnier than Herod's, partly because it has less serious consequences, but still he is a Mad Sinner: although he deserts Mahound regularly, his pride will not let him worship Christ; deprived of the sanity of true belief, his irrationality leads him to choose death rather than salvation, and his mad adherence to Mahound in the hour of need results in death and damnation.

4   The Unholy and Holy Wild Man

> I was the brother of dragons, and the companion of
> ostriches. My skin is become black upon me, and my bones
> are dried up with heat. My harp is turned to mourning,
> and my organ into the voice of those that weep.
>
> Job 30:29–31

The "wild man" — he who lives, for whatever reason,
in the wilderness beyond the bounds of civilization — is one
of the most compelling figures in medieval art and literature.[1]
Essentially human in form, the wild man is set apart from
his civilized counterpart by any combination of the following
characteristics: discolored skin, usually black; long body hair
covering all but his hands and feet; a great beard; dress of
foliage or skins; some physical deformity such as bestial facial
features; unusually great or small size; the inability to speak
or even reason; rough, even churlish behavior; supernatural
power over wild animals; a diet of roots, berries, or raw
flesh; a solitary habitation — often a cave — in the desert or
forest far from men.

Many of these characteristics are derived from Nebuchad-

---

1. Useful literary treatments include R. W. Ackerman, "Arthur's Wild
Man Knight," *RPH* 9 (1955):115–19; Bernheimer, *Wild Men*; Arthur Dick-
son, *Valentine and Orson* (New York: Columbia University Press, 1929);
"Hairy Anchorite" 1 and 2. Two books include useful summaries of
Bernheimer's and Dickson's works as well as providing new material: Ben-
son, *Art and Tradition*, pp. 62–90, and Neaman, "The Distracted Knight,"
chap. 5. On the wild man in art, see Benson's and Bernheimer's books;
Anderson, *The Medieval Carver*, pp. 98ff.; and V. Raimond S. van Marle,
Iconographie de l'art profane au moyen-âge et à la renaissance, 2 vols. (The
Hague: M. Nijhoff, 1931), 1:183–87. See also plates 7 and 11–16.

nezzar; perhaps others come from folklore's May King and Green Man, from Enkidu in the epic *Gilgamesh*, from Celtic tradition, and from such biblical characters as Adam and Eve, Esau, Ishmael, Elijah, and John the Baptist.[2] Classical tradition provided satyrs, fauns, and other *homines silvestres* in abundance; and the Alexander legends, confirmed by Prester John's apocryphal letter to the Byzantine emperor, popularized the belief that India was inhabited by large numbers of wild people. One of them is described in the Middle English *Prose Alexander*: he was "als mekill [great] als a geaunte. And he was rughe of hare all over, and his hede was lyke till a swyne, And his voyce also." [3] His great lust, demonstrated by his attacking a naked woman, convinces Alexander that he is not human, so the poor man is burned (plate 11).

Such strange creatures, often listed in encyclopedias and bestiaries,[4] provoked considerable debate on their actual existence, their relationship to man, and their possible salvation. The popular legend of Saint Paul the Hermit asserts that wild men exist and can be saved: apparently Saint Anthony,

2. See Benson, *Art and Tradition*, pp. 62–72; Bernheimer, *Wild Men*, chaps. 2–3 and passim; C. J. P. Cave, *Roof Bosses in Medieval Churches: An Aspect of Gothic Sculpture* (Cambridge: Cambridge University Press, 1948), pp. 65–68; H. D. Ellis, "The Wodewose in East Anglian Church Decoration," *Proceedings of the Suffolk Institute of Archaeology and Natural History* 14 (1912):287–93; Lady Raglan, "The 'Green Man' in Church Architecture," *Folklore* 50 (1939): 45–57; "Hairy Anchorite" 1. 199–210; and Robert Withington, *English Pageantry*, 2 vols. (Cambridge: Harvard University Press, 1918, 1920), 1:70–76 and passim. On the association of the Latin *silva* ("forest"), the wild man's habitation, with ideas of chaos, primitivism, and bestiality in medieval philosophy, see Brian Stock, *Myth and Science in the Twelfth Century: A Study of Bernard Silvester* (Princeton: Princeton University Press, 1972), pp. 81, 100–102, and passim. The biblical tradition of the wild man will be considered further below.

3. J. S. Westlake, ed., EETS, os 143 (1913), pp. 89–90. For classical and Indian traditions, see Bernheimer, *Wild Men*, pp. 85–95.

4. See Bartholomeus 18. 84; Isidore, *Etymologiae*, 11. 3. 21; Vincent of Beauvais, *Speculum naturale*, in *Speculum quadruplex sive speculum maius*, 4 vols. (Douai, 1624; reprinted Graz: Akademische Druck (1964–65), 19. 102; T. H. White, trans., *The Book of Beasts* (London: Jonathon White, 1954), p. 36 and note; and Bernheimer, *Wild Men*, pp. 90–91.

seeking Paul in the desert, met "a dwarfish figure of no great
size, its nostrils joined together, and its forehead bristling
with horns: the lower part of its body ended in goat's feet." [5]
Anthony asked the creature what it was: "Mortal am I, and
one of the dwellers in the desert, whom the heathen worship,
astray in diverse error, calling us Fauns, and Satyrs, and
Incubi. I come on an embassy from my tribe. We pray thee
that thou wouldst entreat for us our common God who did
come, we know, for the world's salvation." Such a creature,
acknowledging God, is clearly more praiseworthy than most
dwellers in cities. Augustine evades any pronouncement on
whether wild men and other fabled monsters exist, but he
neatly solves the theological issue:

> Whoever is anywhere born a man, that is, a rational,
> mortal animal, no matter what unusual appearance he
> presents in color, movement, sound, nor how peculiar he
> is . . . no Christian can doubt that he springs from that
> one [Adam's] protoplast. . . . Wherefore, to conclude
> this question cautiously and guardedly, either these things
> which have been told of some races have no existence at
> all; or if they do exist, they are not human races; or if
> they are human, they are descended from Adam [and can
> be saved]. [*CG* 16. 8 (2:326–28)]

It is not the outward image of God that makes the man, but
the inward image—reason; the wild man who lacks reason is
a beast. Some writers, however, felt that the wild man was
neither beast nor human but rather a devil. This belief, encouraged by the Christian habit of turning pagan deities such
as satyrs and fauns into devils, was stimulated by Jerome's
gloss on Isaias 13:21, which describes the evil inhabitants of
the desert: "But wild beasts shall rest there . . . and ostriches
shall dwell there, and the hairy ones [*pilosi*] shall dance
there." According to the gloss, the beasts and ostriches are
demons, and the "pilosi" are "hairy wild men, and also in-

---

5. *Desert Fathers*, pp. 45–46.

cubi, or satyrs, or certain kinds of demons." [6] The similarity
between pictorial representations of devils — who are often
black and shaggy — and those of wild men must have de-
graded the latter's moral status even further.

So flamboyant and morally ambiguous a figure as the Wild
Man plays many roles in medieval culture. He can be a
heraldic device, a symbol of eroticism, or a pageant figure. He
is a common drôlerie in medieval manuscripts, and he appears on many English roof bosses and baptismal fonts. As a
Brahmin or a Christian hermit, he represents the ascetic life
of virtue; as a friend to Saracens in the Charlemagne romances, he embodies the deformity of heresy or vice. Like
Dangiers in the *Roman de la Rose,* he can be a frenzied
opponent of romantic love; like Yvain, Lancelot, or Tristan,
he can be a victim of it.[7] At times he is a subhuman foe of
wandering knights, like the "wodwos, þat woned in þe
Knarrez" whom Gawain fights; sometimes he is human but
utterly alien to the normal world of men, like the deformed
Giant Herdsman who rules the beasts in *Yvain.* He might be
wild in appearance and churlish in behavior but otherwise
an ordinary member of society, like the wild man in *Aucassin
et Nicolette*; perhaps only a slight deformity, like that of Sir
Groinge Poire Mole, or a name, like that of Sir Dodinel le
Sauvage, marks him as a wild man.[8] He might be mad, like

6. *Glossa ordinaria, PL* 113:1252. For a late medieval classification of
wild men as demons, see Neaman, "The Distracted Knight," pp. 203–11.

7. See Bernheimer, *Wild Men,* passim; Williams, "Hairy Anchorite" 1.
211–25; Benson, *Art and Tradition,* pp. 74, 84–86; and, on the courtly wild
man, see Neaman, "The Distracted Knight," chaps. 4–5. Neaman rightly
points out that the Arthurian Wild Man–Knight never suffers from love-
madness in its strictest medical sense — that is, his love is never the immediate and only cause of madness. For a good poetic treatment of the
Wild Man–Lover, see "I must go walke þe woed so wyld," in *Secular
Lyrics of the XIVth and XVth Centuries,* ed. Rossell Hope Robbins, 2d ed.
(Oxford: Clarendon Press, 1955), no. 20.

8. J. R. R. Tolkien and E. V. Gordon, eds., *Sir Gawain and the Green
Knight,* 2d rev. ed. Norman Davis (Oxford: Clarendon Press, 1968), l. 721;
for Groinge Poire Mole, see Ackerman, "Arthur's Wild Man Knight," pp.
115–19.

Yvain or Merlin Silvestris; he might be sane, like many hermits and Sir Orfeo, despite their apparent madness when compared to the civilized norm. Wild men vary infinitely in form, powers, and significance; but all are alike in one respect at least: their association with the wilderness has made them, for good or ill, unlike other men who dwell in the security of civilization and order.

This chapter is concerned with only two of the many manifestations of the wild man: the Unholy Wild Man, who goes mad because of his own sin and who lives in the wilderness as a beast until his guilt is purged; and the Holy Wild Man, whose flight to the desert and whose primitive, superficially bestial life there are usually inspired by the desire for sanctity and spiritual perfection. These two conventional figures, who differ from the typical wild man in that they are initially civilized and wholly human, have been discussed briefly in chapter 2 in relation to their prototype Nebuchadnezzar; here they will be considered on their own as important literary conventions. Like other wild men, these two figures share the trappings of madness inherited from Nebuchadnezzar: a wild, bestial appearance; a beast's diet of grass or flesh; a flight to the wilderness that is mad by the standards of civilization; persistence in solitude; and often friendship with wild beasts.

The superficial similarity between the Holy and Unholy Wild Man can be deceptive, however; travelers in the wilderness often mistake saints for devils or beasts, and Sir Orfeo's actions and appearance resemble the mad Merlin's. One important distinction between the Unholy and the Holy Wild Man is that the former invariably is truly mad, having lost all use of reason as he endures the suffering that punishes and purges his sin. The Holy Wild Man, on the other hand, is at least capable of reason, although the precise degree of his sanity may be in question; he may well be mad by normal standards in that his love of God prevents him from acting "reasonably" like other men, valuing life, comfort, and kindred. From the secular point of view it is insane to forsake worldly pleasures for almost intolerable hardship, and throughout history one man's saint is another man's idiot.

Nevertheless, the Holy Wild Man is not totally and continuously without the use of reason, as the Unholy Wild Man is. A related distinction between the two is that the Unholy Wild Man typically has no choice about his condition and way of life, while the Holy Wild Man voluntarily chooses the life of the wilderness in the hope that he will be perfected by his willing subjection to God and to all misfortunes and temptations he may send. The Unholy Wild Man is driven mad by God's grace so that he may suffer and eventually be saved; the Holy Wild Man chooses to be a fool so that he may be wise. But for both the wilderness serves a similar function; through its torments, which punish, purify, or test the wild man, lies the path to salvation. This chapter, then, will consider how an understanding of the moral implications of the wilderness, of wildness, and of real or apparent madness can lead to a fuller appreciation of such works as *Ywain and Gawain*, the *Life of Merlin* attributed to Geoffrey of Monmouth, and *Sir Orfeo*.

THE UNHOLY WILD MAN: YWAIN AND MERLIN

Throughout this study we have seen that madness is often both caused by and emblematic of sin, and the discussion of Nebuchadnezzar's insanity showed the symbolic and aesthetic value of portraying the madness of sin as a bestial life in the wilderness, the life of the Unholy Wild Man. One of the best examples of the Unholy Wild Man is Ywain, whose failure to keep his word to his wife leads to his loss of her, to madness in the wilderness, and finally to acknowledgment of his sin and to a series of good deeds that atone for his fault and restore his lady to him. I shall here be concerned primarily with the Middle English romance *Ywain and Gawain*; but occasional reference to its French source (Chrétien's *Yvain*) and the independent Welsh version (*The Lady of the Fountain*) will help clarify the English poet's view of Ywain's madness.[9]

9. The texts cited are these: Albert B. Friedman and Norman T. Harris, eds., *Ywain and Gawain* (fourteenth century), EETS, os 254 (1964); *Yvain:*

First I should like to consider the causes of that madness. After marrying Alundyne and undertaking to defend her marvelous fountain against all challenges, Ywain is persuaded to leave her for the glory of jousts and tournaments. His decision disturbs his wife, who permits him to go only after he promises to return within a year. She then gives him a magic ring to ensure that neither imprisonment nor sickness will interfere with his faithful return. Preoccupied with his chivalric triumphs, Ywain forgets his promise until the year is past. Then, during a banquet in his honor, a lady rides into the hall; she courteously greets everyone but Ywain, whom she accuses of betraying his wife by breaking his word. Seizing Ywain's ring, she departs; and Ywain, grief-stricken, suddenly goes mad. Such are the initiating circumstances of his madness, and they point to a chain of causes. Most immediately, it is grief that drives him mad: "For wa he wex al wilde and wode" (l. 1650). Considered medically, this passion produces excess melancholy and deprives Ywain of reason, after which — like other melancholy madmen — he wishes to shun men's sight by flight into the forest. But less immediate causes are more important: his own moral fault — lack of truth — and the loss of Alundyne's ring, which punishes that fault and induces his madness.[10]

---

le Chevalier au Lion (ca. 1170), text of W. Foerster, introduction by T. B. W. Reid (Manchester: Manchester University Press, 1942). English translations are from W. W. Comfort, trans., *Arthurian Romances* (London: Dent, 1914); *Owein and Lunet, or the Lady of the Fountain* (ca. 1350), in *The Mabinogion*, trans. T. P. Ellis and John Lloyd (Oxford: Clarendon Press, 1929), vol. 2. Line references in the text are to Middle English and Old French versions.

10. Critical opinion on the nature of Yvain's fault varies considerably: Alfred Adler, in "Sovereignty in Chrétien's *Yvain*," *PMLA* 62 (1947):281–305; Julian Harris, in "The Role of the Lion in Chrétien de Troyes' *Yvain*," *PMLA* 64 (1949):1143–63; and John Finlayson, in "*Ywain and Gawain* and the Meaning of Adventure," *Anglia* 87 (1969):312–37, argue that he falls through pride. His rudeness and selfishness are stressed by Joseph J. Duggan in "Yvain's Good Name: The Unity of Chrétien de Troyes' 'Chevalier au Lion,'" *OL* 24 (1969):112–29. Maxwell S. Luria, in "The Storm-making Spring and the Meaning of Chrétien's *Yvain*,' *SP*

The importance of truth as a virtue in fourteenth-century English literature, and especially in *Sir Gawain and the Green Knight*, has been fully documented by J. A. Burrow.[11] He shows convincingly that truth — faithfulness to a person or an ideal, the keeping of promises, personal integrity — is often seen as that virtue which presupposes and maintains all other virtues and without which no true excellence can exist. Hence, failure to meet even the slightest legitimate obligation is a breach of truth and a violation of both Christian and chivalric ideals, involving dishonor (from the chivalric perspective) and sin (from the Christian one). A similar emphasis on the crucial importance of truth characterizes *Ywain and Gawain*, distinguishing it from the French and Welsh versions and supporting the common critical view that English romances tend to be more moral and didactic than the French.[12] Whereas Chrétien's work begins with a lament for the debased state of love in these latter days, and the Welsh story has no

---

64 (1967):564–85, notes that Yvain has a serious "spiritual failure" but does not specify what that failure is. C. R. B. Combellack, in "Yvain's Guilt," *SP* 68 (1971):10–25, argues that Yvain's fault is simple forgetfulness, not the pride usually suggested. Norris J. Lacy, in "Organic Structure of Yvain's Expiation," *RR* 61 (1970):79–84, describes his fault as failure to keep his word; and Dieter Mehl, *The Middle English Romances of the Thirteenth and Fourteenth Centuries* (London: Routledge & Kegan Paul, 1969), pp. 183–85, offers support for my belief (reached independently) that Ywain in the English romance falls through lack of loyalty. Although articles on the French romance are often somewhat applicable to the Middle English version, there are substantial differences between the two poems that frequently invalidate for *Ywain* conclusions based on *Yvain*.

11. *A Reading of Sir Gawain and the Green Knight* (London: Routledge & Kegan Paul, 1965), pp. 42–50 and passim.

12. See Margaret Adlum Gist, *Love and War in the Middle English Romances* (Philadelphia: University of Pennsylvania Press, 1947), chap. 1; James H. Blessing, "A Comparison of Some Middle English Romances with the Old French Antecedents" (Ph. D. diss., Stanford University, 1959), chap. 10; and Mehl, *Middle English Romances*, pp. 5, 19, 21, and passim. For an analysis of the pattern of changes between *Yvain* and *Ywain*, see Blessing's dissertation; Friedman and Harrington, *Ywain and Gawain*, pp. xvi–xxxiv; and Norman T. Harrington, "The Problem of the Lacunae in *Ywain and Gawain*," *JEGP* 69 (1970):659–65.

authorial comment at all, the English poet starts with a long
lament for truth, honored in Arthur's court but shunned
now:

> þai tald of more trewth þam bitwene
> þan now omang men here es sene,
> For trowth and luf es al bylaft;
> Men uses now anoþer craft.
> With worde men makes it trew and stabil,
> Bot in þaire faith es noght bot fabil;
> With þe mowth men makes it hale,
> Bot trew trowth es nane in þe tale.

[ll. 33–40]

This opening sets up expectations that the romance will deal
with truth, and further changes from the French strengthen
these expectations. For instance, here the messenger denounces Ywain as "Traytur untrew and trowthles" (l. 1626),
making her point twice over, but there is no corresponding
accusation in the French or Welsh. The recovered Ywain
seems to realize that breach of troth leads to disgrace and
madness: having sworn to defend Lunet against the false
steward, he fears he must leave Gawain's family to the ravages
of the giant Harpin unless the battle can take place early
enough for Ywain to rescue Lunet afterward. If he breaks his
word to her, "oiþer he sold hymselven sla / Or wode ogain
to þe wod ga" (ll. 2377–78). Chrétien's Yvain shares this recognition (*Yvain*, ll. 4080–82), but at other times he takes the
ideal of truth very lightly, as when he deceitfully offers to
promise to marry the daughter of the lord of Pesme Aven-
ture (*Yvain*, ll. 5750–54). The English poet alters the story:
Ywain staunchly refuses to wed the girl even though he
might be imprisoned, and thereby he avoids putting himself
in a position where he might have to break his word.

Such changes enhance the English poet's emphasis on truth
as the most important virtue, and a further change confirms
the point. As Lunet's accusation suggests, it is Ywain's breach
of troth that leads to his purgative madness, and the connection between this sin and its punishment is made clear by

the English poet's novel treatment of Alundyne's ring and its retrieval. In Chrétien's work Laudine gives Yvain a magic ring: "No true and loyal lover can be imprisoned or lose any blood, nor can any harm befall him, provided he carry it and hold it dear, and keep his sweetheart in mind." [13] As in the English version the ring's powers depend on the lover's remaining true, but the point is not greatly stressed by Chrétien. When Yvain has missed his time, the messenger comes to chastise him for his many faults, and finally she demands the ring: "Senseless and deprived of speech, Yvain is unable to reply. And the damsel steps forth and takes the ring from his finger, commending to God the king and all the others except him, whom she leaves in deep distress. And his sorrow grows on him: he feels oppressed by what he hears, and is tormented by what he sees. He would rather be banished alone in some wild land. . . . But he would rather go insane than not take vengeance upon himself" (p. 216 [ll. 2774ff.]). Fearing madness, he leaves the feast. Then—after a good many lines—"such a storm broke loose in his brain that he loses his senses" (p. 216 [ll. 2804–05]). He stays in the wilderness, mad, until his cure.

In the Welsh version, the relationship of ring to madness is even more confused. Although the countess never gives Owein any ring that we know about, a maiden comes to Arthur's court, takes away Owein's ring, and leaves. Then Owein remembers the countess with sorrow, but he continues his meal and goes home to sleep. "And next day in the morning he arose. Not to the courts of Arthur did he set out; but to the uttermost ends of the world, and to desert mountains. And so he continued wandering until his clothes were all worn out, and until his body was wellnigh wasted away, and until long hair grew all over him." [14] Although Owein is clearly upset, he may not be completely mad; since he is eventually cured of exhaustion and a bestial appearance rather than of madness, as in the English and French versions, his wildness

13. Comfort, *Arthurian Romances*, p. 214 (ll. 2596–613).
14. Ellis and Lloyd, *Mabinogion*, 2:55.

might be more penitential than insane, and his journey in
the wilderness might be to find the countess, who lives at
the ends of the world. Clearly, then, there is no logical connection between the ring and Owein's wildness, let alone his
madness.

The English romance is far clearer about the ring's role in
initiating Ywain's madness. Its significance is defined more
precisely than elsewhere: Alundyne gives a fuller account of
its powers than Laudine, and she particularly stresses that
Ywain must remain true if the ring is to be effective:

> In nane anger sal ȝe be,
> Whils ȝe it have and thinkes on me.
>
> .   .   .   .
>
> It es na preson ȝow sal halde
> Al if ȝowre fase be manyfalde;
> With sekenes sal ȝe noght be tane,
> Ne of ȝowre blode ȝe sal lese nane;
> In batel tane sal ȝe noght be,
> Whils ȝe it have and thinkes on me;
> And ay, whils ȝe er trew of love,
> Over al sal ȝe be obove.
>
> [ll. 1529–30, 1533–40]

But of course Ywain does fail in truth, as we have seen, and
the messenger comes to court, denounces him, seizes the ring,
and disappears. So grief-stricken "þat nere for murning wex
he mad" (l. 1640), Ywain blames himself "for myne owen
foly" (l. 1647) and promptly goes mad:

> An evyl toke him als he stode;
> For wa he wex al wilde and wode.
> Unto þe wod þe way he nome;
> No man wist whore he bycome.
>
> [ll. 1649–52]

Here there is a causal relationship between the loss of the
ring and Ywain's madness that was absent in the French.
There Yvain's madness is gradual, beginning before the ring

is taken and becoming complete only after much tortured self-examination and the flight to the forest. But here Ywain shows no signs of insanity before losing the ring, and he goes quite mad shortly thereafter as he stands stunned in the court. The sudden onset of his distemper, reminiscent of Nebuchadnezzar's sudden madness in the halls of Babylon, bothers the editors of the English poem, who feel that Ywain's madness is psychologically justified by his lengthy self-castigation, while "madness comes upon the restrained, phlegmatic English hero as though it were a sudden physiological disorder." [15] I think the English poet had good reason for making Ywain's madness so unexpected and swift. From the start he has emphasized the importance of truth, and the ring becomes a symbol of that virtue. To some extent a ring is a natural symbol of truth and integrity, for it has the circle's perfect roundness and, like that other great token of truth, Gawain's pentangle, it is endless. The poetic context strengthens the ring's natural connotations: Alundyne gives Ywain the ring specifically to ensure that he will be able to remain true, and she stresses that it will protect him from suffering and sickness only so long as he is true to his wife and his obligations. With this meaning for the ring in mind, the English poet seems to have made Ywain go mad so suddenly after losing the ring in order to show that his madness is the moral consequence of his breach of truth rather than the product of the excessively fine sensibilities that characterize the French hero. Such, at least, is the best explanation for many of the English poet's changes in the story: the addition of the messenger's denunciation of the "untrew and trowthles" Ywain, the omission of Chrétien's reference to Ywain's lack of sense *before* the ring is taken, the abbreviation of the hero's meditation on his guilt after the seizure of the ring, Ywain's sudden madness while he is still in the hall, and finally the alteration of Chrétien's statement that Yvain stole a bow and arrow while he still had enough wit — "S'ot tant

15. Friedman and Harrington, *Ywain and Gawain*, p. xxxiv.

de san" (l. 2819) — to the clearly mad Ywain's acquisition
of weapons "on a day als Ywayne ran" (l. 1657). Both Chrétien
and the English poet see Ywain's madness as having a physiological and psychological cause, the passion of grief; but the
English poet is chiefly concerned that we see the ultimate
cause of Ywain's madness — its moral justification — as his
violation of truth. And he effects this aim by linking Ywain's
purgative insanity with the loss of the ring that symbolizes
truth. Only by adhering to what the ring represents — faith
to his wife, perhaps also his chivalric and Christian duty to
defend the weak rather than to seek glory in tournaments, as
he seems to have done — can Ywain be truly a man, truly
sane. His defection renders him less than human, or at least
less than the romantic ideal; if truth is a condition for life
well lived, for man as he should be, then lack of truth is
fitly punished by madness, that token that all is not what it
should be, that man is no longer in the image of God, that
integrity is gone. Violation of truth releases Ywain from the
protection of the ring and of reason, and symbolic suffering
and sickness are free to come upon him.[16]

In the forest Ywain lives the subhuman life typical of the
Unholy Wild Man. Naked, ugly, he roams the wilderness "als
it wore a wilde beeste" (l. 1654). He shoots deer with his captured bow and lives on

> . . . rotes and raw venysowne;
> He drank of þe warm blode,
> And þat did him mekil gode.
>
> [ll. 1668–70]

16. Perhaps the loss of the ring not only permits a general sort of sickness
to attack Ywain (cf. l. 1535) but even contributes specifically to the form
of that disease, madness: the stone in the ring may be a sapphire, a gem
which frees the imprisoned, staunches blood, and brings victory, just as
Alundyne claims (ll. 1533, 1536–37). More important, it also prevents
"malyncoly passiouns" and "sorrow and dred," which are the immediate
causes of Ywain's madness, as we have seen. See the Peterborough Lapidary
in Joan Evans and Mary S. Serjeantson, eds., *English Medieval Lapidaries*,
EETS, os 190 (1932), pp. 101–02.

That Ywain drinks blood, an English addition, emphasizes his bestiality: the lion too drinks the warm blood of a doe (l. 2030). But this detail does more than evoke "the horror of savagery" which Neaman notes; since such a remedy was commonly prescribed for melancholy madness, it ought to cure Ywain if his disease were of the body only.[17] But the remedy fails, and by including this bit of medical lore, the English poet may be indicating that Ywain's madness is largely spiritual and will respond best to a spiritual cure.

The meaning of Ywain's wildness is partially defined by the contrast between his state and the condition of three other wild creatures in the romance: the Giant Herdsman, the hermit, and the lion. The Giant Herdsman,[18] "a lathly creature" (l. 247) and the very picture of the legendary wild man, appears at first to lack speech and reason (ll. 274–76), but he insists on his identity as a man (l. 279). His task is to care for the wild beasts of the forest, and his power over them is supreme despite their savagery to others:

> Olyve es þare lifand no ma
> Bot I þat durst omang þam ga,
> þat he ne sold sone be al torent.
> Bot þai er at my comandment;
> To me þai cum when I þam call,
> And I am maister of þam all.
>
> [ll. 307–12]

I think we are meant to notice the ugliness of the Giant Herdsman who, though seemingly irrational, claims to be a

17. Neaman, "The Distracted Knight," p. 243; for the use of blood to cure melancholy madness, see chap. 1, n. 59, above.

18. I am not here concerned with possible Celtic or classical sources for such motifs as the Giant Herdsman but rather with their use in the poem. For such sources see Arthur C. L. Brown, *Iwain: A Study in the Origins of Arthurian Romance*, [Harvard] Studies in Philology and Literature, no. 7 (1903; reprinted New York: Haskell House, 1968); C. B. Lewis, *Classical Mythology and Arthurian Romance* (London: Oxford University Press, 1932); and Jean Frappier, *Étude sur Yvain ou le Chevalier au Lion de Chrétien de Troyes* (Paris: Société d'Édition d'Enseignement Supérieur, 1969), pp. 71–131.

man like other men; we are to contrast this superficial ugliness with the moral ugliness and true irrationality of Ywain,
so fair at first. We should notice that the Giant Herdsman
controls dangerous beasts absolutely, while Ywain cannot control even himself; just as the Giant Herdsman's power over
the beasts here signifies his rationality (for man's superiority
to beasts rests in his reason), so Ywain's friendship with the
lion eventually signifies, among other things, his growing self-
mastery. As Ywain learns to control his lion — and it is only
in the last battle with Gawain that the lion does not escape
unsought to aid his master — his spiritual health returns, and
he achieves the self-control he needs to be as much of a man
as even the Giant Herdsman. As Augustine knew, what makes
a man is reason, not form.

The hermit provides another contrast to the wild Ywain.
Presumably having entered the wilderness for religious reasons, the hermit is a Holy Wild Man who treats Ywain with
"charite" (l. 1679) and gives him food; in return, Ywain
brings deer to the hermit, and the two live thus for some time.
Traditionally, Holy Wild Men are aided by food-bringing
animals—Elijah and Paul the Hermit were fed by ravens, and
an otter brought food to a Celtic Saint Paul;[19] in a sense,
then, Ywain is cast here as an irrational creature able to
respond to holiness and charity with faithful gratitude. He
has progressed from utter wildness to some degree of tame-
ness, and his capacity for gratitude, his desire to repay kindness with kindness as he failed to do with Alundyne, indicates
increasing moral stature despite his persistence in madness.
His relationship to the hermit is similar to his lion's later
relationship to him.

Ywain's regeneration is gradual, as the presence of two
moral stages while he is still totally insane would suggest.
And it is some time before he progresses far enough to master
the third wild creature, the lion. First his clinical madness

19. See 3 Kings 17:4–6; Williams, "Hairy Anchorite" 2. 468; and Carl
Selmer, ed., *Navigatio Sancti Brendani Abbatis*, Notre Dame Publications
in Medieval Studies, no. 16 (South Bend, Ind.: Notre Dame University
Press, 1959), pp. 74–75.

must be cured. As Ywain sleeps in the forest, he is recognized
by a maiden who diagnoses the immediate cause of Ywain's
madness accurately:

> In sum sorow was he stad,
> And þarefore es he waxen mad.
> Sorow wil meng a mans blode
> And make him forto wax wode.
>
> [ll. 1737–40]

The Lady of Noroison undertakes to cure him "thorgh
Goddes help" (l. 1749) with an ointment compounded by
Morgan the Wise to cure the "braynwode" (l. 1756). The
maiden anoints Ywain's whole body, and he is cured.[20] He
puts on knightly dress as a token of his newly rational and
therefore human state, but his spiritual cure is not yet complete. Several critics have suggested that Ywain's adventures
after the cure reflect his increasing worthiness of his previous
noble reputation, thanks to his defeat of pride and his growth
in humility, his increased concern for justice and charity, and
his newly acquired ability to reconcile love of adventure with
chivalric responsibility.[21]

20. The peculiarities of Ywain's cure, and particularly the lady's injunction not to waste the ointment and her maiden's disregard of these
instructions, cannot be explained on purely medical grounds. Neaman
claims that all the ointment was used so that all excess melancholy would
be purged ("The Distracted Knight," pp. 235–36), but Chrétien himself
states that the measures taken were unnecessary (ll. 3006–07). Perhaps the
cure is related to the medieval legend of Mary Magdalene's anointing of
Christ; see John 12:3–8, where Judas protests the wasted ointment. Perhaps the poet wished to suggest that as Christ was worthy of Mary's expensive ointment, so will the reformed knight be worthy of the Dame de
Noroison's salve. Alternatively, Frappier may be right in suggesting that,
in the French at least, the maiden's eagerness to cure Yvain and her consequent waste of the ointment are simply comic touches; *Étude sur Yvain,*
p. 42.

21. See Adler, "Sovereignty in Chrétien's *Yvain,*" pp. 281–305; Harris,
"The Role of the Lion," p. 1163; Frappier, *Étude sur Yvain,* pp. 198–209;
Lacy, "Organic Structure," pp. 83–84. Combellack ("Yvain's Guilt," pp.
10–25) and Z. P. Zaddy ("The Structure of Chrétien's 'Yvain,'" *MLR* 65
[1970]:523–40) argue that there is no perceptible progress or purgation in
Yvain's adventures.

Whatever Ywain's adventures after his cure represent, an important part of those adventures and of his regeneration is his relationship to the lion. After all, Ywain's identity is not public until the end; before that, he is known as the Knight of the Lion, bearing a beast's name if no longer a bestial appearance. He may have regained his sanity and his knightly clothes, but the recovery from madness to integrity and truth is not complete until he has regained his proper name. Naturally, much has been said about the lion and its function as a possible symbol of courage, prowess, gratitude, fidelity, perfect knighthood, Christ, and God's grace.[22] Certainly the lion carries considerable and varied symbolic weight in the poem, and an understanding of the lion's role is essential to an understanding of Ywain's regeneration from wildness.

First, as has often been noted, the lion's role as grateful beast reminds us (and Ywain) of Ywain's sin: his ungrateful neglect of his wife. This neglect reduced him to the status of a beast, and it is fitting that he should learn the value of gratitude from one who is nobler as a beast than the forgetful Ywain was as a man. The restoration of Ywain's sanity would mean little unless his moral condition were superior to a beast's. Second, the bestiary lion is noted for compassion and constancy,[23] qualities shared by Ywain's lion; after rescuing the beast, Ywain too exemplifies these virtues in his defense of the weak and his devotion to Alundyne. Once more he learns from a beast how to be a man. Third, the aid the lion gives Ywain may reflect Ywain's new humility and may show God's intervention, but above all the lion represents in the second part of the romance what Alundyne's ring symbolized

22. Ernst Brugger, "Yvain and His Lion," *MP* 38 (1941):267–87; George Kane, *Middle English Literature* (London: Methuen, 1951), p. 79; A. G. Brodeur, "The Grateful Lion: a Study in the Development of Medieval Narrative," *PMLA* 39 (1924):521; Duggan, "Yvain's Good Name," p. 117; Frappier, *Étude sur Yvain*, pp. 212ff.; Adler, "Sovereignty in Chrétien's *Yvain*," pp. 297–98; Harris, "The Role of the Lion," pp. 1148ff.; Finlayson, "Meaning of Adventure," p. 335; Luria, "Storm-making Spring," p. 584.

23. *Book of Beasts*, pp. 7–9.

in the first part — almost supernatural protection against evil for the virtuous man. Before Ywain abused this protection; now he rejects it until external aid is necessary for good to conquer evil. As a symbol of Christ and a substitute for the ring, then, the lion symbolizes that integrity, that ideal of truth, which Ywain formerly violated but now strives to regain. It is as the Knight of the Lion that he is reunited with Alundyne: Ywain finally embodies all the qualities of the Christian knight, and he is now worthy of the ring. According to Dan Michel, "Virtue makeþ man hardi ase lyoun." [24]

But, as I suggested earlier, the lion may also symbolize something quite apart from Christian virtue. As the Giant Herdsman rules his beasts, so Ywain learns to rule his exuberant lion; from being himself a beast or worse, Ywain becomes the ruler of beasts. Again Dan Michel is illuminating: "þe man wes ymad ine zuyche worþssipe and ine zuyche lhordssipe þet he wes lhord of all sseppes [creatures] þet were onder heuene, and to huam alle þinges boʒen. . . . Ac þis lhordssip he leas [lost] be zenne [sin], ne he hit naʒt ayen ne miʒte awynne, bote be uirtue." [25] As Adam lost the mastery of animals by sin, so did Ywain lose even self-mastery; his control of the lion indicates his own virtuous self-control. Finally, the lion is a frequent companion and helper of saints, especially of Holy Wild Men: Macarius had two lions as "little sons"; Paul Helladicus and the solitary Poemen were befriended by lions; and Paul the Hermit and Mary of Egypt were buried by weeping lions.[26] In his relationship to the hermit, Ywain himself was a helpful beast; when he becomes the master of one, he is associated with the elect. Thus the lion is at once his teacher, his protector, and a measure of his triumph over himself. As a reminder of the wildness into which the mad and sinful Ywain once fell and of the noble eminence he eventually attained by embodying the leonine

24. *Ayenbite of Inwyt*, p. 84.
25. Ibid., pp. 84–85.
26. See "Hairy Anchorite" 2. 471, 479; *Desert Fathers*, pp. 51–52, 255–57; and plate 15.

virtues of faithfulness, compassion, and constancy, Ywain's lion is fittingly provided for at the end of the English romance: together with Ywain, Alundyne, and Lunet, he lives happily until death.

Ywain and Gawain may be divided into two sections, two quests, but the ultimate object of both quests is the same: that Ywain may, by his knightly excellence and integrity, be worthy of Alundyne's love. The first section shows a false start: Ywain conquers Alundyne's husband, marries her, and follows Gawain's advice to "hante turnamentes" (l. 1470) so that he may deserve his lady's love and maintain his glory. Ywain leaves his wife against her will — after all, she married him partly so he would defend her fountain and lands — and earns "grete renown" (l. 1575) in tournaments. Hailed by all, he seems to have achieved the goal of meriting Alundyne's love, but his victory is hollow: not only have his triumphs been in chivalric games rather than in the defense of justice, but he betrays his promise as well. Apparently a paragon of chivalry, in fact he is proud of mean accomplishments and faithless.

The second quest is heralded by the messenger's arrival at court during the feast; thus it is that quests are traditionally announced, and what follows may be seen as the true quest of which the first was only a foreshadowing. Ywain's glorious facade is demolished, and he appears to be what he is morally: a wild man, a sinner, a madman. When he saw the Giant Herdsman, he marveled "þat nature / Myght mak so fowl a creature" (ll. 617–18); but Ywain's betrayal makes him even fouler. The wilderness through which he wanders and his bestial appearance reflect his spiritual condition far better than did the court and his former beauty. His degradation begins his purgation, and his regaining of sanity signifies that he has atoned for his fault enough to begin to make conscious reparation. He is now rational and human, but further ordeals and the truly Christian chivalric defense of the wronged are needed to restore him to his name and his wife. When finally he "has his lordship al ogayn" (l. 4022), he has achieved his goal: reason and virtue have conquered madness and sin, and he has gained true human integrity after falling into bestiality and losing even his name. In a moment of self-knowledge unthinkable before his madness, Ywain tells Lunet, "I was a man, now am I nane" (l. 2116); by the poem's end, he has become not merely a man but a lord.

The *Life of Merlin* attributed to Geoffrey of Monmouth deals, like *Ywain and Gawain,* with the purgative madness through which the Unholy Wild Man learns how to be fully human and rational.[27] But the *Life* is a profoundly religious poem rather than a chivalric romance; consequently, its treatment of the madness of sin is richer, and its conclusions about man's best way of life differ considerably from those of the romance. A Christian knight, Ywain must fulfill obligations both to God and to society; but Merlin, a Christian first and a king second, rejects society with a clear conscience in order to live for God and for those willing to share his virtual exile. The poem shows forcefully that even insanity is preferable to the apparent rationality of sinners at court; that unpleasant truths are called madness by the world; and that the Unholy Wild Man, once restored to sanity, may choose to stay in the wilderness of nature to purify himself from the deadlier wildness of man.

Merlin, king and prophet, apparently rules his people well

27. I cite the edition and translation by John J. Parry, *Illinois Studies in Language and Literature,* 10 (1925):243–380; future references will be given in the text. My reading of the poem differs considerably from that of Tatlock in "Geoffrey of Monmouth's *Vita Merlini,*" pp. 265–87. He finds the poem solely comic and suggests that Merlin's madness itself shows that the work is not to be taken seriously; also, ignoring the fact that Merlin was a prophet before his madness (l. 22), Tatlock asserts that Geoffrey made Merlin mad as an excuse for his prophecies. Certainly there are comic aspects of the poem, but I find that occasional comedy seldom precludes serious moral comment in medieval literature. In "The Distracted Knight," pp. 221–29, Neaman offers a reading rather closer to mine. She too takes Merlin's madness as more than a joke or an excuse for prophecy, and she appreciates the significance of Merlin's life in the wilderness after his cure; we disagree, however, on the cause of Merlin's madness and on the time of his cure.

until his three brothers are killed in battle. Grief-stricken, Merlin rages against life's cruelty until he goes mad; "forgetful of himself and of his kindred" (p. 277), he seeks solitude in the forest, living with wild beasts and eating roots, grass, and berries, his sole companion a wolf. Thus Merlin lives and suffers like the mad Nebuchadnezzar, but the causes of Merlin's madness are more complex than Nebuchadnezzar's pride or Ywain's breach of troth. Some immediate causes can be assigned fairly easily: excessive grief and melancholia are the psychological and physiological agents of Merlin's madness as they were with Nebuchadnezzar and Ywain, and one might argue that Merlin sinned in leading too secular a life or in grieving too much for his brothers.[28] But what really maddens Merlin is his rebellion against the pain and apparent injustice of the world and his disgust at human sinfulness masquerading as virtue. Only gradually does he learn that God is just and that pain and suffering are necessary consequences of sin.

Merlin's dual progress from unholy to holy wildness and from rejecting the pain of sin to rejecting sin itself is carefully traced in the poem. He is first driven to the forest by madness induced by the pain of his brothers' deaths; rejecting a world where men die futilely, he seeks the world of nature only to find there the cruelty of beasts and the agony of winter. Once more, the mad Merlin tries to reject pain: "O that there were no winter or white frost! That it were spring or summer, and that the cuckoo would come back singing . . ." (p. 281). He suffers like the Seafarer in that Old English poem, but Merlin, unlike the Seafarer, does not realize why he suffers; wanting true felicity on earth and maddened because he cannot have it, he can only complain. He has exchanged one wilderness for another seemingly as harsh: the madness of war, adultery, and greed for the madness of the Unholy Wild Man.

28. John J. Parry cites two Celtic analogues to the *Life* in which the madman — Lailoken or Suibhne — goes mad because he prevented peace between two armies and was thus responsible for many deaths; "Celtic Tradition and the *Vita Merlini*," *PQ* 4 (1925):193–207.

Finally Merlin's sister Ganieda sends a messenger to find Merlin and charm him with music; cured temporarily as so many madmen are, "Merlin became mindful of himself, and he recalled what he used to be, and he wondered at his madness and he hated it" (p. 285). Newly rational, he is willing to accept the pains of civilization in exchange for the inclement wilderness. But the sight of the courtiers maddens him again, and he tries to return to the forest; presumably the wickedness of men is still intolerable. Ganieda's husband, King Rhydderch, asks Merlin "not to long for the grove or to live like a wild beast, or to want to abide under the trees when he might hold a royal scepter and rule over a warlike people" (p. 285), but the mad Merlin rejects power and gifts, showing that even as a madman he is in some ways morally superior to courtiers.

Since nothing can restore his sanity, Merlin is chained at court. One day he laughs aloud, knowing by his prophetic powers that his sister has been unfaithful. Asked to explain his laughter, Merlin extracts a promise that he be allowed to return to the forest; then he reveals Ganieda's sin, but Ganieda denounces Merlin as completely insane and Rhydderch as a fool to believe him. She tricks Rhydderch into believing her after Merlin has made three more apparently inaccurate prophecies. Having seen his sister's sins and having heard truth denounced as madness, Merlin, mad though he is,[29] realizes that the agonies of winter are preferable to the contagion at court; and he insists on his release according to the bargain. After giving his wife permission to marry someone else, he goes back to the forest, "living like a wild beast, subsisting on frozen moss, in the snow, in the rain, in the cruel blasts of the wind. And this pleased him more than administering laws throughout his cities and ruling over fierce people" (p. 297). Merlin is not yet sane, but he has learned to accept suffering even though he sees it as the better of two evils rather than as good in its own right; that fuller understanding comes only later, with total sanity.

29. Neaman finds Merlin sane from here on; "The Distracted Knight," p. 225.

Merlin learns that his wife is about to remarry, and he prepares a grim wedding present. Mounted on a stag, he leads a herd of goats, deer, and stags to the wedding, where everyone marvels at his control of the beasts. But this control, which he had lacked earlier, hardly indicates sanity here: Merlin immediately kills his wife's new husband with antlers ripped off a stag. Merlin's disgust at an immoral society leads to an act of madness, just as earlier his grief at useless war and death turned him into an Unholy Wild Man. Merlin is caught and brought back to court, where another remedy for madness is tried: he is taken to the marketplace to be cheered up by diversion. But again he sees only the sins and tragedies of human life: he laughs at a beggar who is really a rich miser and at a young man who has bought new shoes, ignorant of his imminent death by drowning. Again Merlin explains his laughter only after he is promised freedom; but this time before he leaves, he tells his sister that although he does not fear winter, he would welcome an observatory in the woods and scribes to write his prophecies. Clearly saner than he was, Merlin is willing to live less bestially even though he no longer resents the ravages of nature; having accepted the wilderness, he begins to adapt it to his purposes. His prophecies, too, reveal his growing sanity: he inveighs against the "rabiem britonum" (l. 580), the madness of greed, warfare, murder, and impiety, against the reduction of man to beast by slavery. Merlin is still mad, but in his madness he reveals the far greater insanity of sin.

When Rhydderch dies, Ganieda consciously chooses the wilderness for the same reasons as her mad brother: worldly happiness is brief, sin abounds, and man's first duty is to God. She states explicitly what Merlin's conduct has shown and what he learns when he is sane again: "Happy therefore are those who remain firm in a pious heart and serve God and renounce the world" (pp. 315–17). Finally Merlin is miraculously cured. Taliesin sings to Merlin of the glory of God's creation, but Merlin responds with a catalog of man's sins. Suddenly a fountain appears, and Merlin drinks and bathes in it. The water cures him as it calms the vapors — presumably melancholy — that caused his madness: "At once he regained his reason and knew himself, and all his madness departed and the sense which had long remained torpid in him revived, and he remained what he had once been — sane and intact with his reason restored" (p. 339). Significantly, his first action is to praise God the Creator; his despairing vision of human evil is supplemented by the restorative knowledge of God's goodness.

In some ways Merlin's story is like the Fall of Man. When Adam and Eve came to know evil by eating the forbidden fruit, they grew bestial in that appetite conquered reason; having unleashed madness, disease, and the torments of cold, wind, and storm, they were cast out into the wilderness in the wild man's cloaks of skin (see plate 16). Only the knowledge of God's goodness and of the coming redemption could mitigate despair.[30] Merlin too comes to know evil when his brothers are killed, and that knowledge maddens him so that he lives like a beast until knowledge of God's mercy restores his sanity and frees him from his preoccupation with man's mad sinfulness. Later, the story of the Fall that first brought sin and madness into the world is suggested more directly. As Merlin sits by the fountain, a madman approaches, foam at the mouth, shouting, threatening to attack. Merlin recognizes the man as Maeldinus, a friend of his youth, and he tells how the man went mad after eating poisoned apples intended for Merlin. Thus the Fall is recapitulated on two levels: the unfortunate Maeldinus mimics the action of Adam and Eve in eating a poisoned apple[31] and going mad because of it; and Merlin, having gained the knowledge of evil, goes mad with the pain of that knowledge. Throughout the poem madness and moral depravity are equated; sin poisons all, and although the relatively innocent Merlin and Maeldinus suffer real madness largely through the sins of others, the

30. According to the *Vita Adae et Evae*, God comforted Adam after the Fall with a vision of man's eventual salvation; see *Apocrypha and Pseudepigrapha*, 2: 140–41.

31. According to the *Apocalypsis Mosis*, Satan poisoned the apple with lust; *Apocrypha and Pseudepigrapha*, 2:146.

sinners who are apparently sane are maddest of all from the Christian perspective: they barter eternal happiness for earthly pleasure.

Merlin's conclusions are theologically sound: it is better to choose suffering in the wilderness than to be contaminated by the vices of the world. His madness teaches him both the spiritual madness of civilization and the value of the wilderness, and so he rejects when sane the courtly life that repelled him when he was mad: "Here shall I remain while I live, content with apples and grasses, and I shall purify my body with pious fastings that I may be worthy to partake of the life everlasting" (p. 347). This is the life of the Holy Wild Man that Merlin commends to Maeldinus: "You must now go on in the service of God who restored you as you now see yourself, you who for so many years lived in the desert like a wild beast, going about without a sense of shame. Now that you have recovered your reason, do not shun the bushes or the green glades which you inhabited while you were mad, but stay with me that you may strive to make up in service to God for the days that the force of madness took from you" (p. 335). Geoffrey seems to be saying that all men are mad and sinful, though some may seem madder clinically than others. But all are Unholy Wild Men in a sense, whether they live at court like Ganieda or in the forest like Merlin. The only way to cure the madness of sin is to take on the trappings of madness voluntarily, to welcome suffering as purgation, and to live the life of the Holy Wild Man far from the corruption of civilization. Such madness to the world is the highest sanity for the Christian.

The Holy Wild Man: Sir Orfeo

As Merlin himself moves from unconscious suffering to conscious penance in the wilderness, so his story provides an appropriate transition from the discussion of the Unholy Wild Man to a consideration of the Holy Wild Man, a figure with as long and illustrious a history as the Unholy Wild Man and at least as popular in religious literature and in life, if not in romance. As I have already indicated, the

first wild men were Adam and Eve, cast out of the garden into
the wilderness, ordered to eat "the herbs of the earth" (Gen.
3:18), and dressed in "garments of skin" (Gen. 3:21) made
by God as a sign of mortality or, more kindly, as protection
against nature's cruelty.[32] In habitation, diet, and dress, the
fallen pair resemble the wild man of art and literature (see
plate 16); like him, they suffer weakness, disease, hunger,
and cold, and this suffering helps atone for their sin. But
Adam and Eve are often closer to the Holy Wild Man than
to his unholy brother. Although they could be considered
mad as a consequence of Original Sin and although their exile
was involuntary, in the Middle Ages they are often described
as consciously penitent, seeking out additional hardships in
the wilderness to pay for their sin. According to the popular
pseudepigraphal Books of Adam and Eve, for example, they
did penance by standing in the rivers Tigris and Jordan for
forty days.[33] Thus, from biblical times on, the life of the
wild man was often associated with punishment and purgation of either original or actual sin. If the acts of penance are
viewed as voluntary, as those of Adam sometimes are, the
wild man is holy; if they are unconscious, as are those of
Nebuchadnezzar, suffering is inflicted by God's grace, and the
wild man is unholy.

Prophets and other holy men in the Bible often share the
life of the Holy Wild Man, though their flight to the wilderness is more often motivated by the desire to avoid the evil of
the cities or to shun persecution than to do penance for their
grievous sins. Thus Elijah, dressed in skins, lived on a desert
mountain with wild beasts, where he was fed by a raven;

32. See *Glossa ordinaria, PL* 113:96; Peter Comestor, *Historia scholastica,
PL* 198:1074; Evans, *Paradise Lost and the Genesis Tradition,* pp. 53, 70,
84, 90, 141, 172. According to Irenaeus, Adam and Eve wore fig leaves as
a gesture of penance, but God mercifully provided clothes of skin instead;
Against Heresies 3. 23. 5, in *Writings,* trans. Alexander Roberts and W. H.
Rambaut, ANCL, 5, 9 (Edinburgh, 1868–69).

33. *Apocrypha and Pseudepigrapha,* 2:134–37. For a medieval text, see
the "Liif of Adam" from the Auchinleck MS, printed in David Laing, ed.,
A Penniworth of Witte (Edinburgh, 1857), pp. 49ff.

and thus many others, according to Hebrews 11:37–38, were persecuted and "wandered about in sheepskins, goatskins, being in want, distressed, afflicted . . . wandering in deserts, in mountains, and in dens, and in caves of the earth." Thus must the truly holy live, their holiness and their way of life looking like madness.

The most important biblical Holy Wild Man is, of course, John the Baptist, a patron saint of madmen: "A voice of one crying in the wilderness: Prepare ye the way of the Lord, make straight his paths. John was in the desert baptizing, and preaching the baptism of penance, unto remission of sins. . . . And John was clothed with camel's hair, and a leathern girdle about his loins; and he ate locusts and wild honey" (Mark 1:3–4, 6). John's reasons for choosing to live in the wilderness are often given as his desire to "fle fro synne" and to teach men "to leave the world, to devote themselves to God." [34] The harsh conditions of his life are stressed in commentaries (the *Cursor mundi* intensifies his resemblance to the Holy Wild Man by noting that he lived on roots and grass; l. 11109); his poor clothing and meager diet signify the ascetic ideal of saints and preachers, and the desert itself represents "the life of the saints set apart from worldly snares." [35] John's example teaches that the life of the Holy Wild Man is both symbolic of sanctity and also the best practical way to achieve it, but his sojourn in the wilderness has another important meaning as well: according to the *Glossa ordinaria,* that particular desert between Jerusalem and Jericho was where "in a figural sense, Adam was overcome by the devil"; "Jesus and John seek what was lost in the desert. Where the devil conquered, there is he overcome; where man fell, there he rises again" (*PL* 114:253 and 179). By preaching penitence

34. *Cursor mundi,* l. 11105; and *Glossa ordinaria, PL* 114:83–84.

35. *Glossa ordinaria, PL* 114:79; cf. 180. Slavonic additions to Josephus emphasize John's character as a wild man; see *Works,* 3:644–45. For the iconographic tradition, see Réau, *Iconographie,* 2. 1. 431ff., and Adolph Napoléon Didron, *Christian Iconography,* trans. E. J. Millington and Margaret Stokes, 2 vols. (London, 1851, 1886), 2:362ff.

and by baptizing in the wilderness, John helped to conquer sin, madness, and the devil and to restore man to the image of God; and his own life taught that the way to keep that image was the penitential life in the wilderness.

With so notable a biblical precedent, it is not surprising that the wilderness soon became populated with Holy Wild Men seeking salvation in solitude with God.[36] According to C. A. Williams, there were several reasons for this flight to the desert. In the earlier centuries of Christianity, a man might go there either to avoid the city's temptations, in which case he might live in a loosely organized monastic community, or to seek spiritual perfection in an ascetic life that would free him from the body's claims.[37] Williams gives many examples of this ascetic life: the would-be saint — Saint Mark the Athenian, Saint Paul the Hermit, Saint Anthony — flees to a remote cave (see plate 14) far from men but close to God; he lives there many years, naked, suffering intensely from the elements, eating grass and roots, tormented by demons and occasionally by wild animals. Finally he earns God's grace: long hair grows over the saint's body to protect him, the demons vanish, he is befriended by animals (see plate 13), and he is fed either by animals or through a miracle — a fresh fountain, a newly grown date tree, bread sent from heaven. When such men are seen by others, they are often thought to be beasts or demons, but in fact they are spiritually perfect.[38]

In the later Middle Ages, these legends of Hairy Anchorites

36. At least two Holy Wild Men consciously emulated the life of John the Baptist: Saint Onuphrius ("Hairy Anchorite" 2. 453) and Saint Godric (Rotha Mary Clay, *The Hermits and Anchorites of England* [London: Methuen, 1914], p. 24). On the desert's symbolic meanings from biblical times on, see George H. Williams, *Wilderness and Paradise in Christian Thought* (New York: Harper, 1962), esp. pp. 1–64.

37. "Hairy Anchorite" 2. 428ff. Those who lived in monastic communities in the desert were not usually Holy Wild Men in a strict sense; but some of them lived a sufficiently solitary and bestial life to qualify.

38. Ibid., 2. passim.

underwent a shift in emphasis: instead of the quest for perfection, the wish to do penance for some remarkable sin became a common reason for men to seek the wilderness.[39]
Typically, such people — Saint John Chrysostom, Saint Macarius the Roman, Saint Mary of Egypt, Saint James the Penitent — live in the desert for some time before yielding to
temptation and committing murder, fornication, gluttony,
and other sins; then, in great sorrow, they lead a still more
ascetic life to earn forgiveness, which is granted after many
years. Presumably this form of the Hairy Anchorite or Holy
Wild Man legend was intended to illustrate the efficacy of a
holy life in the wilderness even for great sinners.

Whatever the reason, such legends were popular even in
romance versions. Some accounts of Pope Gregory's penance
for incest include his long and painful life on a rock in the
sea, and the romance *Sir Gowther* contains a particularly
intriguing variation on the penitential Holy Wild Man.[40]
Gowther, child of a demon father, commits numerous mad
acts of violence against the Church. Finally learning who he
is, he asks the Pope for absolution and is assigned a curious
penance: he must wander in the wilderness without speaking,
eating only food brought to him by dogs, until a miracle
demonstrates his forgiveness. In other words, Gowther must
live the life of the Holy Wild Man and even — by his unnatural silence — feign madness to atone for his earlier spiritual
madness. This he does, both in forest and at court, where he
is taken for a fool, until he is forgiven; then he becomes a
great king, a staunch defender of the faith, and indeed a saint
who cures madmen himself. In one manuscript, Gowther is
even identified as the revered English Saint Guthlac, who
also lived a wild life when young, later atoning for his sins

39. Ibid., 2. 483.

40. See "The Legend of Pope Gregory," in *Legendae Catholicae*, ed.
W. B. D. D. Turnbull (Edinburgh, 1840), pp. 1–67; and *Sir Gowther*, in
The Breton Lays in Middle English, ed. Thomas C. Rumble (Detroit:
Wayne State University Press, 1965). *Sir Gowther* is, of course, a version
of the popular Robert the Devil legend.

by becoming a hermit, a Holy Wild Man.[41] The equation
of the two men is clearly based on the notion that great sins
are properly absolved by a life of overt wildness mirroring
the sinner's moral wildness. He who deforms God's image by
sin must purify himself by becoming as deformed outwardly
as he is inwardly. In some cases, like Ywain's, this purification
takes the form of real madness; in others, like Gowther's, the
deformity of madness is merely assumed as penance.

More specifically religious stories about Holy Wild Men
were also popular in the Middle Ages. Manuscripts of the
Vitae patrum, the most important collection about the desert
saints, are numerous; tales from that work often appear in
homilies, legendaries, and exemplum books, and episodes of
holy wildness were summarily attached to the lives of popular
saints like Mary Magdalene.[42] The life of hermit or Holy
Wild Man was often chosen by English and Celtic saints; the
Ruthwell Cross glorifies such a life, and Clay notes the great
number of solitaries in England, especially in the twelfth and
thirteenth centuries.[43] Many joined religious orders such as
the Cistercians and Carmelites, which established their found-
ations in the wilderness, though not in solitude, and the
idea of the wilderness as a place of potential union with God
was stressed in mystical theology, especially by Meister Eck-
hart. Even those who stayed in villages may have known of
the lure of the desert: in the Middle Ages in England, there
were 500 churches dedicated to John the Baptist, 187 to Mary

41. See *Guthlac A,* ll. 108–13, in *The Exeter Book,* ed. Israel Gollancz,
EETS, os 104 (1895).

42. For the influence of the *Vitae patrum* in England, see Constance
Rosenthal, *The Vitae Patrum in Old and Middle English Literature*
(Philadelphia, 1936); for Mary, see Victor Saxer, *Le culte de Marie Made-
leine en Occident des origines à la fin du moyen âge,* 2 vols. (Paris: Librairie
Clavreuil, 1959), 1:6–9 and passim; see also the Mary Magdalene play in
the *Digby Plays,* and the Auchinleck MS "Legend of Marie Maudelein,"
in *Legendae Catholicae,* pp. 213–57.

43. See Meyer Schapiro, "The Religious Meaning of the Ruthwell Cross,"
Art Bulletin 26 (1944):232–45; and Clay, *Hermits and Anchorites,* p. 28
and passim.

Magdalene, and 162 to Giles, all of them Holy Wild Men.[44]
Langland, a severe critic of so many aspects of medieval
religion, praises Holy Wild Men, their sufferings in the
wilderness, their friendship with wild beasts, and their imitation of Christ (*Piers* B 15. 261–303); such men, he claims,
show everyone how to suffer in poverty and patience, how to
live the ideal Christian life. Such a life in the wilderness may
seem mad to city-dwellers, to those with secular values who
define insanity as deviation from their own norm; and indeed,
some Holy Wild Men may be mad in that they virtuously
allow their love of God to overrule reason. But those who
dwell in the wilderness are in touch with the ultimate realities; they know that from the Christian point of view the
world itself is a wilderness to be endured, a place of trial
where the highest sanity is sanctity, whatever suffering and
apparent insanity that may involve. The madman in the
desert is closer to true health than the sane man who sins in
the city.

The Holy Wild Man and the meaning of his life of exile
in the wilderness are nowhere in medieval literature more important than in *Sir Orfeo* (?1330), rightly praised by J.
Burke Severs as "one of the loveliest and most charming of
all Middle English romances." [45] As many scholars have noticed, this strange and moving adaptation of the Orpheus
legend differs considerably in plot and detail from extant
classical and medieval versions, and the search for a Celtic
source has been unsuccessful as well.[46] So far no one has con-

44. See David Knowles, *The Religious Orders in England*, 3 vols. (Cambridge: Cambridge University Press, 1948–59), esp. vols. 1 and 2; Williams,
Wilderness, pp. 52–64; and Francis Bond, *Dedications and Patron Saints
of English Churches* (London: Oxford University Press, 1914).

45. "The Antecedents of *Sir Orfeo*," in *Studies in Medieval Literature
in Honor of Professor Albert Croll Baugh*, ed. MacEdward Leach (Philadelphia: University of Pennsylvania Press, 1961), p. 187. Line references to
Sir Orfeo in my text are to the Auchinleck MS version, ed. A. J. Bliss, 2d
ed. (Oxford: Clarendon Press, 1966).

46. Articles putting forth the claims of various sources include Severs,
"The Antecedents of *Sir Orfeo*"; George Lyman Kittredge, "*Sir Orfeo*,"
American Journal of Philology 7 (1886):176–202; Constance Davies's three

vincingly explained or interpreted such distinctive elements as Heurodis's sleep under the *ympe-tree,* the emphasis on Orfeo's harsh life in the wilderness, his successful rescue of his wife, and his testing of his steward. The best approach has been suggested by John Block Friedman, who notes that most medieval manuscripts of Virgil, Ovid, and Boethius contain elaborate allegorical glosses, and he has considered a number of these commentaries in an effort to explain the poem. Although I find shortcomings in Friedman's specific application of such evidence to *Sir Orfeo,* he is right to stress its importance.[47]

I am convinced that the poem can be fully understood only when one grasps the traditions that seem to have influenced its conception: the commentaries, the Christian uses of the Orpheus legend, and especially the convention of the Holy Wild Man. As Orfeo's ten years' exile is central structurally, so it is central thematically; and if his life as a wild man

---

articles, "Notes on the Sources of *Sir Orfeo,*" *MLR* 31 (1936): 354–57; "*Sir Orfeo* and *De Nugis,*" *MLN* 51 (1936):492; and "Classical Threads in *Sir Orfeo,*" *MLR* 56 (1961): 161–66; Roger S. Loomis, "Sir Orfeo and Walter Map's *De Nugis,*" *MLN* 51 (1936):28–30; Dorena Allen, "Orpheus and Orfeo: the Dead and the *Taken,*" *MÆ* 33 (1964):102–11; and Bliss's ed., pp. xxvi–xli and lii–lvii. Celtic sources most often suggested are the *Tochmarc Etaine* (see Kittredge and Loomis, and Bliss's contrary views) and Walter Map's *De nugis curialium*; many scholars also posit a lost Old French source.

47. See "Eurydice, Heurodis, and the Noon-day Demon," *Speculum* 41 (1966):22–29, and *Orpheus in the Middle Ages* (Cambridge: Harvard University Press, 1970), pp. 175–94. Friedman's valuable description of the Orpheus figure in art and in the commentaries, published some time after this chapter was substantially completed, has made available much of the material on which my argument was originally based; hence I have reduced the amount of evidence here presented and refer to Friedman's book when possible. However, Friedman and I make quite different use of the commentaries in relation to *Sir Orfeo,* most particularly in that Friedman feels "there is little in the poem to suggest that it should be read as a Christian allegory" (*Orpheus,* p. 190). I would also cite as specific shortcomings his failure to note that the identification of the Fairy King with the Noonday Demon implies that Heurodis was guilty of sloth, his failure to deal convincingly with the implications of the poem's happy ending, and his attribution of lust to the Fairy King.

Table 2
A Comparison of *Sir Orfeo* and Suggested Sources

Virgil/Ovid	Alfredian Boethius	Walter Map	Tochmarc Etaine	Sir Orfeo
Harper	Harper	Knight	Eochaid a king	Orfeo a king
				Heurodis's sleep, *ympe-tre*
				Heurodis's madness
			Defense by armed knights	Defense by armed knights
Death by serpent	Death, cause unspecified	Death of wife	Abduction by Fairy King	Abduction by Fairy King
	Long period of grief			Long period of grief *as* Wild Man
Harping in wilderness after return from Hades	Harping to beasts noted before trip to Hades			Harping to beasts in wilderness before descent
Immediate search	Delayed search	Delayed search	Immediate search	Delayed search for Heurodis
				Wild hunt
		Wife found in valley with ladies	Etaine found in Fairy Mound, with sixty ladies	Heurodis found outside underworld with sixty ladies

Table 2 (continued)

Virgil/Ovid	Alfredian Boethius	Walter Map	Tochmarc Etaine	Sir Orfeo
Orpheus reveals identity and purpose	Orpheus reveals identity and purpose			Orfeo conceals identity and purpose
			Rash promise by husband, early in story	Rash promise by Fairy King
				Fairy King objects to Orfeo's ugliness
Failure	Failure	Success	Success	Orfeo's success
				Testing of steward, disguise

during these years is properly understood, it leads to an exciting new reading of the poem, explaining virtually all the important alterations of the classical legend (see table 2) and also providing a frame of reference within which the poem assumes deeper significance. Certainly there are also Celtic motifs in the poem—the Fairy King and the Wild Hunt, for example; but I think the poem's guiding conception is Christian, and that the apparently Celtic elements, which often convey Christian meanings and might even be Christian in origin, were added to the legend chiefly as appropriate romantic coloration. As Evans has noted, "From each different culture with which it has come in contact Christianity has inherited a fresh body of legend, imagery, and diction in and through which to express itself," [48] and Celtic elements would

48. *Paradise Lost and the Genesis Tradition,* pp. 108–09.

be highly fitting in a poem that gives Christian overtones to a
classical legend and expresses the result as romance.

Perhaps a recognition of the limitations of my approach is
here in order. Basing my reading of the poem on an examination of changes in the classical versions, possible reasons for
those changes as given by the Christian commentarial tradition, and the pattern that emerges, I intend to argue that
Sir Orfeo is shaped by the Christian pattern of Fall, Redemption, and Judgment, although it is explicitly and primarily about Orpheus and is *not* a strictly allegorical poem
in the sense of being continuous allegory or susceptible to
four-level exegesis.[49] The ancient legend has been recast in
such a way that its Christian significance might be more
fully developed and perceived within the mythological frame-
work. In so doing, the poet has used a technique I will call
situational allegory, a mode consciously employed by medieval
scriptural exegetes and explained by the *Speculum humanae
salvationis*: "One thing may sometimes signify the devil,
another time Christ. And we ought not to wonder at this
way of writing, because according to the different actions of
some thing or person, different meanings can be assigned
to them. Thus when King David committed adultery and
murder, he prefigured not Christ but the devil; but when he
loved and helped his enemies, he was a figure of Christ, not
of the devil." [50] In other words, it is *action* or *plot* that matters in this kind of allegory, not people or things in them-

49. In general I am reluctant to assume allegorical meanings in secular
Middle English literature; for a contrary view, see Robertson, *Preface to
Chaucer.* See also articles by E. Talbot Donaldson, R. E. Kaske, and
Charles Donohue comprising "Patristic Exegesis in the Criticism of Medieval Literature," in *Critical Approaches to Medieval Literature: Selected
Papers from the English Institute, 1958–1959,* ed. Dorothy Bethurum (New
York: Columbia University Press, 1960); and see Burrow's convincing discussion of the Ricardian preference for literal and exemplary modes of
meaning: *Ricardian Poetry,* pp. 78–92. Nevertheless, I hope to demonstrate
that there are convincing reasons for recognizing the presence (although
certainly not the dominance) of allegory in *Sir Orfeo.*

50. J. Lutz and P. Perdrizet, eds., 2 vols. (Mulhouse: Ernest Meininger,
1907–09), Prologue, ll. 67–74.

selves; and a coherent story can be told on the literal level without its being forced to take one direction or another by fixed meanings for a character and incident. The resonance of allegorical significance adds richness to people or events without rigidly defining them. Thus the allegory grows from the story being told; the story is not composed primarily to embody the allegory, although it may in places be altered for allegorical reasons as *Sir Orfeo* is altered. Only when allegory is servant rather than master can the story stand on its own as a work of art, and the *Orfeo*-poet excels in this kind of writing; having chosen a good story to begin with, he turns it simultaneously into a romance of captivating charm and into a parable with profound moral and religious significance.

The Christianization of pagan myth certainly has ample precedent in the Middle Ages. Augustine argued that theological truths might be found in pagan dress and that Christian poets might adapt pagan literature to their own purposes just as the Israelites used Egyptian gold and silver.[51] It was to this end that Lactantius, Fulgentius, Berchorius, and other Ovidian commentators retold and reinterpreted the old myths, and that Boccaccio wrote his *Genealogia deorum gentilium*, justifying his aims thus: "The old theology can sometimes be employed in the service of Christian truth, if the fashioner of the myths should choose. I have observed this in the case of more than one orthodox poet in whose investiture of fiction the sacred teachings were clothed." [52] Usually such poets made their allegorical intent quite explicit, of course; but Boccaccio implies that sometimes *only* the "investiture of fiction" is provided, and some manuscripts of the *Gesta Romanorum* circulated without appended morals even though the tales were clearly intended to carry religious inter-

51. *On Christian Doctrine*, trans. D. W. Robertson, Library of Liberal Arts (Indianapolis: Bobbs-Merrill, 1958), pp. 75–76 (2. 40); for the influence of this passage in the Middle Ages, see pp. xiii–xiv. For the use of classical *exempla* in sermons, see Owst, *Literature and Pulpit*, pp. 179ff.

52. In *Boccaccio on Poetry*, trans. Charles G. Osgood, 2d ed., Library of Liberal Arts (Indianapolis: Bobbs-Merrill, 1956), p. 123 (*Genealogia* 15. 8).

pretations.[53] I do not in any case intend to argue that *Sir Orfeo* was written primarily for didactic ends; surely the poet wished first to tell a good story as well as he could. But he may have known one of the common Christian interpretations of the story, or he may have seen the Christian implications for himself. He may then have shaped the material into entertaining fiction suitably ornamented with romantic touches, but fiction that nevertheless conveyed sacred teachings. To write a romance that could stand on its own as romance, but that would carry religious overtones for those seeking *sentence* as well as *solaas,* might well appeal to so gifted a poet as the author of *Sir Orfeo.*[54]

There is also some evidence that *Sir Orfeo* might have been regarded as a religious, or potentially religious, poem in the Middle Ages. Three extant manuscripts — the Auchinleck MS, Harley 3810, and Ashmole 61 — include it, and an analysis of their contents indicates that the poem was not out of place beside overtly religious and moral works. The Auchinleck MS, compiled around 1330, contains forty-four items, many of them religious: a verse paraphrase of the apocryphal Life of Adam and Eve, five saints' legends, five Virgin poems, a Harrowing of Hell dialogue, some psalms, a translation of the Pater Noster, and numerous moral poems, one of which immediately follows *Sir Orfeo* and will be discussed later.[55] There are also many romances, some of which (e.g. *The King of Tars, Amis and Amelion*) are religious in tone. The first manuscript bound in Harley 3810 contains an early fifteenth-

53. Ed. Herrtage, p. xiii.

54. Of course, allegory itself was seen as pleasurable as well as informative: see Edgar de Bruyne, *The Esthetics of the Middle Ages,* trans. Eileen B. Hennessy (New York: Frederick Ungar, 1969), p. 77; and Robertson, *Preface to Chaucer,* pp. 52–64.

55. For information on the three MSS, see Bliss's ed., pp. ix–xv, and the relevant catalogs; for contents and scribal attributions of the Auchinleck MS, see the catalog by Sir Walter Scott in Laing, *A Penniworth of Witte*; Eugen Kölbing, "Vier Romanzen-Handschriften," *Englische Studien* 7 (1884):177–201; A. J. Bliss, "Notes on the Auchinleck Manuscript," *Speculum* 26 (1951):652–58. The survival of three MSS of the poem suggests that it was very popular.

century text of *Sir Orfeo* and five other pieces, all moral or religious. And Ashmole 61, compiled at the end of the fifteenth century, contains mostly moral pieces (instructions to children, a poem on the proper governance of man), romances, and religious pieces (a Crucifixion poem, saints' lives, hymns). Readers of this manuscript might have been guided toward a religious interpretation of *Sir Orfeo* by the preceding poem — a meditation on Christ's wounds as defenses against the seven deadly sins (fols. 150v to 151r); the romance is then followed by a poem beginning, "Vanyte off vanytees All is vanitee." If my reading of *Sir Orfeo* is correct, it too deals with the lessons to be learned from Christ's passion and with the vanity of temporal goods. Thus evidence from the manuscripts suggests that their compilers may have thought that *Sir Orfeo* had moral and religious overtones.[56] In any case, regardless of what the poet intended to do with his poem or of what compilers had in mind, I believe that the reading offered here is one that an educated medieval reader might easily have deduced for himself.

The key to the poem is Orfeo's long sojourn in the wilderness as a Holy Wild Man; on that section my whole interpretation is based, and there my argument is strongest. But I shall begin at the beginning, for it is the first part of the poem that explains *why* it is necessary for Orfeo to go into the wilderness, why the classical Orpheus's immediate descent to hell has been postponed for a very important ten years.

56. Perhaps the compiler of the Auchinleck MS, which contains the best text of the poem, was himself responsible for the romance as we have it. This MS, probably written by six closely collaborating scribes at a London bookshop in the 1330s, seems to have been planned, arranged, and supervised by one man — perhaps Bliss's Scribe 1, the man responsible for many of the religious and moral pieces, for *Sir Orfeo,* and for other romances that are religious in tone. Loomis suggests that this man is, in his handling of translations from the French, responsible for many skillful alterations and substitutions; whether or not *Sir Orfeo* is itself a translation, this scribe may have created many of its distinctive features. See Laura H. Loomis, "The Auchinleck Manuscript and a Possible London Bookshop of 1330–1340," *PMLA* 57 (1942):595–627, and Kölbing's article cited above. Bliss lists the pieces ascribed to Scribe 1 (Kölbing's Scribe α).

The first section of the romance tells how King Orfeo, the greatest harper of all, loses his beloved wife Heurodis, fairest of women. One spring day, she takes two maidens

> in an vndrentide
> To play by an orchard-side,
> to se þe floures sprede & spring,
> & to here þe foules sing.
>
> [ll. 65–68]

They sit beneath "a fair ympe-tre" (l. 70), and Heurodis sleeps until afternoon as her maidens watch. She wakes into madness:

> Sche crid, & loþli bere [outcry] gan make:
> Sche froted hir honden & hir fet,
> & crached hir visage — it bled wete;
> Hir riche robe hye al to-rett,
> & was reueyd [hunted] out of hir witt.
>
> [ll. 78–82]

Orfeo finally calms her, and she tells him that they must part: while she slept under the tree, the Fairy King came with his company, took her to see his kingdom, and finally returned her to the orchard, warning her that tomorrow he will carry her off forever; if she resists or fails to meet him at the tree, he will tear her in pieces. Orfeo and a thousand knights guard Heurodis the next day at the *ympe-tre*, but she disappears from their midst, "wiþ fairi forþ y-nome" (l. 193). The whole kingdom mourns her loss.

This account differs considerably from classical versions: in Ovid, Eurydice gathers flowers, is bitten by a snake, and dies; in Virgil, she is wandering in the meadows when the rustic Aristaeus attacks her lustfully, and as she flees, she steps on the serpent and is killed. Heurodis, like her classical counterpart, goes out to enjoy the beauties of spring, but she falls asleep under a tree, has a vision of the Fairy King, goes mad, and is later carried off alive by that king. Why might the poet have made these changes? Friedman rightly suggests the relevance of medieval commentaries for finding the answers.[57] According to the Boethian tradition, Orpheus represents the intellect, Eurydice is sensuality, and Aristaeus is virtue, which Eurydice shuns. Henryson provides the common moral:

> Bot quhen we fle outthrow the medow grene
> Fra vertew, till this warldis vane plesans,
> myngit with cair and full of variance,
> The serpentis stang, that is the deidly syn,
> That posownis the saule without and in;
> And than is deid, and eik oppressit doun
> Till warldly lust, and all our affectioun.[58]

As Friedman says, Eurydice is "fair prey for Satan," and some medieval commentaries equate either Aristaeus or the serpent with the devil.[59] Friedman continues to derive the poet's invention of the Fairy King from manuscript illuminations of Eurydice's slayer as a draconopede or man-headed serpent; he finds Heurodis blameless, her attacker being motivated by the lust characteristic of the devil in pseudepigraphal and rabbinic tradition; and he suggests that Heurodis's *undrentide* abduction identifies her captor as the noonday demon of Psalm 90:3. I disagree with the first two suggestions, as will become evident, and I would draw different conclusions from his final point.

The Boethian reading of the Orpheus legend strongly resembles the allegorical interpretation of the Fall first ex-

57. "Eurydice, Heurodis, and the Noon-day Demon," pp. 22–29; see also *Orpheus*, pp. 89–145, on the commentaries.

58. "Orpheus and Eurydice," ll. 438–44, in *Poems and Fables of Robert Henryson*, ed. H. Harvey Wood, 2d ed. (Edinburgh: Oliver & Boyd, 1958). The lateness of Henryson's poem (late fifteenth century) does not prevent it from being an excellent example of the Boethian tradition in the Middle Ages. In such moralizations — which derive more from Boethian commentaries than from Boethius himself (see Friedman, *Orpheus*, pp. 90ff.) — Orpheus is a type of the sinner who returns to his past sins or is perverted by his sensuality.

59. *Orpheus*, pp. 181–82.

pounded by Philo and adapted by Origen, Ambrose, Augustine, and later fathers.[60] For them, Adam is reason, intellect,
or the spirit; Eve is sense, the heart, or fleshly desires; the
serpent is the devil who contrives Eve's fall by tempting her
with sensual pleasures. Since the Orpheus legend and the
Fall share a cast of man, woman, and serpent; a plot in which
the woman falls by the serpent; and the same allegorical interpretations, it is hardly surprising that one story should be
associated with the other, as indeed happens in one of Berchorius's interpretations of Ovid: "The serpent (i.e. the devil)
bit this new bride (the newly created Eve) through temptation while she was gathering flowers (or, while she sought
the forbidden apple). Through sin he killed her, and at last
he sent her off to hell." [61] Thus the Orpheus legend may be
seen as a pagan vehicle for the Fall story, and the *Orfeo*-poet
could easily have drawn similar conclusions.

If the loss of Heurodis is analogous to the Fall of Eve and,
more generally, to the loss of the soul through sin, the
changes in the classical legend become intelligible. In the
poem, it seems innocent enough for Heurodis to enjoy the
flowers in the orchard, and there is no explicit condemnation
of her conduct, unless the result of that conduct — her falling
into the power of the Fairy King — is so construed. But in
Boethian tradition, Eurydice's enjoyment of the garden is
compared to the soul's delight in fleshly pleasures, and there
is considerable evidence to show that walking about in
gardens was often interpreted as a sign of moral fault. Proser-

60. See Evans, *Paradise Lost and the Genesis Tradition*, pp. 71–77.

61. *"Ovidius Moralizatus"* (*Reductorium morale XV. ii–xv*), ed. D. van
Nes (Utrecht: Instituut voor Laat Latijn der Rijksuniversiteit, 1962), p.
147. Friedman also cites this passage and comments that Eurydice is remarkably like Eve, but he does not develop the similarity. Since the
"Ovidius Moralizatus" is almost certainly several years later than *Sir
Orfeo*, Berchorius was presumably not known to the *Orfeo*-poet. But the
poetic *Ovide Moralisé*, used by Berchorius, might well have suggested to
the *Orfeo*-poet the identification of Eve and Eurydice as well as the
identification of Orpheus and Christ; C. de Boer, ed., *Verhandelingen der
Koninklijke Akademie*, 37 (Amsterdam, 1936), bk. 10, ll. 466–85 and bk. 11,
ll. 177ff.; see also Friedman, *Orpheus*, pp. 124–26.

pina's gathering of flowers signifies love of temporal goods, according to Berchorius, and therefore the devil was able to carry her off to hell.[62] Chaucer too comments on the moral significance of enjoying nature: Melibee "for his desport is went into the feeldes hym to pleye" (CT 7. 968), and this seemingly harmless pleasure results in the wounding of his daughter Sophia and the beating of his wife, Prudence. Prudence allegorizes the incident: "Thou hast ydronke so muchel hony of sweete temporeel richesses, and delices and honours of this world, that thou art dronken, and hast forgeten Jhesu Crist thy creatour. Thou ne hast doon to hym swich honour and reverence as thee oughte" (CT 7. 1409–12), and therefore the world, the flesh, and the devil have been able to "entre in to thyn herte . . . by the wyndowes of thy body" (CT 7. 1419). Overindulgence in the joys of nature implies neglect of duty to God, and sensual pleasures open the soul to the devil; medieval gardens and orchards might be dangerous as well as pleasant. Heurodis's delight in the garden seems harmless, but the consequences belie her innocence; like Melibee, she leaves the garden in frenzied grief, for she has put herself into the devil's power. Heurodis intends nothing wrong, but her lack of caution leads to disaster nonetheless; the pleasures of the garden demand the agony of Orfeo in the wilderness.

Her fault is defined by another change in the classical story: whereas Eurydice was bitten by a snake, Heurodis simply falls asleep beneath the *ympe-tre* — an act that makes her attendants slightly uneasy, for we learn that they "durst hir nouȝt awake" (l. 73), and the implication is that they feel they *should* awaken her. Why did the poet introduce Heurodis's sleep beneath the tree into the legend, and why did he intimate, through the maidens' concern, that such sleep was dangerous? Given the similarity between the allegorical interpretations of the Orpheus legend and of the Fall and given the presence of the apple in Berchorius's commentary, Heurodis's *ympe-tre* may well have been added to signify the Tree of

62. *Ovidius Moralizatus*, p. 92.

Knowledge,[63] to help identify Heurodis as a kind of Eve
who loses her love and her happiness in a paradisal setting
as she sleeps by the tree. Through Eve and the tree, all men
lost their peace and happiness; through Heurodis and the
ympe-tre, all the inhabitants of Traciens suffer lasting grief
and the loss of their king and queen.

But the tree itself is not dangerous: Heurodis's maidens sit
beneath it with her and are not harmed, nor indeed was the
biblical Tree of Knowledge pernicious in itself.[64] Eve earned
death by disobedience, and the comparable incident in *Sir
Orfeo* is Heurodis's falling asleep, another detail lacking in
classical versions.[65] We have seen that Heurodis's wandering
in the orchard may be morally suspect; and her later sleep
heightens the implicit condemnation. Her enjoyment of natural beauty, morally neutral in itself, yet seems to indicate
her forgetfulness of other obligations; her love of sensual
pleasures; her tendency, in short, to the spiritual sin of sloth,
the most deceptive of sins since it often seems to be no sin
at all. Cassian suggests that wandering to and fro is an early
sign of sloth, and sleep is a later one; Dan Michel too thinks

63. D. M. Hill notes that the dangerous tree in romances is generally
comparable to the tree of the Fall, but he does not develop the similarity;
"The Structure of 'Sir Orfeo,'" *MS* 23 (1961):136–53. A. M. Kinghorn
agrees that Heurodis is careless to fall asleep under a tree; "Human Interest
in the Middle English *Sir Orfeo*," *Neophil* 50 (1966):359–69. The tree and
its possible Celtic, classical, and Christian sources have been much discussed: see Bliss, pp. xxxv–xxxvii; Davies, "Classical Threads in *Sir Orfeo*,"
p. 161; and M. B. Ogle, "The Orchard Scene in *Tydorel* and *Sir Gowther*,"
RR 13 (1922):37–43.

64. According to some versions of the Fall, God intended Adam and
Eve to eat from the tree eventually; see Evans, *Paradise Lost and the
Genesis Tradition*, pp. 79ff.

65. Friedman finds the source of this detail in illuminations showing
the serpent biting Eurydice beneath a tree. He suggests that in some of
these pictures Eurydice is asleep, but the plates he includes are not convincing: Eurydice could as easily be falling from the bite as asleep
(*Orpheus*, pp. 182–83). Another possible explanation for Heurodis's sleep
must not be overlooked: conceivably the poet has her fall asleep as an
excuse for her vision.

the slothful man "loueþ . . . to ligge and resti and slepe." [66]
For Chaucer, anyone who sleeps at an unreasonable time is
guilty of sloth: "And certes, the tyme that, by wey of resoun,
men sholde nat slepe, that is by the morwe, but if ther were
cause resonable. For soothly, the morwe tyde is moost con-
venable a man to seye his preyeres, and for thynken on God,
and for to honoure God, and to yeven almesse to the povre"
(*CT* 10. 706–07). It is precisely in the morning that Heurodis
falls asleep, and she is allowed to "ligge & rest take" (l. 74)
until noon is past, although we know of no reasonable cause,
in Chaucer's terms. Melibee's delight in the fields was a
token of his sloth and spiritual drunkenness; Heurodis's
spiritual drunkenness leads to sleep, a deeper state of sloth.
Indeed, if the *Orfeo*-poet wanted to depict the course of
sloth in Heurodis, he could hardly have done better. The
slothful man, forgetful of his obligations to God, characteris-
tically delights in worldly pleasures and falls into somnolence;
he may then become desperate or completely mad, he attempts suicide, and he is finally damned.[67] So Heurodis goes
into the orchard, falls asleep, awakens in a state of profound
grief and madness in which she rends her flesh as though
she would kill herself, and is finally carried off by the Fairy
King to remain forever in the underworld.

Both the classical Eurydice and Eve died, literally or metaphorically, through a serpent, but Heurodis is seized by the
Fairy King. There are several possible reasons for this change.
Medieval commentators, as we have seen, identify the serpent
of the classical and biblical stories as the devil, and illuminations show these devils as draconopedes, while Eve's serpent
occasionally has a human face.[68] But Friedman's contention

---

66. *Desert Fathers*, pp. 230–31; and *Ayenbite of Inwyt*, p. 31.

67. On the slothful man, see *Ayenbite of Inwyt*, pp. 31–34, and Chaucer's
Parson's Tale, *CT* 10. 676–726. For an exemplum on sloth with considerable relevance to *Sir Orfeo*, see the story of Isboseth, in *Ancrene Riwle*,
pp. 120–21.

68. See Friedman, *Orpheus*, pp. 183–84; see also Evans, *Paradise Lost
and the Genesis Tradition*, pp. 181–82 and 196–97.

that "it would not be a far step from the man-headed draconopede to the King of the Fairies formed as a mortal man"
seems unsatisfactory. It is far more likely that the poet knew
of the devil's frequent disguise: "Satan transformeth himself
into an angel of light" (2 Cor. 11:14). In this form Satan had
several encounters with Eve. In the *Life of Adam and Eve,*
Satan grew angry at the human couple's penitence, so he
"transformed himself into the brightness of angels" [69] and
successfully tempted Eve to leave her penance. The *Orfeo*-
scribe himself copied a version of this incident into the Auchinleck MS; if *Sir Orfeo* was indeed a creation of the London
bookshop, or if the scribe himself had a hand in its composi-
tion, the figure of Satan as an angel of light may well have
influenced the transformation of serpent to man.[70] The related idea that Satan tempted Eve in Eden as an angel, and
often as an angel of light, is common in medieval drama: the
Cornish *Ordinalia,* the *Ludus Coventriae* Fall pageant, and
the Norwich B play all record it.[71] Presumably the *Orfeo*-poet
did not know these works, but Satan's disguise as an angel of
light was clearly familiar in the period.

If Heurodis fell through sloth, there is another reason for
the appearance of the Fairy King: sloth is traditionally associated with the attack of the noonday demon, as Friedman
points out.[72] Heurodis's vision occurs at some time around
noon (l. 75), and if Friedman is right in conjecturing that
undren-tide refers to late morning, then Heurodis is taken by
the Fairy King at the same time on the next day. In any case,
it is at noon that the Fairy King first appears to Heurodis,
and he looks exactly as the noonday demon should. Accord-

69. *Apocrypha and Pseudepigrapha,* 2:136.

70. On the compilation of the Auchinleck MS, see above, n. 56.

71. Markham Harris, trans., *Ordinalia* (Washington, D.C.: Catholic Uni-
versity of America Press, 1969), p. 8; Block, *Ludus Coventriae,* p. 23, l. 238;
Norwich B l. 40, in *Non-Cycle Plays and Fragments,* ed. Norman Davis,
EETS, Suppl. Text 1 (1970), p. 14.

72. *Orpheus,* pp. 186–89. Friedman inexplicably does not find Heurodis
guilty of sloth.

ing to the *Ancrene Riwle,* the demon responsible for the most
dangerous temptations of all — the hidden, spiritual temptations — is the demon of sloth: "David calls him *the noonday
devil,* 'the bright, shining devil,' and St. Paul *the angel of
light,* for into such he often turns himself and shows himself
to many" (p. 100). The outstanding attribute of the Fairy
King is brightness: his shining company is dressed in white
and mounted on white steeds, and the king himself is so
bright that later Orfeo can hardly look at him (ll. 415–16).
The Fairy King's crown is made "of a precious ston / — As
briȝt as þe sonne it schon" (ll. 151–52), and his country is
always as bright as noon (l. 372). The noonday demon, the
angel of light, the Fairy King with his crown and land as
bright as the sun — surely they may be one and the same. And
the noonday demon, sloth, whose fair appearance beguiles
men into thinking they do no wrong — surely he is a fit creature to capture Heurodis, forgetful of the orchard's dangers.
The poet's reasons for transforming the serpent into the Fairy
King should be evident: Heurodis's sin of sloth indicates that
her abductor should be the brilliant noonday demon, and her
similarities to Eve suggest that the angel of light should seize
her. That the shining devil should appear as the Fairy King
is quite appropriate: first, because the traditional Fairy King
shares the deceptive otherworldly glamor befitting the angel
of light; second, because a Fairy King is more natural to romance than a devil; third, because the Fairy King, according
to the Christian theory that all pagan divinities and demigods
are actually demons, is himself as deadly a devil as the most
monstrous denizen of hell.

In the first section of *Sir Orfeo,* then, the classical legend is
modified by certain changes which contribute both to the
romantic flavor of the poem and to its religious and moral
overtones. Heurodis is not finally Eve, nor is she the soul, but
she is a *figura* of both; she is a real woman, but in certain
specific ways she suggests specific aspects of Eve and the soul,
and the poet seems to have gone out of his way to emphasize
these similarities so that the poem might acquire more uni-

versal significance.[73] The loss of paradise, the loss of the soul
to sin and damnation, and the loss of a beloved wife are three
tragic events the poet has combined in the loss of Heurodis,
and it is this loss that justifies and demands Orfeo's long
suffering as a Holy Wild Man in the heart of the poem.

After Heurodis's disappearance, Orfeo renounces his kingdom and, dressed in a pilgrim's *sclauin*, enters the wilderness
to suffer for ten years. The contrast between his former power
and present misery in the wilderness is movingly described
(ll. 228–80): he who had elegant robes now wears leaves and
grass; he who owned castles and lands now sleeps in snow
and moss; instead of courtiers, his companions are wild
worms; instead of rich foods,

> — Now may he al-day digge & wrote
> Er he finde his fille of rote.
> In somer he liueþ bi wild frut,
> & berien bot gode lite;
> In winter may he no-þing finde
> Bot rote, grases, & þe rinde.
>
> [ll. 255–60]

His sufferings make him ugly, and his beard grows to his waist.
Sometimes he plays his harp, attracting wild beasts and birds,
but they leave him as soon as he stops. Sometimes he sees the
Fairy King hunting with his company; sometimes he sees
hosts of armed knights or knights and ladies dancing. At last
he finds Heurodis hawking with other ladies; neither dares to
speak, but she weeps at his suffering; Orfeo puts on his
sclauin, takes his harp, and follows them through a rock to
the underworld.

Once again, the poet has deviated from his classical sources.
Orfeo is now a king, not merely a harper; and such incidents
as his renunciation of his kingdom, his pilgrim's dress, the
great emphasis on his suffering, his ten years' exile as a Holy

---

73. For the concept of *figura*, see Erich Auerbach, "Figura," in *Scenes
from the Drama of European Literature* (New York: Meridian Books,
1959), pp. 11–76.

Wild Man, his ugliness, his glimpses of the Fairy King and his retinue, and his meeting with Heurodis are all peculiar to *Sir Orfeo*.[74] Why were these changes made? [75] The best explanation is that the poet wanted to turn Orfeo into a Holy Wild Man whose attributes and actions are those of one Holy Wild Man in particular — Christ; again the classical legend is overlaid with Christian meaning couched in mingled religious-romantic imagery.

This interpretation of the poem depends on a traditional view of Orpheus at least as old as the Boethian concept of him as a sinner returning to his old sins: the identification of Christ as the True Orpheus, first made in early Christian art and literature and continuing at least through the fifteenth century.[76] Throughout the Middle Ages, there are two major reasons for associating Orpheus and Christ: first, both are able to tame wild beasts by music, a power which in Christ's case includes reforming wicked men by his words; second, both are able to restore the dead to life. As a twelfth-century sequence on the Redemption puts it, just as the brazen serpent raised in the desert saved the Israelites, so

> Our Orpheus brought forth
> His bride from the kingdom of Hell,
>   Placing her in the kingdom of Heaven.[77]

74. As Severs points out, in Alfred's *Boethius* Orpheus spends some time in the wilderness before going to Hades; "The Antecedents of *Sir Orfeo*," pp. 191–92. In Virgil and Ovid, Orpheus retires to the wilderness *after* his trip to Hades.

75. Severs thinks the poet wanted to arouse pity for the forlorn Orfeo; "The Antecedents of *Sir Orfeo*," pp. 198–201. Several critics note that Orfeo goes into the wilderness to die, to be purified (his fault apparently being the assumption that happiness can last), or both; see James K. Knapp, "The Meaning of *Sir Orfeo*," *MLQ* 29 (1968):263–73; Kinghorn, "Human Interest in *Sir Orfeo*," 362; and Kenneth R. R. Gros Louis, "The Significance of Sir Orfeo's Self-Exile," *RES* 18 (1967):245–52.

76. For artistic representations of both Christ and Orpheus as the Good Shepherd and as a harper taming wild beasts, see Friedman, *Orpheus*, pp. 38–85.

77. G. M. Dreves and C. Blume, eds., *Analecta hymnica medii aevi*, 55 vols. (Leipzig: R. Reisland, 1886–1922), vol. 8, no. 30. These two reasons for

According to Virgil, Ovid, and Boethius, of course, this is a false parallel: Orpheus failed to rescue Eurydice permanently. Apparently there were some classical versions of the legend with a happy ending,[78] but we need not assume that Christian writers knew them: after all, if part of the similarity between Orpheus and Christ rested on their descents into hell, then, since Christ was successful, Orpheus may have been seen as successful too. Thus many Ovidian commentaries report not only the standard tragic ending with its Boethian moralization but also an alternative version in which Orpheus is a figure of Christ and the story — or at least its allegorical interpretation — ends happily. Thus a richly glossed thirteenth- or fourteenth-century French manuscript of the *Metamorphoses* reports both Christ-Orpheus's musical skill and his success: "Orpheus is the type of Christ, who provided himself a wife, Eurydice (i.e. the soul); but she descended into hell by the serpent's tooth (by the advice of the devil disguised as a serpent). Orpheus (Christ) descended with his lute (the prophets' preachings) to the dead in the world (sinners) — or perhaps he spoke so sweetly (he preached) to the dead, that he brought her back from death (he converted many)." [79] Thus Christ-Orpheus rescued sinners both on earth and in hell by the power of his song, and later the passage equates Orpheus's martyrdom on the mountain to Christ's death on the Cross. A similar interpretation by Berchorius resembles that suggested by *Sir Orfeo*: Eurydice is at once Christ's bride, the soul, and Eve; and Christ's love for his spouse is stressed:

> Allegorically, say that Orpheus, son of the Sun, is Christ, son of God the Father. From the beginning he guided Eurydice, or the human soul, through charity and love;

---

comparing Orpheus and Christ are given as early as Clement of Alexandria (d. 215), who argues against them: *The Exhortation to the Greeks*, ed. G. W. Butterworth, LCL (London, 1919), pp. 9, 11.

78. See C. M. Bowra, "Orpheus and Eurydice," *ClassQ* n.s. 2 (1952):113–26; and Peter Dronke, "The Return of Eurydice," *C&M* 23 (1962):198–215.

79. Cited by F. Ghisalberti, "*L'Ovidius Moralizatus* di Pierre Bersuire," *Studj Romanzi* 23 (1933):44–45.

because of his particular privilege, at the start he was married to her. But the serpent (the devil) bit this new bride (the newly created Eve) through temptation while she was gathering flowers (or, while she sought the forbidden apple). Through sin he killed her, and at last he sent her off to hell. Seeing this, Orpheus (Christ) chose to descend to hell himself, and thus he regained his wife (human nature). He brought her forth from the kingdom of shadows, singing this passage from Canticles 2: Arise, make haste, my love, and come.[80]

In these and other Ovidian commentaries, the identification of Orpheus as Christ is firmly established, and it is found in all interpretations of the myth including a happy ending. One of the most important differences between *Sir Orfeo* and the major classical versions is Orfeo's success; in the light of the commentaries, this fact strongly suggests that Orfeo may be taken as a type of Christ.

In the first part of *Sir Orfeo,* then, Orfeo played the part of Christ as defined by Berchorius: although a devoted husband, he could not prevent his wife's abduction even as Christ could not save Adam and Eve until the proper time.[81] The second part of the poem brings us to that proper time; while the classical Orpheus was able to descend to hell immediately, Christ (except in the commentaries) was not: he had to become incarnate and endure much suffering first. Similarly, Orfeo must undergo ten years as a Holy Wild Man before redeeming his wife. And for the *Orfeo*-poet, as for theologians,

80. "Ovidius Moralizatus," p. 147. See also the poetic *Ovide Moralisé* 10. 477–85 and the fifteenth-century prose *Ovide Moralisé,* ed. C. de Boer, *Verhandelingen der Koninklijke Akademie,* 61 (1954):264.

81. The significance of Orfeo's length of exile, ten years (1. 492), is uncertain; perhaps it indicates his fulfillment of the law even as Christ came to fulfill the law (Matt. 5:17); perhaps, in that ten is the number of perfection, it indicates his perfection through suffering. For the significance of the number, see Vincent Hopper, *Medieval Number Symbolism, Its Sources, Meaning, and Influence on Thought and Expression,* Columbia University Studies in English and Comparative Literature, no. 132 (New York: Columbia University Press, 1938), pp. 34, 44–45, 87, and 92.

this suffering is crucial: happy endings are usually paid for one way or another.

If Orfeo is seen as Christ, many details peculiar to *Sir Orfeo* may be explained. As Christ is king of heaven, so is Orfeo king of Traciens. Orfeo's renunciation of his kingdom, a detail with no classical counterpart, resembles Christ's decision to forsake heaven in order to rescue mankind, although of course the resemblance is not perfect: there is no indication that Orfeo is consciously setting out to find his wife. Christ's decision to become incarnate is often shown as the renunciation of heavenly glory for poverty on earth; thus a fifteenth-century lyric has Christ contrast his great power and comfort in heaven with his misery on earth, where he came

> . . . of grett love . . .
> The to delyuer out of this wrechidness
>
> .   .   .   .
>
> Borne in bedlem, lappyd and laide in strawe
> Ine a powur howse wher bestys ete ther mete
>
> .   .   .   .
>
> Poorly a-rayed in clothes bare and thyne
>
> .   .   .   .
>
> Thus longe I lyvid, passyng frome place to place,
> Bare-fotyd, caplese, wythout syluer or gold.[82]

In similar fashion the barefoot Orfeo leaves his court in poverty, moved by grief and love.

Orfeo leaves as a pilgrim, dressed in the rough, hairy mantle or *sclauin* adopted by penitential pilgrims and worn by Christ on the road to Emmaus.[83] The *sclauin*, reminiscent of the wild man's hairiness, corresponds figuratively to the coats of skin that Adam and Eve put on as tokens of mortality, weakness, and penitence, and that Christ too put on when he become incarnate, as Augustine notes.[84] Orfeo's

82. *Religious Lyrics of the XVth Century*, no. 109.

83. For Christ's dress as a pilgrim, see *Holkham Bible Picture Book*, p. 144, and Réau, *Iconographie*, 2. 2. 562.

84. *Confessions* 7. 18–19 (*Writings*, 1:106).

coat bears the same meaning: he leaves court to suffer and die (ll. 212–17). The garment also signifies pilgrimage; and while the object of Orfeo's pilgrimage is obscure, Christ's object was the Redemption. The idea that all human life is, in essence, a pilgrimage was extremely common in the Middle Ages, and the metaphor applies to Christ as well: Deguileville's *Le pelerinage Jhesucrist* (ca. 1358) characterizes Christ's life as a long, tiring, painful, and expensive pilgrimage; Nicholas Love (ca. 1410) praises Christ for taking on the hardships of "a pilgryme and a straunger"; and in a lyric Christ describes himself as "a sely pylegrym, þet ferr habbe i-souȝt." [85] Whatever Orfeo's motives, his actions are clearly Christlike.

Orfeo spends ten years in the wilderness before he finds Heurodis, and similarly Christ's pilgrimage involved his sufferings in a double wilderness. In one sense, all of Christ's life was spent in the wilderness of this world, "the wilderness through which you are travelling together with God's people towards the land of Jerusalem, that is, the Kingdom of heaven," according to the *Ancrene Riwle*.[86] But the wilderness into which Christ descended is also a very specific place, the wilderness between Jericho and Jerusalem inhabited by demons, beasts, and Holy Wild Men like John the Baptist. There Christ went to be baptized, and there the Holy Ghost descended to lead him into the solitude of the deeper desert

85. J. J. Stürzinger, ed., *Le pelerinage Jhesucrist* (London, 1897), esp. ll. 728ff. and 10380ff.; Love, *The Mirrour of the Blessed Lyf of Jesu Christ*, ed. Lawrence F. Powell (Oxford: Clarendon Press, 1908), p. 86; *Religious Lyrics of the XIVth Century*, no. 36. See also F. C. Gardiner; *The Pilgrimage of Desire* (Leiden: E. J. Brill, 1971).

86. *Ancrene Riwle*, p. 92. Christ's great sufferings are also stressed in the Auchinleck MS "Harrowing of Hell," copied by the *Orfeo*-scribe: see text in David Laing, ed., *Owain Miles and Other Inedited Fragments of Ancient English Poetry* (Edinburgh, 1837), p. 7. See also interpretations of the Good Samaritan parable in which Christ is the Samaritan wandering in the desert and rescuing man: *Mirrour of Mans Saluacionne*, p. 19; *Piers* B 17. 47ff.; and Ben H. Smith, *Traditional Imagery of Charity in "Piers Plowman,"* Mouton Studies in English Literature, vol. 21 (The Hague: Mouton, 1966), pp. 74–93.

to suffer and to be tempted. The first part of this journey is
described by Nicholas Love in terms remarkably like those
used for Orfeo's stay in the wilderness (ll. 227–64):

> And so the lorde of all the worlde gothe all that long
> weye bare foote and allone. . . . Gode lorde, where ben
> ȝoure dukes and erles, kniȝtes and barouns, horses and
> harneises . . . ? Where ben the trumpes and clariouns
> and alle othere mynstralcie and herbergeres and pur-
> veyoures that schulde goo byfore, and alle othere wor-
> schippes and pompes of the world as we wrecched wormes
> vsen? Be not ȝe that hiȝe lorde of whose ioye and blisse
> heuene and erthe is replenesched? Why than goo ȝee thus
> sympilly, alone and on the bare erthe? Sothely the cause
> is for ȝe be not at this tyme in ȝoure kyngdom, the which
> is not of this world. For here ȝe haue anentisshed [hum-
> bled] ȝoure self, takynge the manere of a seruant and
> not of a kyng.[87]

Christ's sufferings in the desert before his baptism and his
entrance into the wilderness as humble servant rather than
king comprise interesting parallels to Orfeo's life, but there
are other comparisons far more important for the poem. According to some theories of the Atonement, it was in the
desert that Christ, the second Adam, repaired the damage of
Original Sin and redeemed mankind. The saving brazen
serpent raised by Moses in the desert prefigures Christ's
sufferings in the wilderness as well as his death by the Cross.

According to the Bible, Christ went into the wilderness
after his baptism; among wild beasts he fasted forty days, and
then the devil tempted him to change stones to bread, to
leap from a pinnacle of the temple, and to worship the devil
and thereby gain the whole world (Matt. 4:1–11, Mark 1:13).
These events assume tremendous importance for writers like
Irenaeus and Ambrose, who accept the doctrine of recapitula-
tion — that the Atonement was effected by Christ's whole
life, not merely by his death; that Christ's life was closely

---

87. *Mirrour of the Blessed Lyf of Jesu Christ,* p. 85.

parallel to Adam's but that Christ acted throughout as Adam should have done; and that the temptation in the wilderness was especially important because Christ's resistance to temptation canceled out Adam's sin, so that man was redeemed there even though he was not yet led from hell.[88] Ambrose gives an especially full account of this doctrine in explaining the significance of Christ's stay in the wilderness. His fasting was designed both to teach men how to suffer and to counteract the Fall, to "atone for Adam's sinful tasting of the apple" (4. 6). Other parallels too are important:

> We ought to remember how the first Adam was cast out of paradise into the desert in order to notice how the second Adam returned from the desert to paradise. . . . Naked of spiritual graces, Adam covered himself with the leaves of a tree, while Christ, naked of earthly things, did not want bodily clothing [or, clothes of flesh]. Adam was in the desert, and in the desert was Christ also, for he knew where to find the damned soul that he would call back to paradise after atoning for its error. . . . But once man in paradise had lost his way, being without a guide, how could he remember that lost pathway out of the desert unless he might have a guide? [4. 7–8]

Christ was to guide man back to paradise, but first he had to defeat the devil, partly by causing the devil to tempt him unjustly, partly by causing the devil to allow the Crucifixion, and partly by refusing to give in to temptation. The devil attacked Christ with the weapons that felled Adam — gluttony, avarice, and pride. But Christ conquered these and thus nullified Adam's sins (4. 17–33). In short, "Jesus had to go into the desert to challenge the devil; for if he had not fought, he would not have conquered for me; mystically [he fought there] to free Adam from exile" (4. 14). According to

---

88. For Irenaeus, see *Against Heresies*, esp. 5. 21. 2, in *Writings*; for Ambrose, see Gabriel Tissot, ed., *Expositio evangelii secundum Lucam*, Sources Chrétiennes, nos. 45 and 52 (Paris: Editions du Cerf, 1956–58), 4. 6–4. 33; additional references to Ambrose will be given in the text.

such views, known widely in the Middle Ages,[89] the Temptation is a necessary part of the Redemption, and the Atonement could not have happened without the desert, without Christ's life as a Holy Wild Man. This does not imply that the Crucifixion was unnecessary, but rather that the suffering in the wilderness was central. Overcoming the temptations squared things with God, and Christ's virtue and death settled the devil's claims, just or unjust.

From this perspective, Orfeo's sufferings take on greater significance. He too suffers hunger, his meager diet of roots and grasses causing emaciation (ll. 262, 325, 459). He too is alone except for wild beasts and the demonic fairy troops. Perhaps he too is tempted: the Fairy King's hunt, the armies, and the dances may be painful reminders of the regal life Orfeo renounced and to which he might easily return. More important, perhaps, is Orfeo's renunciation of gluttony (he eats only what the desert provides), of avarice (he sacrifices rich possessions, keeping only his harp), and of pride (he gives up his title and his former personal beauty). Like Christ and the Holy Wild Man, he defeats temptation by his ascetic life in the wilderness, and therefore he finds what he seeks — Heurodis — in the desert; just as Christ, according to Ambrose, knew where to find lost souls. One major difference between the classical and English versions may thus be explained: Orpheus did not find Eurydice until he reached Hades, while Orfeo finds Heurodis in the wilderness (ll. 303–30). But just as Christ's success in the wilderness was only part of the Redemption, so Orfeo's preparation by suffering does not suffice to win his wife; a journey to the underworld is needed for that.

Other aspects of Orfeo's life in the wilderness are reminiscent of Christ's life. Hairy, blackened, eating roots and grass,

---

89. See Evans, *Paradise Lost and the Genesis Tradition,* p. 103; *Stanzaic Life,* ll. 5237ff.; Hastings Rashdall, *The Idea of Atonement in Christian Theology* (London: Macmillan, 1920), passim; and Gustaf Aulén, *Christus Victor: An Historical Study of the Three Main Types of the Idea of the Atonement,* trans. A. G. Hebert (London: SPCK, 1953), chaps. 2–5.

enduring the ravages of nature, Orfeo lives as a wild man; although we know he is sane, anyone might assume that he is as mad as Nebuchadnezzar.[90] Perhaps Heurodis herself thinks so when she weeps "for messais þat sche on him seiȝe" (l. 325). As we saw in chapter 2, the *Miroure of Mans Saluacionne* compares Christ's suffering in life and on the Cross to Nebuchadnezzar's torments as a madman in the desert; Nebuchadnezzar's bestiality signifies that Christ was treated as a beast by the Jews.[91] In fact, Christ's very nature renders him kin to the wild man: as a man who leads the life of a beast incorporates within himself two levels of creation, two natures, so Christ, both man and God, has a dual nature. Thus the *Cursor mundi* writes that anyone would be amazed to see a man changed into a beast:

> Men miȝte sey selcouþ [strange] he ware
> But selcouþer a þousande folde
> Is þis childe I haue of tolde
> Boþe is god & mon be riȝt
>
> [ll. 9856–59]

When the shepherds find a sheep in Mak's cradle, it should be less surprising than finding God as a child in the manger.[92] Since Christ's nature is dual in this sense, he may fitly be represented by other things with dual natures — Nebu-

90. Thus Finlayson and D. M. Hill find Orfeo quite mad and comparable to such indisputable madmen as Yvain and Merlin; such critics see the similarities between Holy and Unholy Wild Men but not their important differences: "*Ywain and Gawain,*" p. 334; and "The Structure of 'Sir Orfeo,'" pp. 144–50.

91. Christ was also thought to be a madman, although in rather different circumstances from Orfeo's. His disciples and the crowds thought him mad when performing miracles (Mark 3:21, John 7:20), and Herod Antipas thought him mad for refusing to testify in his own defense (Luke 23:8–11). The medieval drama popularized this humiliation of Christ as a fool; the theological point seems to be that those who accuse Christ of madness and then condone his death are far madder than he despite their worldly wisdom and his refusal to be worldly wise.

92. *Secunda Pastorum,* in *Wakefield Pageants.*

chadnezzar, the griffin, the centaur, the Sagittarius.[93] Christ's dual nature may also be illustrated by Orfeo, whose progress from king to wild man is analogous to the progress from God to man.

In the wilderness, Orfeo tames wild beasts with his harping, which is so excellent that it could be "on of þe ioies of Paradis" (l. 37). As we have seen, it was partly because of Orpheus's ability to tame beasts that he was originally identified with Christ; if Orpheus "from wild, savage creatures made irrational men gentle and mild and calmed their behavior," so too was Christ's "new song" able to reform the most vicious men.[94] The precise nature of Christ-Orpheus's musical power was interpreted in many ways. Often the "new song" represents Christian teachings — Scriptures, preaching, the Sacraments, the Ten Commandments, the Twelve Articles of Faith. Or it may symbolize right conduct: the tautness of the harp's strings indicates the hardships of the true Christian life, and the harp itself is the eloquence of reason and conscience.[95] Sometimes too Orpheus's harp is identified with

93. For the griffin, see Dante, *Purgatorio* 29. 106–14 and commentaries, and Réau, *Iconographie*, 1:88; for the identification of Christ with the Sagittarius, see Philippe de Thaun's *Livre des Créatures*, ll. 680–727, ed. and trans. Thomas Wright, in *Popular Treatises on Science Written During the Middle Ages* (London, 1841); and G. C. Druce, "Some Abnormal and Composite Human Forms in English Church Architecture," *Archaeological Journal*, 2d series, 22 (1915):183–86. Christ the Centaur is sometimes shown shooting an arrow down a dragon's throat to signify the Harrowing of Hell — see M. D. Anderson, "The Iconography of British Misericords," in G. L. Remnant's *A Catalogue of Misericords in Great Britain* (Oxford: Clarendon Press, 1969), p. xxxvi; Remnant provides several examples of the shooting centaur in his catalog.

94. John de Ridevall, *Fulgentius Metaforalis*, ed. Hans Liebeschutz, in *Studien der Bibliothek Warburg* 4 (1926):123; and Clement of Alexandria, *Exhortation*, p. 11.

95. On the symbolism of Orpheus's and Christ's music, see *Gesta Romanorum*, pp. 138 and 443; Gregory, *Morals on the Book of Job*, 2:510; the fourteenth-century Ovid MS described by Ghisalberti, "L'Ovidius Moralizatus," p. 45; the poetic *Ovide Moralisé* 10. 2556ff.; Berchorius, "Ovidius Moralizatus," pp. 148–49; the prose *Ovide Moralisé*, p. 264; Henryson, "Orpheus and Eurydice," ll. 508, 546.

David's, having the power of curing madness;[96] in this case, it is fitting that Heurodis, rendered mad by her vision and then metaphorically possessed by the Fairy King, should be freed by Orfeo's music.

Orpheus's harp is also interpreted as signifying Christ's seven last words on the Cross, "sept chansons moult piteuses" sung by the agonized Christ "pour la redempcion et le salut [du] lignaige humain." [97] The sweet power of this song is described in the *Miroure of Mans Saluacionne*:

The xxiii chapitle seith ȝow / crist was nayled on rode tree
And prayed for his crucyfiours / of his inneffable pitee
Jubal fynder of musik / figured this thing properelye
ffinding in tubalkaym hamers / the tunes of melodye
So crist as he was ruthfully / hamered apon the croce
Songe to his fadire of heven / In a full swete voice
So swete and faire was it / and full of all dulcoure
That it convertid thre thouzand / men in that ilk one houre
[p. 6]

This passage combines the ideas that Christ's words are the music and that the Cross itself, to which Christ was hammered and on which he was stretched with ropes, is the harp; similarly, the *Glossa ordinaria* claims that David's harp could cure madness "because it was a figure of Christ's cross, made of wood and stretched strings, which he carried and which even then put demons to flight" (*GO* 2:417). As Orfeo's harping charms the beasts and frees Heurodis from hell, so the music of Christ's preaching and of his death on the Cross leads men from sin and hell.[98] For both Orfeo and Christ, the harp — taken literally or figuratively — is the passport to hell and to the recovery of what was lost.

96. Poetic *Ovide Moralisé* 10. 2922–31. Friedman discusses the identification of Orpheus with David; *Orpheus*, pp. 148–55.

97. Prose *Ovide Moralisé*, pp. 264–65.

98. For Orpheus and Christ as musicians and symbols of resurrection, see Kathi Meyer-Baer, *Music of the Spheres and the Dance of Death: Studies in Musical Iconology* (Princeton: Princeton University Press, 1970), pp. 68–69, 257–68, 272–76, and 313–19.

As befits a wild man, Orfeo becomes extremely ugly during his exile: he is dressed in grass, emaciated, scarred (l. 262),
his rough beard reaching to his waist (ll. 265–66), black in
color (l. 459), so ugly that the Fairy King thinks him quite
unfit to be seen with Heurodis (ll. 458–62). This ugliness is
not mentioned in any classical sources, and although an
English poet writing of Orfeo's ten-year stay in the wilderness
might logically and realistically comment on his ugliness
and give him the physical characteristics of a wild man,
nevertheless Orfeo's ugliness may be more than romance convention.

Many early church fathers believed that the incarnate
Christ had been ugly. According to Isaias's prophecy of the
Suffering Servant: "So shall his visage be inglorious among
men, and his form among the sons of men. . . . There is no
beauty in him, nor comeliness: and we have seen him, and
there was no sightliness, that we should be desirous of him:
Despised, and the most abject of men, a man of sorrows, and
acquainted with infirmity: and his look was as it were hidden
and despised, whereupon we esteemed him not. Surely he
hath borne our infirmities and carried our sorrows: and we
have thought him as it were a leper, and as one struck by God
and afflicted" (Isa. 52:14; 53:2–4). When this passage is accepted as literally true, as it is by Augustine and many
others,[99] the implication is that Christ "took upon himself the
burden of all human wretchedness and misery, with intent
to heal it, and concentrated also in his own person all the
hideousness of physical deformity, with intent to transfigure
it. According to this doctrine, diseases of the soul should have
been outwardly typified by the deformity of the body, and our
blessed Lord would have been the most hideous of the children of men."[100]

The idea that Christ was ugly disturbed many theologians,

---

99. See *CG* 18. 29 (2:432–33); see also Tertullian, *Apologetical and Practical Treatises,* trans. C. Dodgson, LF, 3 vols. (Oxford: John Henry Parker,
1842), 1:252–54, note F, on the tradition of the Ugly Christ in the early
fathers.

100. Didron, *Christian Iconography,* 1:265.

especially because the Messiah is described in Psalm 44:3 as "beautiful above the sons of men." The fathers reconciled these contradictory opinions in one of three ways. First, Christ's ugliness might be relative rather than absolute; compared to God, his corporeal appearance was ugly, but he was still more beautiful than men.[101] Second, Christ was ugly in appearance but excellent in worth; therefore, he was ugly to those who did not value his teachings but beautiful to those who loved him. Thus, for Tertullian, the fact that Christ's tormentors mocked and killed him proves that they found him ugly:

> These were the words of men who even despised his outward appearance, so far was his body from being of human comeliness, not to speak of celestial glory. . . . The very sufferings, the very revilings tell the tale: the sufferings proved his flesh human, the revilings proved it uncomely. . . . How could he, as he said would happen, be despised and suffer, if in that flesh there had shown any radiance from his celestial nobility? [102]

The third and most common way to reconcile ugliness with beauty is to believe that Christ was beautiful but that his sufferings — in the desert and in the Passion — made him ugly; his ugliness is directly related to his mission of Atonement. Thus Origen notes that Christ was beautiful before and after his sufferings but ugly while they lasted; and Irenaeus claims that when the Word shone through him, Christ was beautiful, but sometimes the Word had to remain "quiescent, that He might be capable of being tempted, dishonoured, crucified, and of suffering death." [103]

With the rise of the Arian heresy, this early emphasis on the ugly humanity of Christ was displaced in the orthodox

101. Ibid., 1:265–70.
102. *Treatise on the Incarnation*, ed. and trans. Ernest Evans (London: SPCK, 1956), chap. 9 and p. 126n26. See also Origen, *Contra Celsum*, trans. Henry Chadwick (Cambridge: Cambridge University Press, 1953), 6. 76–77.
103. Origen, *Contra Celsum* 6. 77; Irenaeus, *Against Heresies* 3. 19. 2–3.

Church by Christ Pantocrator, divine, majestic, and beautiful.
But the ugly Christ survived in art; according to Didron,
there are extant several diptychs pairing an ugly, bearded,
exhausted Christ on the Cross with a beardless, young, beautiful Christ in Glory after the Resurrection.[104] During the
thirteenth century, however, artistic and literary emphasis on
the suffering and ugly Christ again became dominant. Didron
cites a superb example of the Ugly Christ in a fourteenth-
century French Bible illustrating the Crucifixion: " 'Jesus is
entirely naked,' says the commentary, 'and his skin is ugly
and discoloured, because he bore our sins in his own body:
Christ is here not only bearded, but entirely naked, and the
colour of his skin is red; he is poor, human, and ugly." [105]
The same idea is reflected in a fifteenth-century complaint
spoken by Christ:

> Payne of my traveylle a-pered in my face;
> Men myght perceyve yf thei listed to be-hold.
> Watch & grett labur, sharpe honger, thrust & cold
> fful ofte me brought so feble & so lowe,
> That myne owen mother sum tyme dyd me not knowe.[106]

Christ was made ugly and almost unrecognizable by his sufferings for man; so too does Orfeo become ugly and, upon his
return to his kingdom, unrecognizable, through his sufferings
for Heurodis.

The ugliness of Christ and Orfeo indicates the extent of
their sufferings and arouses pity in others: we have seen Heurodis's tears, and the point of late medieval emphasis on
Christ's agony was to make sinners grieve at his sacrifice and
determine to be worthy of his love. But this ugliness has
another important purpose as well: had Orfeo not been able
to pass as a lowly minstrel, and had Christ not appeared to

---

104. Didron, *Christian Iconography*, 1:270–78.

105. Ibid., 1:276; see also Réau, *Iconographie*, 2. 2. 36–37.

106. *Religious Lyrics of the XVth Century*, no. 109. See also Nicholas
Love, *Mirrour of the Blessed Lyf of Jesu Christ*, p. 230; and John Algrinus
(d. 1237), *Commentarium in Cantica*, PL 206:84–85.

be mortal, corruptible, and human, they would never have been able to rescue the souls they sought.

According to many theories of the Atonement, when man fell, he put himself in the devil's power. Whether or not the devil's dominion was just — the point was hotly disputed — man could be freed only by a champion who would defeat the devil on his own ground by inducing him to abuse his power.[107] By tempting a sinless man and receiving him in hell, the devil would undo his power over men. The devil led him to fall by a sort of trick: he lied to Eve about the apple's danger, he disguised himself deceitfully as a serpent or an angel, and he used God's own creation, the apple, to trap man. Man could justly be redeemed by a similar trick worked by God: Christ would come to earth disguised as a mortal, poor and weak. Moreover, the simple expedient of having Mary marry Joseph would deceive the devil into thinking that Christ was normally conceived and corrupted by Original Sin.[108] Thus deceived, the devil could be made to tempt Christ in the wilderness, where he tried to discover whether Christ was God or man. There the devil would be convinced that Christ was human, and he would then permit the Crucifixion. The devil would be lured by the bait of Christ's manhood only to be caught on the hook of his divinity.[109]

Christ's ugliness, then, was part of a disguise to trick Satan, and its importance is emphasized by the choice of the death of the Athenian King Codrus, one of the few nonscriptural stories in the *Speculum humanae salvationis,* as a type of the Crucifixion.[110] Codrus, whose people were fighting the Dorians, asked Apollo's oracle who would win; the answer was that whichever side killed the opposing leader would surely

107. For an account of each major theologian's views, see Rashdall, *The Idea of the Atonement,* passim; for a briefer summary, see Evans, *Paradise Lost and the Genesis Tradition,* pp. 175ff.

108. See *Cursor mundi,* ll. 10783–94, and Ambrose, *Expositio . . . secundum Lucam* 4. 12.

109. For this commonplace, see *Stanzaic Life,* ll. 6337–424.

110. See *Miroure of Mans Saluacionne,* p. 88, and *Gesta Romanorum* (no. 41 in Latin versions), p. 517.

lose. The Dorians heard of the oracle and ordered that Codrus be spared, but Codrus disguised himself as a slave and, unrecognized by the Dorians, was slain, thereby saving the Athenians. Christ too so loved his people that he disguised himself in humble flesh so that the devil would take him and thus be overcome.

Thus Orfeo in the wilderness is a fitting *figura* for Christ in the world. Both renounced their kingdoms to undertake a kind of pilgrimage as Holy Wild Men; both suffered greatly and grew ugly in their pain. Both were tempted, but both persisted in a penitential life which was finally rewarded by success. Both charmed wild things with the harp; and both were able, by means of their harping and their disguising ugliness, to descend to the underworld.

The final section of *Sir Orfeo* deals with Orfeo's recovery of his wife and his kingdom. Dressed in his *sclauin* and carrying his harp, Orfeo enters the brilliant underworld, so beautiful and shining that it looks like paradise. When Orfeo claims to be a minstrel, he is admitted to the castle, where he finds the unearthly beauty of the place undercut by a ghastly human landscape: all around lie

> folk þat were ȝider y-brouȝt,
> & þouȝt dede, & nare nouȝt
> Sum stode wiþ-outen hade,
> & sum non armes nade,
> & sum þurth þe bodi hadde wounde,
> & sum lay wode, y-bounde. . . .
>
> [ll. 389–94]

There are bodies of people strangled, drowned, and burned, and women dead or mad in childbirth — all seized by the fairies. And there too is Heurodis, asleep under an *ympe-tre*.

Orfeo enters the hall, where he can hardly look at the bright king and queen. The king challenges him: no one else has ever been "so fole-hardi man" (l. 426) as to come without being summoned, but Orfeo defends himself as a "pouer menstrel" (l. 430) who seeks out all lords. He then plays for the court; and the king, delighted, promises him whatever he wants as a reward. Naturally Orfeo asks for Heurodis, but the king objects; she is so beautiful and Orfeo so ugly that it would be "a loþlich þing" (l. 461) to see them together. But when Orfeo reminds the king that a royal lie would be even worse, he lets them return to Traciens (or Winchester) together.

No one recognizes Orfeo, so he borrows clothes from a beggar and goes into the city, where people marvel at his strange appearance: his hair is long, and his beard hangs to his knees. Orfeo meets his steward in the street and asks for aid; the steward offers to share what he has, for all harpers are welcome for Orfeo's sake. At dinner Orfeo plays; the steward recognizes the harp and asks where the minstrel found it. When Orfeo replies that he found it in the wilderness next to a body torn by wolves and lions, the steward is overcome by grief at Orfeo's suffering and "vile deþ" (l. 548). Orfeo reveals himself and praises the steward's loyalty; he and Heurodis are restored to throne and happiness, and the steward reigns after them.

Once again there are elements here which the classical versions lack: the unnatural brilliance of the underworld; the strange inhabitants of the place, seemingly frozen between life and death, many of them mad; Orfeo's disguise as a minstrel, and his refusal to say who he is or what he wants right away; the rash promise; the king's objection to Orfeo's ugliness; Orfeo's success; his disguise as a beggar in Winchester; the testing of the steward. We have already seen that some of these changes can be explained if the poem is seen as a Christianization of the classical legend: Orfeo's disguise represents Christ's, for the devil would never have let him enter had he known who he was; the happy ending reflects Christ's success in redeeming mankind. I would like to speculate on related explanations for a few other oddities, with the warning that these suggestions are far less certain than my previous ones.

The brightness of the underworld and its inhabitants should recall the brilliance of the noonday demon and the illusory beauty of earthly pleasures. It was by yielding to the apparently innocent pleasures of sloth that Heurodis fell, and in the underworld she fitly sleeps beneath the *ympe-tre*, immobilized in the moment of her sin. Man fell by the tree, and by the tree he was saved; we are reminded of the instrument of the Fall so we may appreciate the justice of redemption by the tree — the Cross, Orfeo's harp. Perhaps the tree is related to still another instrument of redemption, Orfeo himself; several medieval works use a grafted tree, an *ympe-tre*, to signify that dual nature of Christ so important to my interpretation of the poem and of Orfeo and Christ as Holy Wild Men.[111]

As for the human inhabitants of the underworld, Dorena Allen argues that they are not dead but rather *taken* by the Fairies to the underworld, which she sees as the Celtic land of the living dead.[112] Perhaps the poet is representing hell as the Celtic Otherworld, just as he transforms the devil into a Fairy King; such changes would be natural in a romance. But the underworld need not be Celtic here: certainly Christian souls in hell might be "þouȝt dede, & nare nouȝt" (l. 390) in that they are eternally alive to torment.[113] Nor is the idea

---

111. Smith, *Traditional Imagery of Charity*, pp. 60–62. Some scholars assume that the underworld in *Sir Orfeo* is definitely the Celtic Otherworld, but I am not convinced: see Bliss, pp. xxxviii–xxxix, and Howard R. Patch, *The Other World* (Cambridge: Harvard University Press, 1950), pp. 46n40 and 243.

112. "Orpheus and Orfeo," pp. 102–11. Her evidence is not entirely convincing in that much of it comes from relatively recent folklore, and her medieval sources for the "taking" of humans involve the fairies' substitution of a changeling for their human victim; there are, of course, no changelings in *Sir Orfeo*.

113. Henryson describes his hell — which is clearly classical/Christian — as inhabited by souls whose ambiguous status corresponds to that of the living dead:

> Quhat creature cumis to dwell in the
> Is ay deand, and nevirmoir sall de.
>   ["Orpheus and Eurydice," ll. 315–16]

Perhaps Henryson knew *Sir Orfeo* or a similar version: although his interpretation of the legend is in the Boethian tradition, he includes such

that madmen have already been captured for the underworld (ll. 394, 400) exclusively Celtic: Dante suggests that sinners who betray their guests continue a bodily existence on earth, while their souls are in hell.[114] Thus the soul can be separated from the still living body in Christian tradition, and if the *Orfeo*-poet saw madness as a consequence of sin and as possession, he might well have placed some of these lost souls in hell. Whatever the sources of the *Orfeo*-poet's hell — and I suspect that Celtic, classical, and Christian elements are fused — it is singularly chilling in its combination of deceptive beauty and horror.[115]

The Fairy King's rash promise and his objection to Orfeo as a fit spouse for Heurodis may merely be appropriate romance motifs added for aesthetic reasons. There are, however, religious overtones if Orfeo is taken as Christ. The rash promise might be related to the devil's rashness in permitting the Crucifixion, through which he unknowingly admitted into hell the one man who could lead forth the souls of the just; certainly the Fairy King's comment on Orfeo's having come uninvited (ll. 421–28) suggests his suspicion that Orfeo should not be there at all. The king's reluctance to let Heurodis go might reflect Satan's refusal to believe that the ugly Christ was really God's son and entitled to redeem mankind; according to the trick theory of the Atonement, the devil's inability to recognize Christ lost him his sovereignty over sinners. Orfeo's insistence that the king keep his word is a legalistic appeal comparable to that made by Christ to the devil in the Auchinleck MS "Harrowing of Hell" and in

---

elements as Eurydice's seizure by the Fairy Queen (l. 125; Friedman too notes this parallel: *Orpheus*, p. 198); the living dead; and a hint that the story might end happily, at least on a moral level, in some circumstances (ll. 616–27).

114. *Inferno* 33. 117ff.; cf. Chaucer's *Man of Law's Tale*, where Donegild is chided: "Thogh thou heere walke, thy spirit is in helle!" (*CT* 2. 784).

115. On classical elements in the underworld, see Davies, "Classical Threads," pp. 165–66. For the view that ll. 387–404 are simply a clumsy interpolation, see Bruce Mitchell, "The Faery World of *Sir Orfeo*," *Neophil* 48 (1964):155–59.

other versions of the Atonement.[116] These parallels are ad-
mittedly doubtful, of course; Orfeo's success in regaining his
wife and the disguise he adopts to do it may well have made
the similarities between Orfeo and Christ so clear that the
poet felt free to embellish the story with romance motifs designed solely to entertain and create suspense.[117]

Strong Christian parallels appear again at the very end of
the poem when Orfeo regains his kingdom.[118] Orfeo's decision
to test his steward and his disguising himself to do it suggest
Christ's testing of his disciples after the Resurrection. One
such parallel is found in John 21:1–4: the risen Christ appeared to Peter at the sea of Tiberias, but Peter did not
recognize him. Finally Peter knew Christ, who then tested
his love and committed to him the care of the faithful on
earth (John 21:15–18). Similarly Orfeo is not recognized by
his steward for a long time, and after the steward has proved
his faith and love, he is made heir to the kingdom. Far more
important is Christ's testing of two disciples on the road to
Emmaus (Luke 24:13–21), especially as that event was interpreted in the Middle Ages. As the disciples walked to Em-

116. Christ's argument is that Satan has false possession of mankind
because he bribed man with an apple and apple tree that belonged to God:

> How may thou on ani wise
> Of other mennes thing mak marchandise?
> Seththen thou boughtest him with min,
> With resoun schuld Ich aue him.
>
> [*Owain Miles:* "Harrowing," p. 9]

117. Of course, not every detail even in an explicitly allegorical story is
allegorically important: see Robertson, *Preface to Chaucer*, pp. 299ff.

118. Several critics find the testing of the steward a fitting end to the
poem; see Severs, "The Antecedents of *Sir Orfeo*," pp. 199–202, and Bliss,
p. xliii. H. M. Smyser, however, thinks the romance should end with
Heurodis's recovery; *Speculum* 31 (1956):134–37 (review of Bliss ed.). Hill
("The Structure of 'Sir Orfeo,'" pp. 138 and 141); Gros Louis ("Sir Orfeo's
Self-Exile, p. 252); and Knapp ("The Meaning of *Sir Orfeo*," p. 273) think
that the test enables the romance to affirm the value of loyalty as well as
of love in the face of adversity.

maus, they met Christ disguised as a pilgrim; they told him of their grief at Christ's death and their fears that he had not risen from the dead as promised. Christ rebuked their doubts, explained the Scriptures, and finally tried to leave them at Emmaus. But the disciples forced him to accept their hospitality, and as he broke bread they recognized him and were overjoyed. According to Gregory,[119] Christ appears as a pilgrim to pilgrims in order to signify that all human life since the Fall has been a pilgrimage of exiled man toward the heavenly city. The disciples are good men who love Christ but still doubt. When they force their unknown companion to eat with them, they prove their virtue; since they seek occasions to perform works of mercy, they are enabled to aid and recognize their God just as a certain householder who always received pilgrims one day found Christ among them. Clearly this reading, extremely popular in the Middle Ages, is applicable to *Sir Orfeo*. Not only are the concepts of the Fall, pilgrimage, and exile important throughout the poem, but events at the end closely correspond to Luke and Gregory. The steward too fears the death of his lord, whom he loves greatly; he too meets his disguised lord in the street and offers hospitality; he too recognizes his lord at table after having welcomed him as a stranger.[120]

Orfeo's testing also recalls Christ's parables of the faithful servant (Matt. 24:45–51) and of the separation of the sheep from the goats (Matt. 25:34–40); the latter parable figures in

119. Gardiner, *Pilgrimage of Desire*, pp. 30–36, 39–41. For other readings of the parable, see *Mirrour of the Blessed Lyf of Jesu Christ*, p. 273, and *Piers* B 11. 224–37.

120. Orfeo is disguised as a beggar, not as a pilgrim, of course — perhaps because he left as a pilgrim and fears recognition if he returns in the same dress even though his appearance has changed drastically. But the fact that Orfeo disguises himself as a beggar, and that his steward is thereby made a king, finds a curious analogy in Love's *Mirrour of the Blessed Lyf of Jesu Christ*, where Christ is praised because he "bycome a seruaunt to make vs kynges" (p. 86). The steward's grief at Orfeo's supposed "vile deþ (l. 548) suggests the disciples' grief at Christ's degrading death on the Cross.

some readings of the Journey to Emmaus as well.[121] The first
parable describes a situation much like that in *Sir Orfeo*:[122]

> Who, thinkest thou, is a faithful and wise servant, whom
> his lord hath appointed over his family, to give them
> meat in season? Blessed is that servant, whom when his
> lord shall come, he shall find so doing. Amen I say to
> you, he shall place him over all his goods. But if that
> evil servant shall say in his heart: My lord is long a
> coming: And shall begin to strike his fellow-servants,
> and shall eat and drink with drunkards: The lord of
> that servant shall come in a day that he hopeth not, and
> at an hour that he knoweth not: And shall separate him,
> and appoint his portion with the hypocrites. There shall
> be weeping and gnashing of teeth.

Orfeo returns at an unexpected time to find his servant faithful, and his words to the steward echo those of the parable:

> ȝif ich were Orfeo þe king,
>
> .   .   .   .   .   .
>
> & were mi-self hider y-come
> Pouerlich to þe, þus stille,
> For-to asay þi gode wille,
> & ich founde þe þus trewe,
> þou no schust it neuer rewe.
> Sikerlich, for loue or ay,
> þou schust be king after mi day;
> & ȝif þou of mi deþ hadest ben bliþe
> þou schust haue voided, al-so swiþe.
>
> > [ll. 558, 566–74]

In the second parable, the sheep and the goats are differen-
tiated on the basis of their charity; the sheep will be set on

121. Gardiner, *Pilgrimage of Desire*, pp. 40–41.

122. Hill seems to refer to this parable in noting that there are New
Testament echoes in the testing of the steward, but he does not carry
the comparison further; "The Structure of 'Sir Orfeo,'" p. 141.

the right hand of God, inheriting a kingdom as reward, "For I was hungry, and you gave me to eat: I was thirsty, and you gave me to drink: I was a stranger, and you took me in. . . . Then shall the just answer him, saying: Lord, when did we see thee hungry, and fed thee. . . . And the king answering, shall say to them: Amen I say to you, as long as you did it to one of these my least brethren, you did it to me." Orfeo's steward, acting charitably to a man he takes to be one of the least of Orfeo's brothers, in fact receives his lord; he is rewarded with a kingdom.

These two parables, dealing with the Second Coming and the Last Judgment, are appropriately suggested at the end of a poem which recapitulates both the history of mankind and the progress of each human soul. Heurodis is also Eve and the soul lost through sin; Orfeo in the wilderness is also Christ grieving over the sinful human race; Orfeo in the underworld is also Christ harrowing hell and rescuing each soul; his return with Heurodis signifies the resurrections of God and man; and Orfeo's testing of his steward represents the Last Judgment, which will assign every man to heaven or hell. Thus the traditional three comings of Christ can be seen in the structure of the poem. The first coming, as King and Creator in Eden, may be related to Orfeo's kingship and virtue at the start; as Eve's fall demanded that Christ come again to the wilderness of this world, so does Heurodis's abduction require Orfeo's exile. The coming of the ugly incarnate Christ is reflected in the ugly Orfeo's suffering as a Holy Wild Man, his descent to the underworld, and his winning of Heurodis. Finally, Christ's coming as Judge is suggested by Orfeo's testing of his steward. When the poem is seen in this light, the ending is far from anticlimactic. *Sir Orfeo* is a good story, full of *solaas* for those who seek it; but there is a deeper *solaas* in the *sentence,* in the religious overtones of this charming romance which warns how easy it is to fall, reminds us of Christ's love and suffering and triumph, and points the way to salvation — through the love of God and acts of mercy.

At the beginning of the Auchinleck MS, the Fall and the Harrowing of Hell are narrated in explicitly religious poems which emphasize the suffering of the penitent Adam and Eve and of Christ in his work of redemption. In *Sir Orfeo* the same events — the tragic fall, the pains of man's pilgrimage in the wilderness of earth, Christ's suffering, the joy of redemption, the possibility of happiness after the Last Judgment — are told again, veiled in classical legend, romance idiom, and the convention of the Holy Wild Man. Two other lyrics in the Auchinleck MS seem to be related in theme to *Sir Orfeo*, and both express directly and urgently the need for suffering if one wants to be saved.

The lyric that immediately follows *Sir Orfeo* — "þe siker soþe" — describes man's hard lot in this world of sin.[123] Life itself is a sort of bitter pilgrimage, where we "walk mani wil ways / As wandrand wiʒtes." Beset by the world, the flesh, and the devil, man's condition is fearfully unstable:

> Now sounde, now sare,
> Now song, now sites,
> Now nouʒt, now y-nouʒ,
> Now wele, now wouʒ,

until finally death resolves the issue. As Orfeo goes from richness and beauty to the torments of the wilderness, so does everyone in this life; the only answer is to mourn one's sins, to fight the first three enemies so that the fourth, Death, will not have an everlasting victory. The lyric is addressed to those who are in the wilderness with Orfeo; the poem seems to warn that we have not all been saved with Heurodis, that we must temper joy with fear and seek true values, perhaps as a penitent Holy Wild Man.

The other lyric, which precedes *Sir Orfeo* by three items, states forcefully the moral lesson inherent in *Sir Orfeo* and clearly enunciated in "þe siker soþe." It begins with the nostalgic evocation of the romance world:

123. Printed in *Religious Lyrics of the XIVth Century*, no. 27.

Where ben men biforn ous were
That houndes ladden and haukes bere
        And hadden feld and wode
The riche leuedis in her bour
That werd gold in her tresour
        With her bright rode

Thai eten and dronken and made hem glade
With joie was al her liif y-lade
        Men kneled hem bi fore
Thai beren hem wel swithe heighe
With a tvinkling of her eighe
        Her soules were for lore

Whare is that hoppeing and that song
The trayling and the proude gong
        The haukes and the houndes[124]

The deceptive splendor of the life of the past — the hunting, hawking, the beautiful ladies with hair bound in gold,
the feasts and ceremonies, the minstrelsy — all this is reminiscent of the occupations of the Fairy troops in the wilderness, of the beauty of Heurodis's orchard, of the brilliance
of the underworld. Yet in a twinkling of an eye — in a sleep
beneath the *ympe-tre,* perhaps — such pleasures are lost and
the soul is damned:

        Al that wele is went oway
        Her ioie is turned to wayleway
                To mani hard stoundes

The swift change from beauty to pain is like that in the
underworld, where the shining glory of meadows and palaces
is suddenly transformed into horror by the landscape of the
maimed. So tempting are the beauties of earthly pleasure;
so swift is the punishment of indulgence.

The remedy to such a fate is suffering such as that endured
by Orfeo in the wilderness:

124. Printed in Laing, *A Penniworth of Witte,* pp. 119–20.

> Dreighe her man ȝif that thou wit
> A litel pine men the bit
>   With drawe thine aise oft
> ȝif the pine be vnrede
> And thou thenke of thi misdede
>   It schal the think soft.

Man should remember the sufferings of Christ, "Take the rode to thi staf," and dedicate himself to God by choosing willingly a life of pain on earth — perhaps the life of the Holy Wild Man — to avoid sudden damnation, so easily brought on in a moment of pleasure. For any medieval reader of the Auchinleck MS, these two poems, placed so near *Sir Orfeo,* must have seemed to articulate a similar vision of human life, emphasizing the tenuous nature of human existence, the swiftness of retribution, and the penitential value of suffering.

The conventional wild man — both holy and unholy — teaches much the same lesson in all the works examined in the chapter. The garden's joys too often require the agony of the wilderness: as Adam and Eve were cast from one to the other, as Christ suffered in the desert to atone for the sins of the garden, as Heurodis's brief forgetfulness required Orfeo's ten years of pain, so it is with all wild men who learn the price of the pleasures of garden and court. Voluntarily or not, everyone who will be saved must undergo the desert's trials, and those who suffer find grace amid the barrenness. Characters who, like Ywain and Merlin, seek true and lasting happiness at court and in secular values, are spiritually mad, and their moral insanity is both symbolized and purged by suffering in the wilderness that so accurately mirrors the true conditions of earthly life. Those who are driven mad on earth so that they may be purified are blessed to endure their purgatory on earth, unlike the lords and ladies of the Auchinleck MS poem. Still more blessed, however, are those like Orfeo, the saints, and the desert fathers who willingly choose to be mad in the world's eyes so that they may become whole in the wilderness. Theirs is the way of Christ, outcast in the desert, tempted, scorned as mad, suffering all the world can inflict to prove that man is stronger than the world and that true reason is not what courtiers think it is. Leading the life described by Chaucer in "The Former Age," these Holy Wild Men know that the world is but a desolate place, a wilderness, and that he who is honored by the world is more like a beast than the wild man is. Chaucer's "Balade de Bon Conseyl" expresses the call of the desert for Holy and Unholy Wild Man alike, for it is in the true wilderness that they learn what man is and how he should serve God in the wilderness of earth:

That thee is sent, receyve in buxumnesse;
The wrastling for this world axeth a fal.
Her is non hoom, her nis but wildernesse:
Forth, pilgrim, forth! Forth, beste, out of thy stal!
Know thy contree, look up, thank God of al;
Hold the heye wey, and lat thy gost thee lede;
And trouthe thee shal delivere, it is no drede.

5 Conclusions: Thomas Hoccleve

> He that sinneth in the sight of his maker, shall fall into the hands of the physician.
>
> Ecclesiasticus 38:15

> I write of melancholy, by being busy to avoid melancholy.
>
> Robert Burton, *The Anatomy of Melancholy*

Throughout the Middle Ages, as we have seen in this study, disease and madness were frequently associated with sin. By physical and mental suffering, a sinner might be punished on earth in anticipation of his torments in hell, like Herod and other Mad Sinners; he might be both punished and purified, like Nebuchadnezzar, Ywain, and other Unholy Wild Men; or, like Job, Sir Orfeo, and many Holy Wild Men, he might be refined in the fire of undeserved tribulation. Of course, man's trials on earth might include loss of position, of wealth, and of friends as well as loss of health; but disease and especially madness were considered particularly appropriate as punishment or purgation for several reasons. All kinds of disease were viewed as the direct consequence of disobedience to God. Man's disobedience in the Garden of Eden first brought about the enfeeblement of reason (a precondition for madness), consequent loss of control over the body, and disease, facilitated by the newly arisen conflict of the four bodily humours; later, actual sin of the individual might produce further physiological and psychological decay in the sinner. Man was so created that his sin would inevitably carry its own physical as well as spiritual punishment; and, consequently, the cure of disease requires spiritual treatment — confession, prayers, exorcism, intercession of saints — at least as much as physiological or psychological treatment. The body might be cured by earthly medicine, but if the true cause of disease in the soul were not cured, the sufferings of both body and soul would persist in eternity if not on earth.

Madness was considered an especially appropriate consequence of sin: first, because sin involves a disorder in the soul which is fitly manifested as a disorder in the mind; second, because insanity and possession by the devil — and therefore by sin — were often equated; and third, because reason, the image of God in man, is destroyed both in sin and in madness. The sinner thus willfully brings upon himself madness, bestiality (for reason is all that raises man above the beasts), or both, as in the case of Nebuchadnezzar, the spiritual father of later madmen. Of course, not all who seem mad are so from a religious point of view; Holy Wild Men, in their acknowledgment of the frailty of man and in their disdain for the good opinion of the world, illustrate the highest moral sanity. Yet most men are sinners, and most men are mad in the sight of God if not before men. He who values worthless things and rejects true riches will always be called mad by some; the madman is defined in part by society and by its conception of what things ought to be desired. Ywain at Arthur's tournaments and feasts is sane to Gawain and mad to God, or at least to Alundyne; while Ganieda, in her false denial of adultery, is mad to the wild Merlin and sane to the corrupt court. In the Middle Ages, the definition of madness was looser and more inclusive than it is now, and both important definitions — that of the world and that of God — appear frequently in literary treatments. The dominant religious view, as we have seen, was that all sin was mad, and that most madmen were sinners; desert saints and Holy Wild Men whose way of life seemed inhuman and mad were in reality sane in soul and often in mind, while their accusers — like Herod accusing Christ — were the true madmen.

In concluding this study of madness in the Middle Ages, I should like to take a somewhat different approach from those I followed earlier; instead of focusing on the characteristics and

significance of disease or on the most common conventional
representations of madness, I should like to look briefly at one
author who writes more extensively about madness, disease,
and their moral significance than any other medieval literary
figure. Thomas Hoccleve (ca. 1368–1437), a minor but much
underrated poet whose writings deserve more attention than
they can be given here, is a fifteenth-century Robert Burton,
whose work includes many of the commonplaces and conventions of madness discussed in this study.[1] In his fascination —
perhaps one might even say obsession — with the topics of
madness, melancholy, and disease, Hoccleve combines considerable scientific and medical knowledge with traditional moral
and religious attitudes toward madness and disease as punishment for sin and as earthly purgatory far preferable to the
pains of hell. The result is a series of portraits of madmen,
melancholics, and diseased sinners so detailed, vivid, and realistic that they are generally taken to be autobiographical; if
they are — a question I will discuss later — then Hoccleve is
the first English writer I know of who describes his own madness.[2] Regardless of whether the content of his poems is truly

1. Citations to all of Hoccleve's poems except the *Male Regle* are to
Works: The Minor Poems, ed. F. J. Furnivall and I. Gollancz, rev. ed.
Jerome Mitchell and A. I. Doyle, EETS, es 61, 73 (reprinted in 1 vol., 1970);
and *Works: The Regement of Princes and 14 Poems*, ed. F. J. Furnivall,
EETS, es 72 (1897); I have repunctuated the text and omitted editorial
final *e*'s. The text of the *Male Regle* is from Eleanor P. Hammond, ed.
English Verse between Chaucer and Surrey (Durham, 1927; reprinted
New York: Octagon Books, 1965). Hoccleve, who claims to have known
Chaucer (*Regement*, ll. 2077–79), spent most of his life as clerk in the
Office of the Privy Seal; he may have intended to become a priest, but his
alleged marriage closed that door to advancement.

2. On autobiographical questions in Hoccleve, see Jerome Mitchell,
Thomas Hoccleve: A Study in Early Fifteenth-Century English Poetic
(Urbana: University of Illinois Press, 1968), chap. 1; see also Ian Robinson,
Chaucer's Prosody: A Study of the Middle English Verse Tradition (Cambridge: Cambridge University Press, 1971), pp. 197–99, for the view that
what matters in Hoccleve's poetry is not its truthfulness but its convinc-
ingness. On the problems of autobiography in the period, see George Kane,
The Autobiographical Fallacy in Chaucer and Langland Studies (London:
H. K. Lewis for University College, 1965). I hope to examine late medieval
autobiographical, pseudo-autobiographical, and first-person narrative in
a subsequent study, which will contain further material on Hoccleve.

autobiographical, Hoccleve is one of the first authors to describe his own life poetically in terms of the conventional attitudes toward madness and disease discussed in previous chapters, and this combination of literary convention, scientific knowledge, and alleged autobiography provokes some interesting speculations with which to close a discussion of madness in the Middle Ages.

I should like to begin this examination of Hoccleve's poetry by demonstrating his preoccupation with the relationship between sin and disease and with God and Mary as spiritual and physical physicians, a preoccupation which recurs in most of his religious poems and which lays the groundwork for his writings on melancholy and madness. In one such religious poem, the "Inuocacio ad patrem," Hoccleve asks God to pardon those whose sins manifest their "seek feeblenesse" (l. 128); and in a poem "Ad Spiritum Sanctum," he prays,

> Come on, confort of our soules seeknesse,
>   And ay reedy in our necessitee!
> Of wowndes leche, helpere in distresse,
>   O, come now foorth, strengthe of our freeltee,
>
> .   .   .   .
>
> O, oonly helthe of our mortalitee. . . .
>
> [ll. 43–46, 58]

The oil of the Virgin's mercy soothes and cures men's wounds:

> That licour our wowndes greuous & sore
>   Serchith, and is our ful curacion;
>   That is the way of our sauuacion. . . .
>
> ["De Beata Virgine," ll. 17–19]

A poem translated from the French of Deguileville is attributed to Hoccleve by Furnivall; the prevalence of imagery of sin and disease would certainly lend credence to this attribution, for, as we shall see, Hoccleve frequently chose to translate texts including these ideas. This poem, "The epistle of grace sent to the seek man," begins with Grace's admonition to the sinner: he is oppressed by "malady" (l. 9), death's servant, and the disease has been caused by the sinner's negligence of proper "gouernaunce" (l. 20), of keeping body and soul strictly obedient to God. The sick man's lust has so corrupted him that he needs "a fleobotomye" (l. 28), and his corrupt humours must be purged by sweat and tears in penance. Only by confession to Grace and by strict penance and amendment can the sick man be cured of his physical and spiritual illnesses. Tears of contrition and hard labor for God will purge both the evil humours of the body and the sins which oppress the soul.

Hoccleve's tendency to see disease as the product of sin and to see a full confession as necessary to the cure of physical disease is illustrated by his selection of works for translation. One of the sources of the *Regement of Princes* (ca. 1412) is the pseudo-Aristotelian *Secreta secretorum,* an extremely popular medieval compendium of medical, moral, and physiognomic knowledge.[3] This work emphasizes the interdependence of soul and body, and it advocates for continued good health the observance of the mean in all things; some versions specifically urge the prince to exemplify the seven cardinal virtues so that he might be both healthy and a good ruler.[4] Hoccleve's *Regement,* treating the sins and virtues in the text proper and incorporating some of the medical and moral lore into the seemingly autobiographical Prologue, is less dependent on the *Secreta* than on other works,[5] but that he should choose to translate parts of the *Secreta* is indicative of his affection for the concept that physical health, salvation, and virtue are intimately connected.

This affection is illustrated particularly well by the two tales from the *Gesta Romanorum* which Hoccleve translated for the *Series.*[6] The first is the tale of *Jereslaus' Wife,* an analogue

3. For the popularity of the *Secreta secretorum,* see Mitchell, *Hoccleve,* pp. 24–25.

4. See especially Yonge's translation in *Secreta secretorum,* ed. Robert Steele, EETS, es 74 (1898), pp. 145ff. and passim.

5. See Mitchell, *Hoccleve,* pp. 24–31.

6. The *Series* includes (1) the *Complaint,* (2) the *Dialogue with a Friend,* (3) the tale of *Jereslaus' Wife,* (4) dialogue and prose moralization, (5) *Lerne for to Dye,* (6) further dialogue, (7) the story of *Jonathas and Fellicula* with prose moralization, and (8) an envoy to Lady Westmoreland.

of Chaucer's *Man of Law's Tale*. Possibly Chaucer's use of the story influenced Hoccleve's selection, or perhaps his motive was solely to please women, as he claims in the *Dialogue* (ll. 799–826); but it is at least as likely that the denouement of the story, with its emphasis on the disease produced by sin and on confession as a cure, moved Hoccleve to translate it. In this version, the virtuous empress is wronged most grievously by her brother-in-law, a knight, a thief, and a shipman; after many tribulations, she retires to an abbey and earns fame as a healer. Her betrayers, afflicted with leprosy, blindness, palsy, gout, and madness, come to her unknowingly for a cure. She extracts a full and contrite confession before healing them miraculously and revealing herself. The second tale includes similar events: Jonathas, betrayed and robbed by the courtesan Fellicula, first suffers for his sins of the flesh by becoming leprous after eating a strange fruit and by losing the flesh from his feet in a hot stream. Cured by a second fruit and a second stream, he goes to take vengeance on Fellicula; setting himself up as a physician, he cures many people before Fellicula falls ill and summons him. He orders her to make a full confession, but she complies not from contrition but from the desire to be cured. Jonathas then gives her the fruit of leprosy and the water of decay, and she dies miserably. In both stories, the wronged sufferer is restored to happiness — an idea which clearly appealed to Hoccleve, who writes of himself as a sufferer and sometimes as a wronged one; more important, the sinners are afflicted with punitive diseases, and only by a proper confession may they be cured.

The same ideas occur in Hoccleve's best-known poem, the *Male Regle* (ca. 1406), but the character of the work as a begging poem involves the parody rather than the straightforward statement of these themes.[7] Smitten by disease both of body

7. I follow Mitchell's dating of the poems. For an excellent discussion of the *Male Regle*, see Eva M. Thornley, "The Middle English Penitential Lyric and Hoccleve's Autobiographical Poetry," *NM* 68 (1967):295–321. She relates Hoccleve's use of the imagery of sin and disease to the conventions of the penitential lyric, and she finds the poem more conventional than autobiographical. She considers the poem a parody of religious and

and purse, Hoccleve undertakes a full confession of his excesses
to the god of Health. The invocation to Health has clear religious implications based on the double meaning of *salus* as
physical (and perhaps financial) well-being and as spiritual
salvation, and the double-edged humor of the poem depends
on Hoccleve's persistence in asking for the first kind of health
rather than the second. He laments his rebellious youth and
his willfull disdain for Reason's counsels of moderation; he
confesses his submission to the seven deadly sins[8] and admits
that his excesses in the tavern have led to physical illness and,
more predictably, to "the penylees maladie" (l. 130). To restore his lost health Hoccleve knows that he must make a full
confession of his sins against "god, his freend, & eek him self"
(l. 168), and he does so with great detail and subtle distinction, thereby fulfilling the requirements of telling "why &
where, how & whenne, / and how ofte . . ."[9] and of discrim-
inating between sins of word, thought, and deed.[10] For example, Hoccleve confesses that he often grew belligerent in his
cups but was too cowardly to speak insults aloud, let alone to
fight (ll. 161–76).

Thus Hoccleve formally fulfills the three parts of confession:
he describes his sins as openly as one could wish, he claims to
be motivated by extreme contrition (l. 403), and he hopes to
amend and to make restitution (ll. 369–408). In each part, however, his confession is imperfect. In describing the circumstances of his sins, he indulges in the accusation of others, even
naming names when he attacks Prentys and Arondel (l. 321);
this was explicitly forbidden in confessional manuals.[11] He
expresses contrition for the wrong reason: instead of regretting

---

courtly love complaints, and she relates it to the confessional form without, however, noting the *Male Regle's* explicit violation of the spirit of
the three parts of confession.

8. See Thornley, "Hoccleve's Autobiographical Poetry," for the enumera-
tion of the sins in the poem.

9. See John Mirk, *Instructions for Parish Priests*, ll. 1299–300.

10. See Arthur Brandeis, ed., *Jacob's Well*, EETS, os 115 (1900), pp. 293–
95.

11. Ibid., pp. 83 and 170ff., esp. pp. 180 and 182.

that he has offended God, he wants health and money back, and confession seems the proper way to get it. The fallacy is exposed in *Jacob's Well*: "Thou schalt noȝt haue sorwefull mynde in þin herte for þi good & for þi gold, but for þi synne, and noȝt for þi bely" (p. 170). The conscious irony of the poem hinges particularly on Hoccleve's proposal for reformation: he is willing to refrain from lust of the flesh (lechery, gluttony) and pride of life (his desire to be called "maister" — ll. 201–05), but his plea for money (ll. 409–40) indicates his persistence in lust of the eye, avarice. Lest we miss the point, Hoccleve underscores it by his final words:

> By coyn I gete may swich medecyne
> As may myn hurtes all þt me greeue
> Exyle cleene, & voide me of pyne.
>
> [ll. 446–48]

"Coyn" replaces the "grace" or "absolution" which we might expect in a truly penitential poem; even though gold, as Chaucer's physician knew (*CT* 1. 443–44), might be an efficacious cure for several diseases, including melancholy.[12] It is an earthly cure of the purse, not a spiritual one of the soul, which Hoccleve seeks in this parody of confession. Having made a confession so like Fellicula's in his later *Gesta Romanorum* translation, he could hardly expect a cure either of purse or of body, if his distress was indeed real; and he seems to have received no cure despite the charm and skill of the *Male Regle*.[13]

12. See Zilboorg and Henry, *History of Medical Psychology*, p. 139. Avarice was traditionally associated with melancholics; see *Saturn and Melancholy*, pp. 284–86 and passim.

13. Mitchell (*Hoccleve*, pp. 3–4) doubts that Hoccleve was really poor. Questions of autobiography are considered in Mitchell's first chapter; while there is undeniably a fair amount of accurate autobiography in the poems — references to the Privy Seal, to Hoccleve's co-workers, to the amount of his annuities — I think there is rather less than Mitchell would find, particularly in the details of Hoccleve's quite conventional youthful follies in the *Male Regle*. The question of Hoccleve's madness will be discussed below.

In the *Regement of Princes* (ca. 1412), the first poem to deal explicitly with melancholy, Hoccleve's purse and body are still sick; and the more serious tone of this later poem, contrasting sharply with the flippancy and wit of the *Male Regle,* inclines the reader to believe that Hoccleve might really have been in financial straits and that he may have suffered from severe fits of depression. The Prologue begins with Hoccleve's sleepless night, occasioned, according to proper medical theory, by the oppressiveness of "thought" (l. 7), by which he means something like morbid anxiety or melancholia. The *Secreta secretorum* warns against "ouer myche thoght," which may be correlated with "Wakynge moche . . . , grete drede, moche doutynge . . . , goodis of fortune gretly to covete . . . , or myschaunces to remembyr" (p. 248) as causes of severe bodily harm. According to Bartholomeus, melancholia may be caused by "passyons of the soule, as of besynes & grete thouȝtes" (7. 6); conversely excess melancholy produces "colde & wakynge and heuynesse . . . besy thoughtes & sourenes of mouth" (7. 3), delusions and anxiety (4. 11), and "inordynat wakynge, & anguysshe foloweth . . . and besy thoughtes encrease, & rauynge & vnresonable suspecyons" (7. 9). Caught in this vicious circle, Hoccleve indulges in a Boethian meditation on the false felicity and uncertainty of this world, and these thoughts almost drive him mad as they did Merlin. Hoccleve's state the next morning is that of the textbook melancholic: desiring solitude and hoping to shun joy (ll. 85–98), he goes into the fields where he wanders in a mental condition near to madness. He describes the plight of the thoughtful man:

> Whan to þe þoghtful whiȝt is tolde a tale,
>   He heeriþ it as þogh he þennes were;
> Hys heuy thoghtes hym so plukke & hale
>   Hyder and þedir, and hym greue & dere,
> þat hys eres auayle hym nat a pere;
>   He vnderstondeþ no þing what men seye,
>   So ben his wyttes fer gon hem to pleye.
>
> þe smert of þoght, I by experience
>   knowe as wel as any man doþ lyuynge;

His frosty swoot & fyry hote feruence
And troubly dremes, drempt al in wakynge,
My mayzed heed sleeplees han of konnynge,
And wyt dispoylyd, & so me be-iapyd,
þat after deþ ful often haue I gapid.

[ll. 99–112]

Unawareness of what goes on about him, intense anxiety, chills and fever, waking delusions, the desire for death: all these are typical of the melancholic as Bartholomeus describes him (4. 11; 7. 6).

When Hoccleve meets the Beggar, the Beggar understandably thinks him mad because of his failure to respond (ll. 124–26), and when he has succeeded in arousing Hoccleve, he tells him

I fonde þe soul, & þi wyttes echone
ffer fro þe fled, & disparpled ful wyde;
Wherefore it semeþ, þe nediþ a gyde,
Which þat þe may vnto þi wyttes lede.

[ll. 208–11]

The Beggar, desiring to cure Hoccleve, follows many of the therapeutic recommendations of medieval physicians; he provides us with our first fictional account of psychiatry, and, as the Church would require, he combines mental and spiritual medicine. Recognizing Hoccleve as a melancholic (l. 217), the Beggar cautions him against wandering alone, insists upon speaking with him, and urges him to tell "the verray cause of þin hyd maladye" (l. 262), be it fear of losing riches, poverty, or love. Melancholy is the devil's weapon to lead men to despair (ll. 267–80), and the Beggar realizes that he must encourage Hoccleve to tell his troubles so that they may be remedied and — at least as important — so that he may be diverted from his grief, a standard treatment for melancholy madness.[14] When Hoccleve is unwilling to talk at first, the

14. See the discussion of treatment for madness in chap. 1. Chaucer uses the same techniques in dealing with the Black Knight's grief; *BD* 548–51.

Beggar tries to encourage him by telling of his own life, which
closely resembles Hoccleve's as described in the *Male Regle*:
both men haunted taverns in their youth and indulged in
lechery and other sins, both ran off like cowards when tavern
brawls started, and both suffered from the poverty which the
Beggar, at least, acknowledges as a token of God's grace
(*Regement*, ll. 596–672). Hoccleve at last confesses the cause
of his grief: he is quite poor, and he goes in dread of losing
the little he has — he would rather die. The Beggar encourages
Hoccleve: he will not lose his money, and even if he did, poverty would not be so unpleasant; Hoccleve should realize that
the rich of this world endanger their souls, and God has
written, "Whom so I loue, hym wole I chastyse" (l. 1260). The
Beggar tells diverting stories, both from his own life and from
history, to prove that honest poverty is no disaster; but despite
Celsus's recommendation that melancholics be taught to rejoice in apparent misfortune, the remedy does not work for
Hoccleve. Finally the Beggar makes a practical suggestion: if
Hoccleve busies himself with translating a noble work for
Prince Henry, perhaps both melancholy and fear of poverty
will be cured. Much as Robert Burton was to do two centuries
later, Hoccleve decides to shun idleness and to write so that he
may avoid melancholy, and the *Regement of Princes* proper is
the result.

    In the Prologue, Hoccleve thus paints an accurate and con-
vincing portrait of the melancholic man as described in medical treatises; the use of commonly recognized symptoms and
cures contributes greatly to the realism and vividness of the
account, as a close examination of the text will show. But
Hoccleve seems interested in giving us such a lively and convincing picture not for its own sake, although he must have
known how charming the Prologue is, and not because he himself was really prone to melancholy, although he may have
been. Rather, the melancholic character Hoccleve is a delightfully particularized and attractive but still recognizable Boethian Everyman, obsessed with earthly goods and in need
of consolation by the Beggar, an equally concrete and practical
spokesman for Philosophy. Hoccleve is less concerned ulti-

mately with his protagonist's disease than with what that disease signifies in moral terms, and this emphasis is clearly in keeping with the traditional medieval view of madness as well as with Hoccleve's own practice.

Hoccleve's omnipresent preoccupation with sin and disease is important to the *Regement*, but it is more muted and less explicit there than it is in either the *Male Regle* or the *Series*, perhaps because the technique of dialogue involves the stating of two positions — the Beggar's and Hoccleve's — which are never truly reconciled within the poem; the analogy to Boethius's *Consolation* implied above is only partially valid. Hoccleve's behavior and statements illustrate the fearful disease of melancholy and suggest the cause: excessive desire for earthly goods. The Beggar, happy in the poverty which he accepts as fit punishment for his youthful sins and as a token of God's desire to refine him by affliction, indicates again and again Hoccleve's folly in so fearing poverty that he becomes melancholic. But the Beggar's advice is not wholly acceptable to Hoccleve, and so the Beggar must content himself with saving Hoccleve from despair and perhaps from suicide by suggesting the writing of the *Regement*: condoning a little avarice is better than discouraging a man so much that he will take his life.

The Prologue ends suddenly and indecisively, as many medieval debate poems do; the Beggar has put the case for holiness and suffering on earth, and Hoccleve has argued that, for those of us who are not saints, some small measure of security is necessary.[15] As is common in debate poems, both sides are right in their way; one senses that Hoccleve the poet knew that the Beggar was right, but that perhaps neither Hoccleve the poet nor Hoccleve the character could yet be content with accepting earthly trials as medicine for the soul. Hoccleve does not here endorse the easy answer — live for the purse — that he chose wittily in the *Male Regle*, but neither does he accept

---

15. It is tempting to see the Beggar as spokesman for Hoccleve the would-be priest and the character Hoccleve as spokesman for the worldly clerk of the Keeper of the Privy Seal.

the tentative submission to the ways of God which distinguishes the *Series*. Unlike the Beggar, he has not yet been smitten by God, so he cannot yet be reconciled. The tension between the Christian injunction to be mad to the world and the secular desire for prosperity which entails the spiritual madness of sin is strongly felt in the Prologue. It is this tension which may indeed have driven Hoccleve mad a few years after writing the *Regement*.

In the *Complaint* and *Dialogue with a Friend,* which begin the *Series* (ca. 1421–22), Hoccleve's concern with physical and mental disease as the consequence of moral failure receives its fullest expression. These poems — and indeed the *Series* as a whole — have as their central theme the usefulness of physical disorder for recalling men to spiritual sanity. They express the need for a balance between sinfulness, conceived of as a disease curable by repentance and confession, and the despair that excessive consciousness of sin can create; and they teach the need for patience and humility in a world of Boethian mutability where men must rely on true rather than false goods, on virtue and God rather than on money and friends. In the first two poems, we see the movement from the actual physical madness caused by sin and eventually cured by God, to the moral madness of melancholy and despair finally cured by Reason and an actual Consolation, to the complete sanity and rationality of the humbled Hoccleve who is willing to combine the story of his own humiliation with other fictions and with a moral treatise as examples from which other men may profit.

In the *Complaint* Hoccleve describes his difficulty in adjusting to the world after a serious illness — it seems to have been a form of madness — which he claims to have suffered some five years before. The poem begins, as did the *Regement,* with Hoccleve's inability to sleep one autumn night, "so vexyd me the thowghtfull maladye" (l. 21). Again, he is a typical melancholic: the season is that in which the melancholy humour increases; his meditations on death and mutability are characteristic of the melancholic; and his wakefulness and despair — he wishes he might die (ll. 27–28) — are also standard medical symptoms. He finally bursts out with his complaint: busying oneself with the task of writing, as the Beggar knew, is one possible treatment for melancholy. He tells of his illness:

> All myghty god, as lykethe his goodnes,
> visytethe folks alday, as men may se,
> with lose of good and bodily sikenese,
> and amonge othar, he forgat not me:
> witnes vppon the wyld infirmytie
> which that I had, as many a man well knewe,
> and whiche me owt of my selfe cast and threw.
>
> [ll. 36–42]

Everyone talked about his illness, and some of his friends undertook pilgrimages for him, much as Charles VI's queen did for her mad husband. Finally Hoccleve's memory, which "went to pley" (l. 51) during his madness, returned by God's grace; like Nebuchadnezzar, he knew himself again.

But Hoccleve, like Charles, was not accepted by his friends as wholly sane; as "a ryotows person" (l. 67), he was scorned and deserted, and many spoke against him. These speeches indicate many of the attitudes toward madness which we have seen in earlier chapters. Some thought he was of the age when recurrent madness was inevitable (ll. 88–89); as a middle-aged man, he was in the melancholic stage of life, and melancholy madness might be anticipated in one who had already suffered it once. Others felt that hot weather would bring back his illness; summer was considered the most dangerous time for madmen of all kinds. According to others, he "loked as a wilde steer" (l. 120), he rolled his eyes, he carried his head askew, his brain was obviously "bukkyshe" (l. 123), he ran about madly, and he never stopped moving his hands and feet (ll. 127–33). All are standard symptoms of the madman, according to Bartholomeus: "Thyse ben the sygnes of frenesye: . . . woodnes and contynuall wakynge, meuynge and castynge abowte the eyen, Ragynge, stretchynge and castynge of hondes, meuynge & waggynge of heed . . ." (7. 5). In fact, even Hoccleve's suspicions that everyone is gossiping about him could be taken as a sign of extreme melancholy (Bartholomeus 4. 11). Rendered painfully self-con-

scious by his friends' treatment, Hoccleve pathetically prac-
ticed looking sane before a mirror; he also took care not
to speak angrily or impatiently, although he had good
cause, lest people accuse him of losing control again. Mascardus, in his list of symptoms of madness, suggested that
great audacity or shouting in public indicates insanity, and
Hoccleve perhaps felt the same. Hoccleve then pleads for people to realize that one bout with insanity does not imply continued madness: a man may be mad with drink and then become sober, and so may one be frenzied for a short time only.
His friends clearly agreed with Mascardus's tenet that "insanity
is presumed to endure; therefore when anyone is proven to
have been insane, he who claims such a one is now sane must
prove it." [16]
    Hoccleve asserts that God cured him even though no one
else will believe it:

> Right so, thowghe my witt were a pilgrime,
> and went fer fro home, he cam agayne;
> God me voydyd of this grevous venyme
> that had enfectyd and wildyd my brayne.
>
> [ll. 232–35]

His mention of his wit as a pilgrim suggests the penitential
nature of his illness, and the "venyme" could be either a direct
consequence of his profligate living — overeating and drinking
produces "fumosity" which causes frenzy — or the "venyme"
of melancholy and thought, which the Beggar in the *Regement*
warns against (l. 271). Hoccleve is torn between despair at his
friends' mistrust and pleasure that God has cured him; he is
still, at this point in the poem, the sinful victim of melancholy
even though he is no longer wholly mad.
    He then speaks of the cure of his melancholy despair: he read
a *trostbuch* (a book of consolation) lent him by a friend in
which Reason consoled the mournful man by pointing out,

16. For Mascardus, see Pickett, *Mental Affliction and Church Law*, p. 91.

much as the Beggar had done in the *Regement*, the value of
suffering:[17]

> It [tribulation] sleythe man not to them that ben sufferable;
> and to whom goddes stroke is acceptable,
> purveyed Ioye is: for god woundythe tho
> that he ordeyned hathe to blysse to goo.
>
> Gold purgyd is, thou seyst, in the furneis,
> for the fyner and clenner it shall be;
> of thy disease the weyght and the peis
> bere lyghtly, for god, to prove the,
> scorgyd the hathe with sharpe adversitie.

[ll. 354–62]

Just as God cured Hoccleve of his madness five years before, so
Reason fittingly cures the madness of despair which Hoccleve
suffers during the *Complaint*. Hoccleve is now perfectly sane,
and he accepts willingly from Reason the advice which earlier
he shunned when the Beggar offered it. He sees his madness
and his consequent trials as loving punishment sent by God,
and he will take all for the best:

> Thrwghe gods iust dome and his iudgement —
> and for my best, now I take and deme —
> gave that good lorde me my punishement:
> in welthe I toke of hym none hede or yeme
> hym for to plese, and hym honoure and queme;
> and he gave me a bone on for to knaw,
> me to correcte, and of hym to have awe.
>
> he gave me wit, and he toke it away
> when that he se that I it mys dyspent,
> and gave agayne when it was to his pay;
> he grauntyd me my giltes to repent,

---

17. A. G. Rigg has identified this *trostbuch* as the *Synonyma* of Isidore
of Seville; "Hoccleve's *Complaint* and Isidore of Seville," *Speculum* 45
(1970):564–74. One autobiographical touch added by Hoccleve is his giving his own name, Thomas, to the mournful man of the *Synonyma*.

and hens-forwarde to set myne entent
vnto his deitie to do plesaunce,
and to amend my synfull governaunce.

[ll. 393–406]

Hoccleve the character, and perhaps Hoccleve the poet as
well, has moved from the total rejection of adversity in the
Male Regle, through the tension between following God's way
and man's in the *Regement,* to utter acceptance of God's will
in the *Complaint.* The adversity which he feared in the *Regement* has come, and he has survived both the disease and its
melancholy aftermath. The publication of the *Series* may have
had monetary motivation — it is intended for the Duke of
Gloucester and dedicated to Lady Westmoreland — but such
considerations are never mentioned in the poem. Like Nebuchadnezzar, Hoccleve lost his wit because of his sins, and he
gnawed on the bone of punishment until he was finally cured
both of his madness and of the later melancholy which bordered on insanity. The *Complaint* tells of the cure of the first
disease and illustrates the cure of the second.

The *Dialogue* shows dramatically that Hoccleve is truly
cured of his melancholy. A friend appears to inquire after his
health, and Hoccleve shows him the *Complaint,* which he intends to circulate. His friend counsels him not to do so — Why
remind people of Hoccleve's madness? — but Hoccleve insists;
he knows that people still think him mad, and he wishes to
tell his story for the honor of God at least as much as to convince men that he's sane. He will, in addition, translate a work
called "lerne for to dye" (l. 206) so that others may not have
his misfortunes. This activity will help make reparation for his
previous sinfulness:

for where my sowle is of vertwe all lene,
and thrwghe my bodyes gilt fowle & vnclene,
to clens it some-what by translation
of it, shall be myne occupation.

[ll. 214–17]

Hoccleve's friend is shocked; he thinks that Hoccleve has gone
mad again to want to do such a thing (ll. 302–04), at least until

he is fully recovered. But Hoccleve, perhaps aware that his apparent madness is now the sanity of true virtue, reproaches his
friend's mistrust. The friend defends himself:

> Of studie was engendred thy seeknesse,
> And that was hard; woldest thow now agayn
> Entre into þat laborious bisynesse,
> Syn it thy mynde and eek thy wit had slayn?
>
> [ll. 379–82]

The friend, of course, is accepting the common view that study
leads to melancholy madness, and he kindly attributes Hoccleve's former insanity to such a neutral cause. Hoccleve, however, knows better:

> Trustith right wel þat neuere studie in book
> Was cause why my mynde me forsook;
> But it was causid of my long seeknesse,
> And othir wyse nat, in soothfastnesse.
>
> [ll. 424–27]

His illness was punishment for the long disease of sinfulness
and melancholy that he suffered from the time of his youth,
and his insanity was a moral consequence, not purely physiological.

The friend is convinced and suggests also that Hoccleve show
his repentance for his alleged crime against ladies in writing
the "Epistle of Cupid," a poem which Hoccleve rightly denies
to be antifeminist. Nonetheless, he translates the tale of
Jereslaus' Wife in praise of good women. By this time, Hoccleve has not only lost his melancholy, he has also lost his bit-
terness against doubting friends; he even sets out to make
reparation for his past sins by writing moral stories. The three
other long poems in the *Series* — the two *Gesta Romanorum*
tales and *Lerne to Dye* — involve the idea that sin deserves
punishment by disease on earth and that such punishment is
infinitely preferable to an eternity in hell. The whole *Series*
is thus united by the theme of the value of suffering and disease which preoccupied Hoccleve throughout his poetic career.

One fascinating question concerning Hoccleve is whether his madness, referred to in the *Complaint* and *Dialogue,* is historical. There are no references to it in the fairly extensive records of his life,[18] and we must assume that, if it did exist, it was brief. Certainly he speaks of it as though it were true, and most critics have assumed that the description of his madness is genuinely autobiographical. If Hoccleve did go mad, I am inclined to think that his insanity was a short but intense fit of depression, something like that which he describes as making him witless in the *Regement,* caused by his inability to reconcile the claims of God — essentially, resignation and patience in the face of adversity — with the desires of man for money and security. Conceivably, too, this tension may have combined with some degree of ill health to cause Hoccleve's remarkable concern throughout his life with sin as a disease and punishable by disease.

But the case is not at all clear; we can hardly believe everything that medieval writers tell us about themselves in their poetry. It is most unlikely that Gower ever met Genius in the forest one May morning, or that the *Pearl*-poet really fell asleep on his daughter's grave and had a wonderful vision, or that Chaucer really had a dream about Fame on the tenth of December and later met a model for the Pardoner as he was going on pilgrimage to Canterbury. It might be argued that no one expects a dream vision or a frame narrative to be autobiographical, while a confession of remarkable cowardice in a tavern or of a fit of madness is so unusual that it could hardly be conventional. But such an argument will not hold. Hoccleve's *Male Regle* is, as Thornley demonstrates,[19] an exceptionally good example of the conventional informal penitential lyric; and its colorfulness and realism may relate it more closely to such works of fiction as the *Wife of Bath's Prologue* or the lively confessions of the seven deadly sins and of Haukyn in *Piers Plowman* (B 5 and 13) than to a true confession from the heart. Similarly, both the *Regement* and the *Series* may

18. See Mitchell, *Hoccleve,* p. 4.
19. "Hoccleve's Autobiographical Poetry,"

represent attempts at a frame narrative much like the *Canterbury Tales* or the *Confessio Amantis,* and if we are willing to divorce Chaucer the poet from Chaucer the pilgrim, and the moral Gower from the Gower who confesses to the madness of love (8. 2860–67), then we must be willing to do the same for Hoccleve in all of his "autobiographical" works.

Many of the details which strike us as most autobiographical in Hoccleve's poetry can, in fact, be interpreted as examples of literary borrowing or convention. For instance, one of the most delightful and apparently idiosyncratic parts of the *Male Regle* is Hoccleve's description of his very limited involvement with "venus femel lusty children deere" (l. 138): he kissed them, but never dared progress much further, for "Of loues aart yit touchid I no deel" (l. 153). This could as easily be an imitation of Chaucer's frequent disclaimers of experience in love (e.g. *TC* 2. 19–21) as a confession of real sexual inadequacy. Hoccleve's complaints of poverty in the *Male Regle* and the *Regement* may similarly be indebted to the genre of begging poems or to the description of Impatient Poverty in the *Prologue* to the *Man of Law's Tale.* His pretentious desire to be called "maister" by the London boatmen in the *Male Regle* could be related to the apparently common wish of learned medieval men to have their knowledge recognized. Thus Langland inveighs against men who want to learn only so they may merit the dignified title of Master (*Piers* B 11. 168–69), and Hoccleve's beloved master Chaucer describes a similar case of pomposity soon to be undercut in the *Summoner's Tale,* where Friar Thomas, having been called "maister," hypocritically denies that he relishes the title (*CT* 3. 2185–88). The *Complaint* itself, as Rigg has shown, may owe a good deal that seems autobiographical to the source for the *trostbuch* described in it, Isidore's *Synonyma.*[20]

These examples, which could be multiplied, bring us to the central question of Hoccleve's madness: Are there grounds for

---

20. "Hoccleve's *Complaint,*" pp. 564–74. Such incidents as Hoccleve's desertion by his friends and his fear of speaking out to defend himself have precedent in the *Synonyma.*

thinking that this too is conventional? I think there are. He is not alone in confessing to madness — Gower, Langland, and the *Pearl*-poet make similar admissions in clearly fictional circumstances — but he is the first writer I know of to write at length and *in propria persona* of a madness that could be real. The question that needs to be answered is: Why would a man write a poem, ostensibly about himself, in which he accuses himself of having suffered madness? I should hope that, by this point in this study, the answer might be obvious: one could hardly find a better or more traditional metaphor for the crippling state of sin which is the subject of the poem, as I have shown. Hoccleve describes his case as one of frenzy followed by a long period of melancholia coming close to madness; and, as we have seen repeatedly, both melancholia and frenzy were traditionally associated with sin. Hoccleve might thus have chosen to refer to a long spell of vice as a period of madness, just as the Beggar in the *Regement* refers to his youthful sins as caused by his "wylde steerissh heed" (l. 604), a description remarkably similar to Hoccleve's own "bukkyshe . . . brayne" (l. 123) and his appearance as a "wilde steer" (l. 120) in the *Complaint*. That Hoccleve's friends shunned him because of his being "a ryotows person" (l. 67) could also suggest a sinful life as well as frenzy.

Of course it is impossible to prove that Hoccleve's poetry is *not* autobiographical, but there are, as we have seen, numerous indications that it *may* not be: many "autobiographical" details in all his poems could easily be conventional or borrowed; the themes of madness and disease are common in his work both before and after his alleged madness; and, given that Hoccleve's description of madness and his attitudes toward madness and disease are traditional, there is ample justification for him to choose madness as the vehicle through which to describe the moral insanity of sin. It is also possible that throughout his works Hoccleve adds pseudo-autobiographical detail both to strengthen his argument by providing experiential authority and to move his readers more effectively, either in the direction of moral reform or of pity and generosity. I think that we cannot assume that either the sins of the *Male Regle* or the madness of the *Complaint* were real, fascinating as the possibility may be. Hoccleve may have used the conventions of madness to describe his own insanity, or he may have used details from his own life to add realism and forcefulness to the topic — the madness of sin — about which he wished to write. We cannot tell which is the case, but it does not matter very much, for the *Complaint* loses little of its interest even if Hoccleve's madness is a fiction.

Whether or not Hoccleve was mad, the unity of the *Complaint* derives from the underlying metaphor of madness. Madness may be a specific physical disease or a spiritual disease with physical consequences; it may be manifested in riotous living, in the loss of reason and in frenzy, and in melancholy and despair. It may represent the sickness of all mankind, the moral disease of a particular sinner, or the physical disease of a specific madman. It may be the madness of the fool who thinks he can ignore God or the apparent madness to the worldly wise of the holy man who uses his own sins as a witness to his shame and an example for others. All these implications are present in the poem, and all these varieties of madness, except for that of the Holy Fool, are one in that they consist in turning away from God and from God's image, reason. It is thus fitting that Hoccleve's first madness is cured by God's grace and the second (that melancholy which pervades the early part of the poem) by Reason itself. It is finally impossible to say which senses of madness are real and which are metaphorical in the poem. Hoccleve may have been sane, choosing to see and describe his sins as madness so that the moral of his poem might be more strongly enforced; or he may, at some point, have been mad, and he may later have seen his madness as the consequence of sin. We can be certain only that Hoccleve was thoroughly familiar with the attitudes and conventions of madness discussed in this study, and such attitudes and conventions are like powerful colored lenses: if we look through them at our own lives, what we see will be distorted by the conventions, and details that do not fit will be filtered out. The same will be true in writing: the conventions will shape our ideas, factual or fictional, to themselves. In such circumstances, it is impossible to say where literature influences life and where life influences literature; all questions of autobiography become obscured, but the strength of the conventions in life and literature is demonstrated forcefully.[21] But these are only speculations. In regard to Hoccleve's *Complaint*, perhaps it suffices to note that — as the shape of the poem, with its double cure of two sorts of madness, and as the language of sin and disease seem to suggest — sin is the worst madness, the only madness that really matters; the myriad shapes which the madness of sin may take are much less relevant to man's soul than sin itself. The proper use of wit is much more important than the analysis of how far, in what ways, and with what consequences wit is perverted. Hoccleve's subject, whatever else it may be as well, is the sinful madness of mankind; it is to cure that disease that he tells his own story, the two other cautionary tales, and the treatise which, in showing men how to die, will teach them how to live sanely.

It is fitting that this book should close with Thomas Hoccleve, a man thoroughly familiar with medieval attiudes toward madness and perhaps personally concerned with the disease, a man who recapitulates the past and anticipates the future in his writings on madness. His view of disease and madness as consequences of sin, his understanding of the interaction of

21. A fascinating example of a man's life apparently being interpreted in accord with convention occurs in the fourth-century Armenian historian Agathange's *Histoire du règne de Tiridate,* printed in Victor Langlois, *Collection des Historiens anciens et modernes de l'Arménie* (Paris, 1867), 1:105–93 (also mentioned in *AM,* p. 156). King Tiridate, Agathange's master, fell in love with a Christian maiden whom he killed when she spurned him. Vengeance seized him as he prepared to go hunting: he was possessed by a demon and driven mad, "semblable à Nabuchodonosor" (p. 150). He seems to have acquired most of that king's symptoms: he took the shape of a beast, lived with wild boars in the wilderness, ate grass, ran naked, and grew long body hair and sharp nails. Finally he was cured by Saint Gregory the Illuminator, after which he acknowledged and honored God. It seems improbable that Agathange is reporting the facts accurately; it is far more likely that the conventional representation of Nebuchadnezzar shaped either the historian's account or his perception of the events, just as New Testament reports of madmen seem to have influenced later accounts of madness and its cure.

soul and body and his resulting emphasis on both the physiological and moral effects of sin, and his appreciation of the value of disease as punishment and purgation are all traditional; we have seen them time and again in preceding chapters. But in treating conventional ideas freshly by using himself as exemplum, in creating the appearance of tortured introspection, in illustrating dramatically the destructive moral tensions experienced by a would-be man of virtue living in the world, and in presenting a detailed study of the melancholic as more than just a sinner, he looks forward to the Renaissance — to *Hamlet,* to Robert Burton, to humoural psychology on the stage, and to the Jacobean preoccupation with madness. Hoccleve, like many who went before him and many who followed, asked the eternal question, "Why do men suffer?" Like all the authors we have mentioned, he found the answer in man's sin — a concept which each age must define for itself; and, like his forerunners, he found the best metaphor, both for suffering and for the sin it purges, in madness.

Index